The Moral Theology
of Roger Williams

COLUMBIA SERIES IN REFORMED THEOLOGY

The Columbia Series in Reformed Theology represents a joint commitment of Columbia Theological Seminary and Westminster John Knox Press to provide theological resources for the church today.

The Reformed tradition has always sought to discern what the living God revealed in scripture is saying and doing in every new time and situation. Volumes in this series examine significant individuals, events, and issues in the development of this tradition and explore their implications for contemporary Christian faith and life.

This series is addressed to scholars, pastors, and laypersons. The Editorial Board hopes that these volumes will contribute to the continuing reformation of the church.

Columbia Theological Seminary wishes to express its appreciation to the following churches for supporting this joint publishing venture:

Central Presbyterian Church, Atlanta, Georgia

First Presbyterian Church, Franklin, Tennessee

First Presbyterian Church, Nashville, Tennessee

First Presbyterian Church, Quincy, Florida

First Presbyterian Church, Spartanburg, South Carolina

First Presbyterian Church, Tupelo, Mississippi

North Avenue Presbyterian Church, Atlanta, Georgia

Riverside Presbyterian Church, Jacksonville, Florida

Roswell Presbyterian Church, Roswell, Georgia

South Highland Presbyterian Church, Birmingham, Alabama

Spring Hill Presbyterian Church, Mobile, Alabama

St. Simons Island Presbyterian Church, St. Simons Island, Georgia

St. Stephen Presbyterian Church, Fort Worth, Texas

Trinity Presbyterian Church, Atlanta, Georgia

University Presbyterian Church, Chapel Hill, North Carolina

COLUMBIA SERIES IN REFORMED THEOLOGY

The Moral Theology of Roger Williams

Christian Conviction and Public Ethics

JAMES CALVIN DAVIS

Westminster John Knox Press
LOUISVILLE • LONDON

Book and cover design by Drew Stevens

First edition
Published by Westminster John Knox Press
Louisville, Kentucky

This book is printed on acid-free paper that meets the American National Standards Institute Z39.48 standard. ∞

PRINTED IN THE UNITED STATES OF AMERICA

04 05 06 07 08 09 10 11 12 13—10 9 8 7 6 5 4 3 2 1

Library of Congress Cataloging-in-Publication Data

Davis, James Calvin.
    The moral theology of Roger Williams : Christian conviction and public
ethics / James Calvin Davis.—1st ed.
        p. cm. — (Columbia series in Reformed theology)
    Includes bibliographical references and index.
    ISBN 0-664-22770-8 (alk. paper)
    1. Williams, Roger, 1604?–1683—Ethics. 2. Christian ethics. I. Title.
II. Series.

BX9339.W55D38 2004
241'.0461'092—dc22   2004044184

To E. B. D.

For thy sweet love rememb'red such wealth brings
That then I scorn to change my state with kings.
—William Shakespeare, Sonnet 29

CONTENTS

ACKNOWLEDGMENTS

This book began as a dissertation written for the Religious Studies Department of the University of Virginia and directed by James F. Childress. One of the most important ethicists working today, Professor Childress is also a wonderful intellectual role model. While others may bow to the temptation to dissolve the complex issues of our day into sound bites for mass media consumption, his work consistently reflects careful consideration, thorough analysis, and a respect for the ambiguous. Professor Childress applied these gifts to his reading of this work, and my argument is stronger for it. He also encouraged the development of these analytical skills in his student, teaching me to engage my scholarship with independence and a deep critical awareness. For any promise I hold as a scholar, I am indebted to his tutelage.

My interest in Puritanism in general and Roger Williams specifically stems from the influence of two other fine teachers. Douglas F. Ottati served as my mentor during my ministerial training at Union Theological Seminary in Virginia. Besides ably providing me with the tools necessary for historical and constructive theology, Ottati satisfied my budding thirst for Puritan thought by introducing me to the likes of William Perkins, Richard Baxter, and Jonathan Edwards. It was Ottati who led me to discover that the works of these Puritan divines were sophisticated enough to warrant contemporary reading. David Little, now of Harvard, first introduced me to Roger Williams in my early days as a doctoral student, when our paths crossed in a couple of seminars he taught at Virginia while serving at the United States Institute of Peace. Little read and commented on an earlier version of this book, and through much of our eight-year friendship he has offered wise, patient, and enthusiastic conversation on issues in Puritan ethics. I blame him for my obsession with this seventeenth-century Puritan deviant.

Other scholars whom I admire and respect have read and commented on drafts of this volume, including Donald McKim and the kind folks on the Columbia Series Board, William Lee Miller, Heather Ann Warren, and my good friend Charles T. Mathewes. In addition, I wish to thank Bruce and Arlene Mentch, the late Alquin Edwards, Evelyn Martin, Richard and Bea Ewing, Colver Presbyterian Church, and the Louisville Institute for financial support at different stages of this project. Much of the material in chapter 5 first appeared in an article I wrote in response to the presidential election of 2000, "A Return to Civility: Roger Williams and Public Discourse in America," *Journal of Church and State* 43:4 (autumn 2001): 689–706; I am grateful to *JCS* and editor Derek Davis for permission to use this material. Finally, I also thank my colleagues in the Religion Department of Middlebury College, especially our chair, Larry Yarbrough, for creating an environment conducive to scholarly pursuits such as this one. What a rare delight it is to do theology in a liberal arts context, often a fitting laboratory for testing the compatibility of Christian conviction with public moral discourse.

Now to attend to debts of a more intimate kind. My parents, William and Kathy Davis, performed not-so-minor miracles to give me the college education that neither of them enjoyed, an education usually out of reach in the economic circumstances in which they managed to raise five children. Just as important to my maturation as a scholar and a human being have been the work ethic and worldview they passed on to me. I give thanks for their love, and I remain prouder of my identity as their son than of anything I have done. And a special word of gratitude to my wife ElizabethAnne, to whom this book is dedicated. Not only has she applied her careful editorial eye to every word contained herein, but she has supported my work in more fundamental ways. Through twelve years of marriage, and all of the fresh challenges, unanticipated vocational changes, and personal tragedy we have lived together, she has been my breadwinner, cheerleader, pastoral counselor, partner, fellow dreamer, and friend. To the greatest blessing of my life, I say thanks.

INTRODUCTION

Because primary credit usually is given to icons a century his junior, Roger Williams seldom receives the attention he deserves as an important early advocate for the political doctrine of religious liberty in America. What is appreciated even less, however, is Williams's importance as a *theologian.* Williams defended religious liberty from an explicitly confessional theological commitment, but his starting point is lost on generations of subsequent interpreters who insist on reading him more as an icon of American political philosophy than as a Christian theologian (when they read him at all). Popular lore casts Roger Williams in the role of agnostic seeker and defender of democracy opposite a Puritan worldview that he rejected as authoritarian and inauthentic. In reality, though, Roger Williams was a Puritan, and a rather orthodox and extreme one at that, with a theological stringency that sometimes made John Cotton and the Massachusetts Bay Colony establishment look like capitulating religious liberals. Contrary to popular perception, Williams did not come to his principles regarding religious liberty and separation of church and state by rejecting Puritan orthodoxy; he developed his thoughts precisely through the lens of Puritan beliefs that he pursued in creative, if unpopular, directions. To ignore the theological dimension to Williams's thought is to overlook the complexity and subtlety with which he understood the relationship between his religious convictions and his political vision. Nonetheless, until relatively recently the theological antecedents to Williams's political thought have been largely neglected, and even now students of this "deviant" Puritan often fail to appreciate the extent to which Williams derived his belief in religious liberty from a moral outlook grounded in the orthodoxy of the Reformed Christian confession.[1]

Teasing out the theological framework for Williams's thought is the primary objective of this book. My foremost intention here is neither to provide a narrative of Williams's life nor to rehearse his pronouncements on the issues of religious liberty and church and state. Both his biography and his political opinions have been recounted *ad infinitum,* and the writings of Ola Winslow, Perry Miller, Edmund Morgan, and Edwin S. Gaustad are still valuable for these purposes. My aim instead is to consider Williams's thought *as moral theology,* to uncover the theological underpinnings on which he built his case for religious tolerance. Recognizing and understanding Williams's sophisticated (if unsystematically presented) theology helps us to see the depth to his teachings on religious liberty and that "wall of separation," but such comprehension also reveals that Williams is important to contemporary debates beyond First Amendment politics. In particular, Williams's thought provides a rich historical resource for Christian thinkers grappling with the relationship between confessional integrity and participation in public moral discourse.

Contemporary theologians disagree over the appropriate role Christian theology ought to assume in the wider moral deliberations of civil society, with some Christian thinkers advocating the "translation" of religious belief into a moral vocabulary accessible to non-Christians while others fear that such adaptation risks the abandonment of a distinctive theological stance. To the standoff between Christian particularists, who argue that the meaning of Christian ethics is bound and limited to its context in the community of faith, and strict universalists, who assert that what is ultimately meaningful in Christian moral discourse is that which can transcend the limits of religious participation, Williams offers a third and middle view. Williams provides a moral vision that maintains both its theological integrity and its potential for conversation and cooperation with other worldviews and traditions outside Christianity. On the one hand, Williams recommended duly famous justifications of religious liberty and particular political constructs that were meant to persuade not just Christians, but all members and leaders of civic society, to the cause of conscience. On the other hand, Williams developed his prescriptions as moral *theology,* within a perspective that took seriously the particular convictions of Christian faith. For Williams these faith convictions could not, and should not, simply be jettisoned in the interest of participating in broader political conversations. Williams demonstrated with his own life's work that the desire for public participation in a pluralistic political ethos did not require the abandonment of Christian belief, and in fact he assumed that such abandonment endangered Christian integrity. From the approach Williams took to negotiating religious belief and public participation, he appears to locate himself somewhere between the claims of the modern strict universalist and the equally modern (though less self-consciously so) radical particularist in Christian ethics. Making Williams available to contribute to this current theological debate between Christian particularists and universalists is another reason for this book.

The categories assigned in this debate, that of "universalist" and "particularist," are admittedly quite broad, their imprecision concealing both differences and agreements important to the issue. Acknowledging the vagueness of these terms, Gene Outka nonetheless offers a typology that is helpful for understanding the claims at stake in this dispute.[2] As typology, of course, Outka's descriptions of the two poles do not match every specific moral program that may align itself with (or be labeled with) the terms "particularist" or "universalist." A type ignores individual subtleties in favor of constructing general representatives for the point of comparison. While typology requires a certain amount of distance and abstraction, it proves a useful exercise for the purpose of isolating crucial differences among broad positions.[3]

For general purposes, then, Outka summarizes the following three claims as important dimensions to the universalist position. First, universalists insist that basic moral beliefs are accessible across cultures through faculties of "reason" or, more specifically, "conscience." Basic moral claims are not completely dependent on the vehicle of "revelation." Second, these basic moral values do not rely on the particular beliefs or practices of communities (including religious) for their justification. Third, these basic moral values are held in common by members of the entire human family, and, in fact, those values that are shared by all persons trump those obligations that are particular to cultural or religious contexts. Outka points out that these universalist assumptions are neither rejected by all Christians nor necessarily hostile to participation in particular communities.

In contrast to these general tenets of universalism, Christian "particularism" may be roughly identified with three "senses" or tendencies of its own. First, particularists often argue an epistemic fallibilism, asserting that the commonalities universalists believe to exist among the moral norms of different cultures and communities are not validated by the evidence of human experience. Diversity and moral disagreement, argue particularists, are more characteristic of the moral landscape of basic human interaction than moral agreement. Second, particularists often insist that moral beliefs and concepts are historically and contextually bound, and thus they may not be translated into general human concepts but must be considered in their historical and cultural forms. Therefore historical and contextual inquiry must be emphasized, not marginalized, in moral theory. Third, some particularists entirely reject the notion of a "human essence," atomistic individualism or otherwise, insisting instead that we are fundamentally social and socialized beings. As Outka explains, this third particularist argument "is captured in the dictum that our sociality goes all the way down."

To these typological construals of particularism and universalism, the moral theology of Roger Williams provides a helpful alternative. In contrast to universalist claims, Williams demonstrates that general moral arguments can be made in the context of distinctive Christian commitments and that the relationship between particular Christian convictions and general moral agreements need not be fundamentally adversarial (that is, one need not always retain the right to trump the other). Akin to a particularist approach, Williams demonstrates a profound dedication to the resources and thought patterns of his Reformed Christian tradition, from which he shows no desire to escape in order to participate in broader moral conversations. Contrary to theological particularism, however, Williams believes engagement in those conversations to be possible from within the particular convictions of Christian faith, because according to his interpretation, the Christian moral tradition already possesses the theological resources necessary to explore bases of morality shared with people outside the faith community.

Appreciating Williams as an alternative to both a universalist's theological amnesia and a particularist's avoidance of public moral discourse depends on reading his thought not as political history but as theology. Williams's pronouncements on religious liberty or any other moral topic cannot be understood properly without reference to this religious foundation. Part 1, then, uses the narrative of Williams's emigration to and subsequent exile from the Massachusetts Bay Colony as context to illustrate the religious convictions that formed the groundwork for his ethics. Chapter 1 challenges the notion, popular among American historians, that Williams was hostile or ambivalent toward Puritanism, arguing instead that his thought is grounded in a Reformed theology indebted to his Puritan context. The second chapter of the book explores the ways in which Williams's theology, particularly his ecclesiology, eschatology, and use of Scripture, played an important role in the development of his thoughts on religious liberty. Each of these doctrines, I argue, depends on a prior commitment to the incarnation as interpretive lens, which provides for Williams's unique contribution to the development of notions of religious freedom.

This book begins with the confessional dimension of Williams's works for three reasons. First, Williams thought and wrote from a Calvinist understanding of himself and the world, so to begin here is to recognize what Williams acknowledged to be foundational to his thought. Second, Williams has been mistaken so often for a champion of liberal democracy in the Jeffersonian mold, or a pragmatic relativist influenced more by disgust over religious persecution in old and New England than by theological conviction, that to begin here is to make some additional effort to correct this misinterpretation. And last, I begin with Williams's confessional stringency because it is only by doing so from the outset that I can most clearly distinguish Williams's project from what contemporary particularists call liberalism. Though Williams's moral theology incorporates claims sympathetic to liberal objectives, clearly Williams begins with the distinctive self-understanding of the Christian community called together by Christ.

Having established the confessional basis of Williams's moral theology, Part 2 moves to an exploration of those theological concepts that allowed

Williams to believe it possible and desirable to engage a broader public in moral conversation and projects. In other words, this second part deals with Williams's moral anthropology, most notably his understanding of pluralism and the roles that human reason, natural law, and human experience play in moral agency. Following a general consideration of his moral anthropology in chapter 3, including a look at how Williams's optimism regarding human moral ability was confirmed by his interaction with Native Americans, chapter 4 explores more intensely the one aspect of moral agency that is famously important to his doctrine of religious liberty: the conscience. In particular I relate Williams's development of the concept to that of John Calvin, William Perkins, William Ames, and John Cotton, arguing that Williams's Reformed theory of conscience contributes to the theological basis of a public ethics that invites moral cooperation between Christians and non-Christians.

With the third part of the book, I move from theological framework to moral content, from the consideration of anthropology to an examination of what might be called Williams's "public ethics." In chapter 5 I consider the substantive content of the morality Williams believed all human beings capable of living by examining what he called "civility." Civility for Williams denoted a stable (though not stagnant) set of moral norms that serve the common good and are necessary for a desirable public society. Williams believed "civility" to represent the possibilities for shared moral ventures in the civic arena, a conviction tested but reaffirmed in his contentious relationship with the Quakers. Using Williams's very public battles with the Quakers in Providence and the surrounding towns as my historical backdrop, I explore this notion of civility and how it symbolized Williams's confidence in the existence of a few generally recognized norms that guide social behavior and provide parameters for public discourse itself.

In the final chapter, I return to the confessional nature of Williams's ethics in order to argue that his openness to moral ventures with a non-Christian public did not threaten the theological integrity of his moral project. Because this is so, he remains a conceptual resource for rethinking the sometimes tired debate between contemporary Christian communitarians and universalists. Williams's moral theology suggests that we can understand Christian particularity to be more compatible with the search for publicly shared moral norms than either of these current camps admits. Thus, as a conclusion to my presentation of Williams's moral theology, I provide a constructive sketch of how, in a contemporary setting, one might begin to imagine a "distinct" Christian ethics with confessional integrity that nonetheless refuses to abandon hope for moral cooperation and real dialogue with persons outside the Christian community—in other words, an outline for imagining public ethics along the pattern Williams offered three centuries ago.

A word about sources: the only extensive collection of the writings of Roger Williams remains *The Complete Writings of Roger Williams,* and with some exceptions it is from this edition that I normally draw in my analysis.[4] The first six volumes of the *Complete Writings* are a reprint of the set first published by the Narragansett Club in the late nineteenth century; to these was added a seventh volume containing treatises undiscovered by the Narragansett Club and a solid interpretive essay by Perry Miller. As any student patient enough to read through a couple of pages from these volumes knows, Williams's prose may be described most charitably as "difficult." Williams often wrote hurriedly, under adverse conditions, and once in England his treatises went straight to press without the benefit of editing. Thus his writings are wrought with punctuation inconsistencies, arbitrary italics, unclosed parentheses, and spelling variants. Combined with the difficulties caused by the Elizabethan script of the Narragansett reproductions, these obstacles at times make reading Williams and following the intention of his thought an exhausting exercise. In order to make my use of Williams's writings more readily available to the reader, I have exercised some editorial discretion in my citations from the Narragansett volumes. I have updated typography, though I usually keep the original spelling. I correct the punctuation variances that, in my judgment, obscure the meaning of the passage. I also have eliminated most of Williams's use of italics, since he seldom applied it with any discretion. I believe these editorial adjustments will make Williams's words more accessible to the reader, which is crucial for demonstrating the difference between the Roger Williams of American folklore and the Puritan who leaps from the pages of his own prose.

I also should say a final word about terminology. Already in this introduction it will not have escaped the careful reader that I prefer to use the term "moral theology," rather than "theological ethics," to describe Williams's project. I have made this choice intentionally, and I do so despite the recognition that "moral theology" brings to mind particular associations in the conventions of contemporary ethical discourse, namely Roman Catholic ethics. One reason I have chosen the term "moral theology," rather than "theological ethics" or even "Christian ethics," is because the former more closely matches how Williams would have understood his own work. "Ethics" was a loaded term for the Puritans, representing the dangerous desire to tear moral guidance from its theological base in order to establish it as an independent discipline on quasi-Aristotelian foundations. Therefore I believe "moral theology" to be the most accurate term, historically speaking, to describe the moral thought of this seventeenth-century Puritan.

I also use the term to describe the thought of this Protestant Reformer out of deference to the power of language to name. The alternative term, "theological ethics," brings with it its own contemporary connotations, associations important for me to avoid given the interpretive corrections I seek in this study of Williams. Part of my objective is to contribute to the emancipation of Williams from the co-opting idealism of American democratic history, restoring him to his rightful place as a theological resource of the Reformed tradition. Given this objective, I seek to emphasize the theological nature of his ethical writings in a way the term "theological ethics" will not allow. For I am afraid that Stanley Hauerwas is correct in asserting that "theological ethics" has acquired a vanilla flavor in the conventions of contemporary moral discourse. Protestant projects that qualify as theological ethics often read as if their theological component is tangential, if not irrelevant, to the moral norms they develop. Although I believe Hauerwas's characterization of theological ethics as a conspiracy between Protestantism and American liberalism to be something of an overstatement, he is right in charging that the term is undiscriminating, for it obscures the important distinctions between different approaches that are called theological ethics just because their authors are Protestants.[5] It is so central to my argument to demonstrate that Williams's ethics is distinct from what particularists usually associate with Protestant liberalism that I want to avoid the use of a term associated with that phenomenon.

Therefore, while I use the term "ethics" occasionally, I prefer to call Williams's overall project "moral theology," for that is what it was, a theological worldview that gave life to a sophisticated understanding of the relationship between Christian conviction and public moral discourse. Williams understood his theological location and identity to be his starting point for thinking on these moral issues, and he justified the extension of their application primarily through theological concepts. In the work of Roger Williams we have more than political history or a philosophical ethics superficially delimited by theological language. Here instead is the work of a master (though largely unsystematic) theologian, who bravely reinterpreted the Calvinist landscape of his Puritan context to give theological warrant to religious and moral tolerance, ecumenical conversation, and civic cooperation. Because this is so, Williams's work is indeed an important historical contribution to Reformed moral theology.

PART I

THEOLOGY

And I believe (dear Peace) it shall appear to them that with fear and trembling at the word of the Lord examine these passages, that the charge of error reboundeth back, even such an error as may well be called the bloody tenent, so directly contradicting the spirit and mind and practice of the Prince of Peace; so deeply guilty of the blood of souls compelled and forced to hypocrisy in a spiritual and soul rape; so deeply guilty of the blood of the souls under the altar, persecuted in all ages for the cause of conscience, and so destructive to the civil peace and welfare of all kingdoms, countries, and commonwealths.

—*The Bloody Tenent of Persecution* (1644)

1

WILLIAMS AND THE
REFORMED TRADITION

Roger Williams was not primarily a champion of liberal democracy and political pragmatism, regardless of how American historians insist on portraying him. Nor was he some sort of nebulous seventeenth-century mystic whose disdain for institutional religion pressed him to advocate religious liberty and found the Rhode Island colony. Roger Williams was foremost a Puritan theologian, and a rather orthodox one at that. Despite his heated religious controversies with the Massachusetts Puritan establishment, Williams remained committed to Puritan orthodoxy, choosing to interpret conventional doctrines with such innovation that they spurred in him a dedication to religious liberty and, as a result, courageous professional and personal choices. The vector of his brief career in the Bay Colony illustrates both his commitment to the Puritan cause and the seriousness with which he took his role as teacher to the church.

"MR. WILLIAMS, A GODLY MINISTER"

Williams most likely was born in 1603 in England, although the precise year of his birth cannot be known for sure because the official record of it burned with St. Sepulchre's Church, the Church of England parish to which he belonged as a child. If the birth date accorded him is accurate, though, his beginnings coincided with the end of the Elizabethan age and the ascension of James I to the English throne. Evidently the growing hostility between Puritans and royalists so characteristic of James's reign—and reaching a flash point during that of his successor Charles I—affected young Roger, for before he was thirty Williams would exhibit the telltale signs that he had gone the separatists' ways.[1] Until that moment not much is known about his life, except that he was raised on Cow Lane in Smithfield, a river town bustling with the blessings and ills of commerce. His own father was a trader (likely in imported cloth), a proclivity that Roger would inherit and which would serve him well in his struggle to make a life in the New England wilderness. Smithfield probably offered to Williams a microcosm

3

of England's religious troubles, for on at least one occasion (and probably more) a Puritan zealot was burned at the stake within sight of Williams's childhood home.[2] Possibly as a result of his hometown exposure to Puritan-minded clergy, Williams evidently experienced as a child that famed conversion experience considered so necessary to Puritan piety, though his conversion to separatism would have to wait for an adult decision some years later.[3]

As a young man not yet twenty he had the good fortune to serve as apprentice and scribe to Sir Edward Coke, England's premier jurist. Accompanying Coke on his business with the Star Chamber, Williams likely had a front-row view of the persecution heaped on English Puritans. From Coke he also acquired the means to enter Pembroke College to study for the ministry in 1624 and, perhaps just as importantly, developed a facility with law and legal argumentation that would augment his theological training. In 1629 Williams finished at Cambridge and, as an indication that he had not yet owned up to the separatism that would characterize his entire New England career, he submitted to the oath of uniformity required of all men entering into the ranks of the Anglican clergy.[4]

Williams never took a parish position, though, opting instead to accept an invitation from Sir William Mashem of Essex to serve as estate chaplain, a move that may indicate that Williams's conscience already was troubled by separatist influences.[5] Williams's assignment to this ministerial post was not unusual for a young clergyman's first appointment, especially if he was committed to the Puritan cause. Puritan graduates of Cambridge often sought out appointments with sympathetic patrons, and Mashem definitely qualified as a Puritan sympathizer. The practice of hiding out within the estate of a sympathizer was soon to become much more difficult, as Archbishop Laud accelerated efforts to eliminate these positions that served as "seedbeds of Puritan dissent."[6] For the duration of his stay, however, Williams found the Mashem estate a safe haven from political reprisals.

While Essex protected Williams from persecution, it did not spare him from another species of suffering—romantic heartbreak. In his first year in Essex, Williams's matrimonial overtures to one Joan Whalley were spurned by her guardians, who thought him socially unworthy to marry into such an upstanding family. He recovered soon enough, however, and in December of 1629 he married Mary Barnard, the daughter of a minister and a handmaid in the Mashem estate. The year 1629 was undoubtedly an eventful one for Williams, with his graduation from Cambridge, the commencement of his relationship with Mashem (who would remain an influential friend during Williams's troubles in New England), and the beginning of his lifelong partnership with Mary Barnard. Additionally, that same year Williams seems to have made some important connections with influential Puritan leaders. With the ascension of Charles I to the throne and the elevation of William Laud to archbishop, the Puritans had been forced to rethink the future of their Christian ministries and ecclesial reformation in England. Many of the Puritans were contemplating a migration to New England in 1629, and Williams met John Winthrop, Thomas Hooker, and John Cotton (his eventual nemesis) at a meeting called in Lincolnshire to discuss just this possibility. Though he was not among the first group to venture to the New World, Williams was moved enough by this meeting to consider a voyage the following year. More interestingly, this same meeting alerted Winthrop and others to Williams's considerable skills as a minister and teacher, so that when he arrived in Massachusetts they enthusiastically welcomed him.

What did not happen at this meeting is just as remarkable, however: Winthrop, Cotton, and the others failed to pick up on Williams's separatist inclinations. Puritanism at the time of the Great Migration was divided into two main flavors, the separatists and a nonseparating variety. Both groups longed for reform and revival in the church, but while the nonseparating Puritans labored to bring that reform to bear in the Church of England, the separatists insisted that cleansing the church required the complete rejection of the Anglican institution. The Plymouth Colony had a particularly separatist hue, while the Massachusetts Bay leaders were overwhelmingly nonseparating Puritans, but the distinction between these two interpretations of the Puritan mission eventually was blurred by the relocation to America, when even the nonseparating Puritans were geographically, theologically, and practically independent of the mother church. Nonetheless the difference was important to the Puritans, for reasons having to do with both ecclesiology and practical politics. Separatists called for a complete renunciation of the Anglican Church—its worship, its rituals, and its jurisdiction. The nonseparating Puritans considered this theologically wrongheaded and politically dangerous, since a rejection of the English Church was effectively a slap in the face of the monarch. Both theologically and politically, Williams's separatism would be a thorn in the side of the Massachusetts establishment for decades.

At Lincolnshire, however, Williams's separatism went unnoticed. In these early conversations with Winthrop and Cotton, Williams may have revealed separatist sympathies, though not unambiguously enough to cause these same leaders to associate him with that plague when he arrived in New England. Nonetheless, it is safe to surmise that by the time Williams decided to make the voyage to the Massachusetts Bay Colony in 1630, he was indeed an avowed separatist.[7] John Winthrop and his companions on the *Arbella* left for New England in the spring of 1630. The Massachusetts settlers were ill prepared for the first American winter they encountered, and so Winthrop, faced with widespread starvation and disease in the colony, sent Captain William Peirce back to England for provisions. When it was fully loaded with reinforcements for the struggling New Englanders, Peirce's ship the *Lyon* set sail from Bristol in December 1630, bringing relief to the colonies as well as several additional emigrants, most notably Roger and Mary Williams.

When Roger and Mary disembarked in Massachusetts in February 1631, John Winthrop recorded in his journal nothing but a favorable welcome, noting that "Mr. Williams, a godly minister," and his wife had arrived in the colony.[8] Williams had already established a reputation as a respectable Puritan clergyman, and he was not long in Massachusetts before his positive standing prompted the offer of one of the most enviable positions in the colony, that of teacher at the Boston church. It was his response to this public acclamation that marked the beginning of his undoing in Massachusetts.

"NEW AND DANGEROUS OPINIONS"

In 1630 John Wilson, the teacher at the Boston church, advised his congregation that he wished to return to England to persuade his wife to join him in Massachusetts. His departure leaving a vacancy at the Boston church, the congregation in 1631 extended an invitation to Roger Williams to assume Wilson's role. Williams's response was certain and, one imagines, disconcerting to those who received it. Williams refused the position at Boston because the congregation had failed to separate itself from the apostate Church of England. Williams had declared himself publicly to be a separatist.

Williams's declaration began a rapid succession of debates and events that precipitated his banishment from the New England colony. At the basis of these controversies lay his disagreement with the New England leaders over the relationship between religious convictions and one's status as a civil citizen. After rejecting the Boston church's offer, Williams left for a position at the church in Salem, which was already suspected of separatist leanings. Evidently the congregation's radical inclinations were sufficiently stymied by its location in the Massachusetts Bay Colony that within the year Williams felt compelled to leave the colony entirely, relocating in Plymouth in August 1631. Plymouth openly espoused separatist ecclesiology and Williams expected to be more comfortable there, and indeed he was, until the contradictions between the colony's separatist commitment and the actions of its citizens began to disappoint him. In particular Williams was bothered by the fact that Plymouth church members often attended Anglican services while in the old country and then returned to their congregations in Plymouth uncensored. To Williams it was an abomination to worship in the impure English church and it violated the principles of separatism. He spoke out repeatedly against such inconsistencies; receiving no satisfaction on his protest, Williams resolved to leave Plymouth in 1633 to return to Massachusetts.

Besides the colony's unwillingness to follow Williams's extreme interpretation of separatism, the other major issue that led him to leave Plymouth and return to Salem was the discomfort he provoked in Plymouth (and soon in Massachusetts) over the question of land rights. While in the Plymouth Colony, Williams had a chance to become intimately acquainted with the local natives, at first through a trading enterprise he initiated with them to support himself, and eventually out of pure affection. Inspired by friendship and principle, Williams began to advocate publicly for the land rights of the Native Americans. Williams argued that the land that the English colonists now occupied did not belong to the king, and thus it was not his to give to the colonies. Instead, the land belonged to the Native Americans, and it was the Americans, argued Williams, with whom the English ought to barter and petition for the privilege to settle on it. The Americans themselves held the right to the land and the prerogative to disperse it to the English, for which they should be fairly and fully compensated. Williams's advocacy of the Americans' land rights evidently was included in the "strange opinions" that Plymouth governor William Bradford attributed to him when he wrote of Williams's souring relationship with his colony.[9] Not long after, his views on the subject would reach the Massachusetts leadership, but for now Williams resolved to leave Plymouth and return to Salem as their teacher.

In the two years he had been in New England, Williams's good reputation had deteriorated as a result of his controversial views on a spectrum of subjects, views that he could not seem to keep to himself, either in Salem or in Plymouth. Within months of his return to their colony, the Massachusetts General Court had taken official notice that Williams was again making waves from his position at Salem. His continued advocacy for the Americans' land rights deeply troubled the magistrates, mainly because it called into question the king's right to grant land in the New World and therefore put the health of the colonies at risk. Public support for Williams's objections would not only bait the crown into retaliating against the wayward colonies by reasserting royal power (which heretofore New England had been largely spared), it also threatened to strip them of the only political legitimacy that protected them from the terrorism of Laud and other enemies in old England. Royal prerogative over land in the English colonies provided the foundation for their charters, and the charters were the only guarantee the colonies possessed that they could continue their Puritan mission in New England unmolested.

Yet the question surrounding land grants was not the only political issue in which Williams found himself embroiled. In November of 1634, some residents of Salem desecrated the royal flag by cutting out the red cross that, they argued, originated with the pope and symbolized the polluted intermingling of things sacred and profane. Most likely Williams was in no way responsible for this particular event, but his separatist teachings were immediately blamed for it. He did not help his cause when he soon aggravated another sore spot, the requirement that all adult male residents take an oath of loyalty, sworn to God, as a condition of citizenship. Williams believed that an oath taken before God was a religious act, and therefore he rejected the use of oaths as profane political insurance of social stability. To require the oath was to prescribe an act of worship as an obligation of citizenship, an act of worship to which many citizens could not conscientiously assent. Williams, then, was concerned for both the scruples of those who could not abide by the religious presuppositions of the oath and (more importantly to him) the principles of those whose religiosity was troubled by being forced to participate in this sacred act in such a profane context. Williams therefore suggested that the oath be eliminated, a preposterous idea to most seventeenth-century Englishmen (especially the Puritans), for the oath was the guarantor of promise keeping. Social stability depended on the oath as a universally recognized promise that bound citizens and servants to their duty to respect the common good. Once again, Williams's objections constituted an attack on a key component to public order and safety and invited the wrath of royal and Laudian power on them.

Deeply troubled by Williams's views on these matters, and perhaps directed by residual irritation on the part of the influential but spurned Boston church, the Massachusetts General Court finally acted against Williams in 1635. That summer the Salem community petitioned the General Court for permission to annex nearby land, but their land grant was denied on the grounds that the Salem church had not sought the counsel of the colony's other churches in its decision to call Williams as teacher. Infuriated, both Williams and selected members of Salem church assaulted the Court with letters, insisting that Williams's call was not the business of the other churches, according to the strictures of Independency. But soon practical wisdom intervened, as both the church and Williams realized that Salem's future would require his dismissal, and so Williams resigned his position at the church. In the fall of 1635 the General Court ruled against his teachings and banished him from the colony.

Williams believed his banishment to be the consequence of the religious intolerance of the Massachusetts General Court and an inappropriate convolution of the colony's religious authorities and its political institutions. He was convinced that he was being persecuted politically on account of his separatist religious convictions. Certainly the Massachusetts magistrates understood the grounds for their sentence differently. In fact, in the official ruling that banished Williams from the Bay Colony, the question of religious separatism hardly factors. Instead, the General Court emphasizes the political ramifications of the views Williams espoused:

> Whereas Mr. Roger Williams, one of the elders of the church of Salem, hath broached and dyvulged dyvers newe and dangerous opinions, against the aucthoritie of magistrates, as also writt l[ett]res of defamacon, both of the magistrates & churches here, & that before andy conviccon, & yet maineteineth the same without retraccon, it is therefore ordered, that the said Mr. Williams shall dep[ar]te out of this jurisdiccon within six weekes nowe nexte ensueing, wch if he neglect to p[er]forme, it shalbe lawfull for the Govnr & two of the magistrates to send him to some place out of this jurisdiction, not to returne any more without licence from the Court.[10]

In disputing the king's right to charter the colonies, threatening political stability by rejecting oaths, and resisting the wide scope of civil authority, Williams's opinions transgressed into the realm of the seditious, at least in the eyes of the New England leaders. In risking the ire of the crown against the colony, Williams committed more than blasphemy; he endangered the health of the political state.

Williams believed, however, that the principal cause of his exile was religious intolerance in the Massachusetts Court, and as a result his banishment (and his interpretation of it) sparked a literary and political career dedicated to exploring a healthier relationship between public safety, civil order, and religious integrity. In early 1636 Williams left the Bay Colony by foot, traveling in the snow of winter past the southernmost boundaries of both Massachusetts and Plymouth. By the time summer arrived, Williams had made his way to the headwaters of Narragansett Bay. With a small band of loyal supporters, Williams here founded Providence, which, along with the other settlements that eventually would be chartered as Rhode Island and Providence Plantations, would host his lifelong experiment in trying to balance theological convictions with a peaceable and tolerant society.

THE BLOODY BATTLE OVER PERSECUTION

At first Providence consisted of little more than the Williams family and a few loyalists. Soon, however, the new settlement became known as a haven for others who were, as Williams believed he had been, "persecuted for conscience's sake." In fact, when its population grew to a number that suggested incorporation wise, the town of Providence codified this freedom as part of twelve "articles of agreement" adopted in 1640. The citizens pledged themselves, "as formerly hath been the liberties of the Town, so still to hold forth Liberty of Conscience."[11] It wasn't long until others were fleeing from Massachusetts to avail themselves of this liberty, and these immigrants had a profound effect on the emerging shape of the new colony. In 1637 Anne Hutchinson wore out her welcome in the Bay Colony by attracting too prominent a following to her antinomian theology. Banished from Massachusetts, Hutchinson and her considerable flock of some eighty households moved to the Narragansett in 1638, occupying the large island of Aquidneck (or Rhode Island) and establishing the town of Portsmouth on its northern end.[12] That same year Samuel Gorton was expelled from the Bay Colony for his rejection of all external authority (religious and civil) and his commitment to Quaker-like belief in the indwelling Spirit. He moved in with Hutchinson's gathering in Portsmouth, but soon he was at odds with them as well. After relocating to Providence, where he quickly managed to aggravate Williams and many of the other citizens, Gorton finally moved on to a piece of land south of Providence, where he helped found the town of Warwick. In 1639 John Clarke (the physician-theologian-turned-ambassador who would prove to be Williams's equal in his importance to the long-term stability of the colony) and others settled on the southern end of Aquidneck Island and formed the town of Newport. These four towns—Providence, Portsmouth, Warwick, and Newport —would eventually form the backbone of the colony of Rhode Island and Providence Plantations.

The towns of Rhode Island barely five years old, Williams soon found himself pressured to return to London to secure an official charter for the colony. Massachusetts and Connecticut were not happy that their problem children continued their wayward behavior just beyond orthodoxy's borders, and periodically the two colonies threatened to divide jurisdiction over the towns between themselves in order to reassert Puritan authority. For this reason, Williams agreed in 1643 to travel back to England to seek a charter from the appropriate commission of Parliament. Williams's journey to England from 1643 to 1644 was fortuitous not only for his Rhode Island contemporaries, but also for the eternal cause of conscience itself, because the return to London provided for the publication of his great treatise for toleration, *The Bloody Tenent of Persecution for Cause of Conscience.*

Soon after he had first arrived at Providence, Williams began to exchange letters with the eminent Puritan pastor John Cotton on the subject of religious toleration. Cotton, who already in England was considered one of the rising stars of the Puritan movement, had emigrated to Massachusetts in the summer of 1633 and quickly established himself as a respected voice in the religious and civic affairs of the colony.[13] Cotton had received the position at the Boston church that Williams had declined, and the natural prominence that came with that position thrust him into the midst of Williams's dispute with the Massachusetts leadership. Though the historical record suggests that Cotton actually tried to arbitrate between

Williams and the Court and avert his exile, Williams regarded Cotton as the driving force behind the General Court's decision to banish him, and thus his chief antagonist in Massachusetts.

This opinion led Williams to initiate an exchange of letters with Cotton, the subject being their disagreement over the issues that prompted Williams's banishment: separation, religious toleration, the relationship between the church and political government, and persecution. One of Cotton's letters in the exchange mysteriously found its way to the printer's press during Williams's stay in London (though Williams denied any complicity in its being made public) and was published in 1643. In it Cotton disavows responsibility for Williams's banishment and in fact argues that Williams exiled himself "from the fellowship of all the Churches" in Massachusetts by insisting on ecclesial separation.[14] He portrays Williams's ecclesiology as an extreme view based on faulty logic and erroneous biblical exegesis; Williams was wrong to assume that the Church of England was hopelessly defiled by "every sipping of the whores cup," and that the only recourse was for faithful Christians to abandon her for separated congregations.[15] By contrast Cotton characterizes his own position as "moderation," maintaining that "the Lord hath guided us [the Massachusetts church leaders] to walke with an even foote betweene two extreames; so that we neither defile our selves with the remnant of pollutions in other Churches, nor doe we for the remnant of pollutions renounce the Churches themselves, nor the holy ordinances of God amongst them, which our selves have found powerfull to our salvation."[16] He asserts with confidence that "the hidden hypocrisie of some will not prejudice the sinceritie and faithfulnesse of others, nor the Church estate of all," and considered it bad theology for Williams to assume otherwise. Finally he openly laments that Williams sabotaged his own ministry in the Bay Colony and in Plymouth in order "to helpe erring though zealous soules against the mighty Ordinances of the Lord" in a crusade against the church.[17]

As soon as Cotton's letter suspiciously leapt from the printer's press in London in 1643, Williams published his line-by-line response, titled *Mr. Cotton's Letter Lately Printed, Examined and Answered*. Claiming to "question not his holy and loving intentions and affections," Williams nevertheless blamed Cotton for instigating his banishment and castigated him for his misrepresentation of the causes behind that exile. He accused Cotton of doublespeak, pleading, "it is no wonder that so many, having been demanded the cause of my sufferings, have answered that they could not tell for what, since Mr. Cotton himself knows not distinctly what cause to align."[18] Cotton claimed that Williams's banishment was a civil sentence imposed for civil reasons, but Williams insisted that he had been politically punished for religious differences. In his letter to Williams, for instance, Cotton unwisely characterized the exile as Williams's self-directed separation from the "society of the Churches" in Massachusetts. Williams seized upon this conflation of the civil and the religious, asking,

> Why should [Cotton] call this a banishment from the Churches, except he silently confesse, that the frame or constitution of their Churches is but implicitly National (which yet they professe against); for otherwise why was I not yet permitted to live in this world, or Commonweale, except for this reason, that the Commonweale and Church is yet but one, and he that is banished from the one, must necessarily be banished from the other also.[19]

Cotton's slip proved, Williams argued, that the reasons behind his civil punishment were religious, and that he rightly understood himself as a victim of the intolerance of a political system that conflated civil and religious interests. Cotton was to blame for this ethos of intolerance, continued Williams, for from the most prominent pulpit in the colony "he publicly taught . . . that body-killing, soule-killing, and State-killing doctrine of not permitting, but persecuting, all other consciences and wayes of worship but his own in the civill State."[20] Furthermore, Williams claimed to have reliable evidence that Cotton, who insisted that he did not have a say in the matter, directly counseled those who were responsible for Williams's banishment.

Williams then launched into a detailed defense of his commitment to ecclesiological separatism, peppering that argument with a principled rejection of religious persecution on religious and moral grounds. Most of *Mr. Cotton's Letter, Examined and Answered* responds to Cotton's rejection of separatism, but Williams believed that the issues of ecclesial separatism and religious persecution were related, if for no other reason than, to his mind, the Massachusetts *civil* government had punished him for his separatist *religious* views. His weave of arguments for separatism and against religious persecution aimed to protect the church from both the infiltration of unregenerate sinners and the encroachment of political authority on the interests of the religious sphere. Cotton considered it "butcherie" to threaten the health of the church with the schism Williams represented, "but if he call that butcherie, conscientiously and peaceably to separate from a spiritual communion of a Church or society," railed Williams, "what shall it be called . . . to cut off persons, them and theirs, branch and root, from any civill being in their territories, and consequently from the whole world . . . because their consciences dare not bow down to any worship, but what they believe the Lord Jesus appointed, and being also otherwise subject to the civill state and Laws thereof."[21] To Williams's mind, religious persecution was morally and theologically abominable, and his debate with Cotton over separatism gave him a platform to begin pressing the equally noble cause of conscience.

This argument for religious tolerance, while presented in piecemeal fashion in the pages of *Mr. Cotton's Letter, Examined and Answered*, would be developed with great detail in Williams's sequel work. With the unauthorized publication of his letter and the appearance of Williams's reply, Cotton himself ripped off an incensed rebuttal, to which Williams in turn felt compelled to respond. The result was Williams's classic apology for toleration, *The Bloody Tenent of Persecution for Cause of Conscience*, published in 1644.

Written as a dialogue between Truth and Peace, *The Bloody Tenent* makes a case for religious toleration by addressing, in excruciating detail, the points Cotton raised in the last salvo in this war of words. Refuting the premise of Cotton's argument for enforced religious uniformity, Williams argued that persecution guarantees neither the conversion of the individual nor the greater civil peace. Rather than converting, said Williams, persecution more often reifies an individual conscience against the opinions of its oppressor, and to try to change a person's conscientious convictions by force constitutes "soul rape." Furthermore, the lack of religious uniformity does not automatically result in civil chaos: "The worship which a State professeth may be contradicted and preached against, and yet no breach of Civill Peace."[22] In fact, argued Williams, a "breach of Civill Peace" is more likely from "that wrong and preposterous way of suppressing, preventing, and extinguishing such doctrines or practices by weapons of wrath and blood."[23] In other words, the employment of persecution as a means of protecting the integrity of faith and tranquility in the social order accomplishes neither, and instead contradicts the evidence of history, experience, and common sense.

If Williams removed the basis in empirical fact from Cotton's defense of enforced religious uniformity by arguing that it does not succeed in converting citizens to faith, he also struck at the heart of the defense by insisting that persecution is contrary to the gospel. "Those Churches cannot be truly Christian," according to Williams, "which either actually themselves, or by the Civill power of Kings and Princes given to them . . . doe persecute such as different from them or be opposite against them."[24] Taking it upon himself to sort the "perplexed and raveled" arguments in Cotton's biblical interpretation, in which "so many things and so doubtfull are wrapt up and intangled together," Williams argued in his own "intangled" prose that persecution violates the spirit of Jesus and the pattern of the early church.[25] In fact, persecution is so contrary to Christian tradition that "if the civill Magistrates be Christians, or members of the Church, able to prophesie in the Church of Christ, then . . . they are bound by this command of Christ to suffer opposition to their doctrine, with meeknesse and gentlenesse, and to be so farre from striving to subdue their opposites with the civill sword, that they are bound with patience and meeknesse to wait if God peradventure will please to grant repentance unto their opposites."[26] Cotton was "directly contradicting the spirit and minde and practice of the Prince of Peace" to attest otherwise. More to the point, in defending persecution in the name of Christianity, Cotton was guilty of perpetuating the substitution of a "bloody tenent" for the true gospel message of peace, and thus by extension was "so deeply guilty of the blood of soules compelled and forced to Hypocrisy in a spiritual and soule rape; so deeply guilty of the blood of the Soules under the Altar, persecuted in all ages for the cause of Conscience, and so destructive to the civill peace and welfare of all Kingdomes, Countries, and Commonwealthes."[27]

The testimony of experience corresponded with the witness of the gospel, to Williams's mind: toleration begets peace, while religious persecution brings violence and instability to the social order. Therefore, he insisted, if non-Christians challenged the peace and welfare of the civil states by offending civil laws, they should be punished, but with regard to the differences in religious conviction they should be tolerated, for only an atmosphere of religious liberty respected both the nature of the human conscience and the spirit of Jesus Christ. *The Bloody Tenent* was published in London in 1644, along with Williams's anonymous contribution to the English Parliament's parallel debate over toleration.[28] The overture to Williams's symphony for religious liberty had been performed.

ROGER WILLIAMS THE THEOLOGIAN

Despite the fact that relatively few scholars have elected to read him this way, it is clear from his dependence on biblical interpretation and theological imagination that Williams considered his struggle for religious freedom in America to be primarily a theological debate. That is, what was at stake for Williams was a religious understanding of the responsibilities of magistrates and ministers, the nature of belief and conversion, and the foundational tenets of a stable society. While a number of influential students of his thought have insisted, contrary to the evidence, that Williams's Puritan religious background lent little influence to the development of his moral positions, an accurate understanding of Williams's thought actually requires that he be considered a moral theologian whose religious presuppositions to a large extent determined his ethical conclusions. Those presuppositions stemmed from a variety of the English Puritanism he shared with his Massachusetts colleagues and opponents; in other words, Roger Williams was a Reformed theologian, in the tradition of John Calvin, Theodore Beza, William Ames, and John Cotton himself.

Far from being a relativist, Williams believed that Christianity—specifically the Protestantism of Calvin, Beza, and Ames—was true and that other religions were false.[29] As Timothy L. Hall explains, Williams enjoyed a certain "confidence in his ability to discern spiritual truth," and this confidence in his faith propelled him to seek religious separation from those he considered to be in error. Williams maintained a respect, even an admiration, for the loyalty to conscience of other religious persons, and he argued for their liberty to pursue their religious beliefs without harassment. But he argued for this civil toleration in spite of his personal conviction that most of the varieties of religions surrounding him were doomed to damnation.[30] Despite his unshakable defense of its adherents' religious liberties, for instance, Williams rejected Catholic Christianity as erroneous and deceptive. He shared the convictions of his Puritan colleagues that the pope was the servant of the devil, that Catholic liturgical practices were idolatrous, and that Catholic belief was wrought with error and fiction. Williams exhibited similar disregard for Islam. Unlike John Locke, Williams was never willing to restrict the religious freedom of Muslims or Catholics, but his defense of their civil liberties did not constitute an endorsement of their religious beliefs.[31] Williams was confident his Puritan faith would render him among those who "raigne with [Christ], eternally admire him, and enjoy him, when he shortly comes in flaming fire to burne up millions of ignorant and disobedient."[32] He was just as confident that Catholics and Muslims, as well as thousands of unsuspecting Anglicans, were destined to be among those "millions" far less fortunate.

No clearer example of the theological impatience that Williams sometimes exhibited toward other religious beliefs exists than his frustration with the Quakers. A detailed account of Williams's run-in with the Quakers must wait for a later chapter, but suffice it here to say that Williams had very little stomach for the inner spirituality and religious deviance of the devotees of George Fox. In his treatise disrespectfully titled *George Fox Digged from His Burroughs* and published late in his life, Williams refuted nearly every major theological tenet of the Quakers, point by point.[33] Ironically, instead of serving as an example of the seriousness with which Williams held his theological convictions, his debates with the Quakers are often assumed to represent the philosophical backsliding of an old man worn out by those who dared take advantage of his defense of tolerance.[34] At no time in his arguments, however, did Williams suggest that the Quakers ought to be disqualified from religious liberty simply because they were heterodox.[35] In fact, the vehemence with which he debated them only illustrates his unwillingness to deny them "soul-freedom"; that is, Williams felt such a need to argue with the Quakers because debate (and not civil restraint) was the only justifiable way to counter their theological error. The point of his diatribes was to make clear that the Quakers were theologically mistaken in their beliefs and dangerous to the integrity of Christian teaching. While he granted their right to religious liberty, Williams utterly rejected the beliefs they would freely exercise.

Scholars also frequently cite Williams's relationship with his Native American friends as evidence that Williams was a religious relativist, possessing so little regard for Puritan theological convictions that he could befriend the "heathen" Americans with little obstacle. To argue this conclusion from his association with the Americans is to misunderstand the basis of his friendship with them. Williams was able to befriend the Narragansetts out of a respect for their shared humanity (a dimension to his theology whose importance we will consider in later chapters), not by an implicit endorsement of their religious beliefs. Although he shared remarkable fellowship with the Narragansett and other Native American tribes, Williams actually disapproved of their religion and frequently removed himself from their presence when they engaged in religious practices. To him the "paganish worship" of the Native Americans "cannot be denied to be a worshipping of Devils, as all false Worship is."[36] Elsewhere he indicated in certain terms that he rejected the religious practices of the Narragansetts:

> I confess to have [i.e., to know about] most of these customs by their owne Relation, for after once being in their Houses and beholding what their Worship was, I durst never bee an eye witnesse, Spectatour, or looker on, least I should have been partaker of Sathans Inventions and Worships.[37]

Williams's affection for his American friends is all the more remarkable when it is considered against his unwavering condemnation of their religious beliefs and practices.

Of course, in the attempt to recover the importance of Williams's religiosity to his moral thought, we do risk overstating his rejection of both Quaker spirituality and Native American religious practice, and my intention is not to portray Williams as an unrelenting religious bigot. Williams was no relativist, it is true, for he enjoyed clear confidence in the truth of his Christian convictions, sometimes to the point of disdain for alternative religious experiences. Yet Williams was theologically humble enough (itself, at times, a Calvinist trait) to realize the dangers in claiming to know too much. He did not claim that his religious tradition had all the answers, and, in fact, he blamed the intolerance of others within his Puritan caucus on their unwillingness to recognize the limits to human knowledge, even theological knowledge.[38] Williams would not entrust the compulsion of "true religion" to the coercive power of the state precisely because he admitted that the ability of any person or group to know with certainty the things of God was seriously limited, and he included himself within the bounds of this epistemological modesty.[39]

Nonetheless, even if Reformed Christians could not always be sure they understood correctly, Williams believed that his theological perspective was the most accurate formulation of true Christian faith, and he based his arguments for religious liberty in the truth of these theological convictions. He insisted that his arguments for toleration were based in Christian conviction, and not simply in international conventions or simple pragmatism.[40] He invoked theological reasons, and he was fond of citing the church fathers as authorities for his arguments.[41] To Williams the justification for religious liberty did not rest in the confession that all religions were ultimately the same, but instead largely in the requirements of the one religion he believed to be true.

ROGER WILLIAMS THE PURITAN

Clearly, then, Williams was a religious thinker, but even this does not say enough, for the religious convictions that informed Williams's moral thought were the product of a specific tradition. "In the area of theological doctrine Williams was a sound, one may even say a conventional, Calvinist."[42] The evidence confirms that Williams was a Reformed Christian theologian, even though he is seldom recognized as part of this tradition. For example, Roger Williams does not receive even an entry in the otherwise comprehensive *Encyclopedia of the Reformed Faith*.[43] In fact, among scholars who otherwise recognize Williams's religiosity, the tendency has been to interpret it by *contrasting* it to Puritanism, rather than by considering him a product of the Reformed tradition.[44]

Despite the lack of recognition, though, Williams's moral theology was based in a religious perspective heavily dependent on the thought of John Calvin, and in this way Williams was at home among his fellow Puritans. Perry Miller helpfully reminds us that at this early stage in the Calvinist tradition, Calvin himself was hardly elevated to the role of theological demagogue.[45] The Puritans considered themselves first and foremost adherents to Scripture, not to a solitary theological figure, and they were unafraid to differ and dispute with Calvin's interpretation of the Bible. As biblical exegetes, the Puritans understood themselves to be part of an interpretive school that included, but was not exhausted by, Calvin. At the same time, the Puritans respected Calvin and adhered to the theological framework they inherited from him, to a greater extent than Miller's characteristic hyperbole suggests. Calvin was more than an afterthought in this budding theological tradition, which valued consistency with him and his disciples in biblical interpretation even if it refused to crown a theological ancestor as its primary loyalty. The Puritans recognized their indebtedness to teachers closer to their generation, like William Perkins and William Ames, and this fact, along with their Protestant penchant for deferring to the counsel of a cloud of witnesses rather than single authorities, led them to regard Calvin as one among many theological divines. But among the many, Calvin was regarded as the pioneering force behind their Reformed faith. Despite Miller's convenient invocation of Thomas Shepard's well-known line—"I have forgot what he [Calvin] hath wrote and myself have read long since out of him"[46]—Puritan theological exegesis frequently invoked Calvin with special authority, alongside Theodore Beza, Perkins, and Ames.

Given his employment of thinkers before him, Williams clearly considered himself a faithful member of the Calvinist theological tradition. He often cited Calvin, as well as others in the Reformed tradition like Beza and John Owen, as an integral part of his moral argument.[47] In his extended discussion of Romans 13, for example, Williams took a text often invoked by the defenders of religious compulsion and used it to argue for the opposite position, justifying his interpretation in part by reference to Calvin's use of the same text. Quoting extensively from Calvin's commentary on Romans, Williams interpreted the Genevan to restrict the scope of Romans 13 to matters of the second table of the law. Insisting that Paul's imperative to civil obedience applies only to social interaction (i.e., relationships between persons in community) and not to religious belief and practice, Williams claimed that he was only agreeing with Calvin, and to further ground his interpretation in the tradition, he also invoked Beza.[48] Additional proof of Williams's affinity with Calvinism is found in the preface of *The Bloody Tenent*, where he declares the objective of that entire book to be a presentation against religious intolerance that is informed not only by Scripture but also by the stalwarts of the Reformed tradition—a list of heavy hitters that featured Calvin and Beza, of course, but that also included John Cotton![49]

Sometimes Williams included the arguments of his Reformed teachers in his own not for support but to assume a critical stance against them, but even this interaction with the tradition indicates his affinity with it. In developing his interpretation of the parable of the Wheat and Tares (one of his favorite biblical references) as an argument against civil persecution of religious dissenters, for instance, Williams admitted that his reading of the biblical story contradicted not only Cotton's but also that of Calvin and Beza.[50] Similarly, when Williams used Calvin's interpretation of Romans 13 against Cotton, he implicitly argued against Calvin's much different stance regarding the relationship between magisterial authority and religious purity in the *Institutes*. One of the central arguments to Cotton's position, that religious diversity is necessarily injurious to the civil order and thus is fair game for civil restriction, was an argument that Calvin also made in his discussion of civil government in the final chapter of the *Institutes*. Calvin emphasized that part of the "appointed end" of civil government was "to cherish and protect the outward worship of God, to defend sound doctrine of piety and the position of the church." To do so was for government to discharge part of its social duty, preventing "idolatry, sacrilege against God's name, blasphemies against his truth, and other public offenses against religion from arising and spreading among the people" and threatening the social order.[51] Cotton ostensibly had adopted Calvin's argument, so that Williams's refutation of Cotton on the question of the social threat of religious dissension was an indirect rejection of Calvin's position, too. Regardless of whether he invoked them to support his position or to critically deconstruct theirs, however, Williams's use of his Reformed predecessors testifies to the fact that Williams recognized them as authorities in the tradition he considered his own.

Williams's affinity with the Reformed tradition is clear not only from his invocation of the authorities of that tradition, but also from the theological dogma he inherited from them and which informs his moral thought. Williams clearly stated his belief in the traditional doctrines of Calvinist Protestantism, including the Trinitarian conception of God, the dual natures of Christ, the reality of original sin, the necessity of grace, the promise of resurrection, and the surety of final judgment.[52] Much of Williams's disagreement with the Quakers revolved around his commitment to these conventional Reformed doctrines and the authority of Scripture, in the face of the Quakers' theological reinterpretations and appeals to the primacy of personal spiritual experience. In addition, several of the points of contention between Cotton and Williams were over the precise interpretation or application of Calvinist tenets of belief. They both accepted as true many of the same doctrinal points, but they interpreted their moral significance for the matter of religious liberty in radically different ways.

The Calvinist doctrine of saintly perseverance is one example of a theological value that Williams shared with Cotton but that generated much different conclusions in Williams's moral thought. Cotton claimed that religious error is dangerous to the spiritual health of the church, and therefore to allow dissenters free civil rein was to put the righteous at spiritual risk. Williams countered by reminding Cotton of the persevering effect of God's grace upon the elect. Cotton's fear, argued Williams, contradicted what the Puritans had long taught, that no human effort can undo the effects of saving grace on God's chosen ones. Salvation is a gift from God to which heresy is no threat, and thus the truly saved have no reason for concern from the propagators of religious error.[53] According to Williams, then, to defend religious persecution in the name of preserving the faith of the chosen makes little sense from a Calvinist point of view.

Similarly, the theological priority perhaps most characteristic of classical Calvinist thought, an emphasis on God's soteriological sovereignty and sufficiency, supported his argument for religious toleration. Williams demonstrated his commitment to the doctrine of *sola gratia* in his debates with the Quakers, when he objected to their doctrine of an "inner light" in part because it seemed to him to contradict the human need for extraordinary grace. For Williams "it was not what man had within him already, and brought into this world with him" that caused the life-altering conversion to faith and true moral goodness, "but the Spirit of God accompanying and blessing the Reading and Hearing of the writings of God preached and opened." In language that Calvin surely would have approved, Williams insisted that "the Heart of man was shut up lockt and barr'd up in willing Ignorance and darkness until the finger of God . . . pick[ed] open . . . the Soul and Spirit of man."[54] This Calvinist emphasis on the priority of grace provided Williams with another argument against religious persecution, when he reminded his fellow Puritans that, from a Calvinist point of view, religious compulsion is pointless, because belief is a phenomenon subject to God's grace, power, and timetable alone. Only God can instill true belief in a human mind and heart, argued Williams. Saving faith is a gift from God given only at God's discretion, and thus religious compulsion does not benefit either the elect or the unregenerate.[55]

Williams's high regard for Scripture, which made him a true child of the Reformation, also influenced his moral arguments. With language that directly mirrors the opening passages of Calvin's *Institutes*, Williams declared that the Bible for him was "the square Rule or Guide according to whose sentence all the Knowledge of God and of our selves . . . [is] to be determined."[56] For Williams Scripture was the primary authority for human knowledge, including moral knowledge. He shared this deference to Scripture with the other Calvinists of his Puritan society, so that the debate between him and John Cotton revolved around not whether the Bible was authoritative in matters of religious tolerance, but only how to interpret it. Respect for scriptural authority also distinguished Williams from his Quaker adversaries, for he counted among the most important topics of their debate the fact that the Quakers subordinated the guidance of Scripture to the movements of individual spiritual experience:

> Either we must subscribe to the Papists and by their pretended Spirit and Church find out and authorize the Scriptures, just as the Foxians say, or else we must with Luther and his Associates, Calvin and his followers maintain Learning [and] study the Scriptures, search the Originals, Copeyes and Translations, and vindicate their Purity and Perfection, their Authority and sole external Direction how to judge of all pretending Christs and Prophets and Doctrines & Churches and Spirits.[57]

Williams considered loyalty to the Bible an inheritance from the tradition of Luther and Calvin and a significant point of contention with the Quakers, but his regard for Scripture also affected his moral disagreements with Cotton and the defenders of religious uniformity.

A careful reading of Williams's treatises, then, reveals that he should be regarded principally as a Reformed theologian, for his ethics is couched in a broad theological framework formed by the Reformed tradition of which he was a part. To argue that Williams operated from a theological perspective, and often defended his moral positions with explicitly theological arguments, does not imply that Williams's attitudes toward religious liberty originated exclusively from direct revelation. As we shall see in subsequent chapters, Williams's theological orientation permitted him to appeal to a number of sources for moral insight, including practical reason and the precedents of human experience. But the larger framework in which Williams understood and interpreted these sources of insight was a perspective grounded in Reformed theology. Rather than dismissing or dissolving it, Williams took this religious perspective for granted and employed it to construct moral arguments that could appeal ultimately to Christians and non-Christians alike.

2

INCARNATIONAL THEOLOGY AND RELIGIOUS FREEDOM

The last chapter labored to show, through historical narrative and theological evidence, that Roger Williams rightly merits regard as an important theologian of the Reformed tradition. Rather than in a convenient pragmatism or uncommitted relativism, his teachings on religious freedom and church and state were rooted in the sources and substance of Reformed theology. Among those few attentive souls who have recognized the Calvinism that informs Williams's thought, several have identified specific doctrinal components of that Puritanism as more influential than others on his political conclusions. Perry Miller insisted that Williams and his fellow Puritans differed on the grounds of biblical hermeneutics, while Edmund Morgan argued that Williams developed from common Puritan tenets a distinctive ecclesiology that alienated him from orthodox Puritans but encouraged his pursuit of religious liberty. More recently, W. Clark Gilpin has suggested that in his eschatology Williams represents a radical innovation of conventional Calvinism.[1] The real focus of Williams's moral theology, however, lies at an even more fundamental level than any of these doctrinal details. What oriented Williams's appeal to the Bible, conception of the church, and eschatological vision was a prior preoccupation with the person of Christ, as both pattern for moral living and divine enabler of the Christian life. More specifically still, beneath Williams's ecclesiology, eschatology, and scriptural interpretation lay an incarnational piety from which he developed his more extended theological and moral claims.

INCARNATION AND SOCIAL COVENANT

What is regarded as a christocentric ethics can take a variety of broad forms. Christocentric ethics may mean, for instance, a theological ethics whose direction is somehow determined by the acknowledgment of Jesus Christ as the modifier of a divine act or attitude toward humankind. Jesus Christ is the "event" in which God reveals God's true disposition and intentions toward human beings. The moral life determined by this christological event, then, may be one concentrated around response to or emulation of that divine disposition. Gratitude, obligation, or an appeal to a "humanizing" spirit may all be the central themes of this type of christocentric piety. The risk to which event christology is especially susceptible, of course, is an overly metaphysical explanation that does not adequately account for the fact that the Christian tradition has regarded Christ not only as divine event but also as historical person. In its focus on metaphysical claims at the expense of the humanness of Christ, event christology may too easily dissolve into a theoretical mechanism for broader philosophical concepts, losing touch with the concrete particularities of the Christian confession.

An alternative approach to christocentric piety regards Christ less as a metaphysical event than as Jesus of Nazareth, the person through whom God provides the normative moral pattern for the Christian community. Christocentric ethics that take seriously the normative pattern contained in Jesus' life and death have enjoyed something of a renaissance in contemporary Christian moral thought. Often employing a narrative ethical approach, "Jesus ethics" argue that Christian moral decision making ought to center on the life pattern offered in the story of Jesus. The Gospels provide first and foremost the story of a person whose character of living and way of dying establish a precedent for moral living for those who would choose to follow him as disciples. This attention to Jesus' life and death as a pattern for Christian discipleship encourages the development of certain virtues and character traits for living and deciding morally. A common problem among contemporary proposals for Jesus ethics, however, is an uncritical selectivity in choosing what is considered normative from the Gospel narratives and larger canonical authorities. Priority awarded to the Gospel narratives over the remainder of Scripture, or the selection of some aspects of the Gospel narrative as more ethically determinative than others, are choices that require explicit (though seldom provided) justification.[2]

By contrast to many contemporary proposals, Williams offered a christological perspective that balanced an attention to the life of Jesus as pattern for moral living with an appreciation for the determinative authority of the more Chalcedonian (or event-oriented) dimensions to Christian teaching on the person of Christ. He was able to maintain this balance because he considered the significance of Christ to the moral life chiefly through the concept of *incarnation*. To Williams, the incarnation of Christ was vital to a proper understanding of the moral life from a Christian perspective. As a conventional Puritan, Williams subscribed to a traditional Reformed substitutionary theory of atonement in soteriological matters, and for this reason the incarnation, the belief that God became human in order to reconcile humanity to God, was an important part of his theology. When he was considering the moral life, however, the incarnation took on even more significance. Not only did the incarnation represent the vehicle by which God chose to impart saving grace to human beings, but it also indicated the nature of the covenant God was initiating with the church and personified God's expectations for human living within that covenant. In other words, the incarnation was vital to Williams's theology because it simultaneously represented God's moral standard and the graceful way God chose to enable the church to pursue that standard.

Williams indicated the importance of the incarnation to his moral theology in his verbal duels with the Quakers, where he rejected his adversaries' notion of a divine "inner light" that exists in every person. Williams insisted that the Quaker theology of inner light denied the historical birth, death, and resurrection of Christ, and by extension human beings' dependence on those events for saving grace.[3] Humanity required the death and resurrection of Jesus in order to be freed from sin, assured of salvation, and empowered to pursue lives of righteousness. Lacking a commitment to these historical doctrines, he argued, the Quakers were guilty of hiding behind this inner light an inordinate confidence in human beings to chart their own salvation. Williams also rejected the Quakers' theology of immanence because of its implications for the substance of Christian morality. To Williams, identifying the Quaker inner light with Christ threatened to dissolve Christianity into nothing more than a nebulous spirituality, denying the reality of Christ's human life and his importance as an authoritative moral precedent. The Quakers' compromise of the incarnation, argued Williams, threatened to undermine the moral pattern God provided in Christ's life and led directly to the antinomian character of their religion he so vigorously opposed.[4] From Williams's perspective, Quaker theology lacked a commitment to the historical events of Jesus' life that underwrote both the assurances of justification and the possibilities of sanctification.[5]

The incarnation was also a central issue at the heart of Williams's disagreement with John Cotton. Both men insisted that the incarnation was vital to understanding Christian theology and morality, but they understood the doctrine's significance for morality very differently. For Williams, the incarnation was the starting point for both Christian theology and Christian morality, because in the person of Christ, God had initiated a relationship with God's chosen people that was starkly dissimilar to the divine relationship with Israel prior to Christ's birth. The incarnation was therefore the lens through which Williams understood all theological, and moral, formulations. The incarnation marked the conceptual beginning of the Christian moral life because it symbolized not only God's intentions for the new covenant Christ represented but also God's expectations for human response. The life of the incarnate Christ established the moral precedent that was normative for all those who would count themselves among his disciples.

Williams regarded Jesus Christ as "holynesse it selfe," "the first Patterne" for moral living.[6] Asking, then, what Jesus would do in a similar situation was a legitimate tactic for Christian morality.[7] Jesus was the Prince of Peace who commended his religious perspective without appeal to violence, and thus the resort to force to advance the claims of Christianity was "so directly contradicting the spirit and minde and practice" of Christ that it was out of bounds.[8] Jesus pronounced blessings on the peacemakers and the persecuted, so that those who "kindle . . . the Fires of persecutions and hunting of Christ's Saints, the Fires of devouring Wars amongst the Nations" on religion's behalf would find themselves "neer to a curse" in God's eyes.[9] "[L]et the Inhabitants of the World judge which come nearest to the doctrine, holiness, povertie, patience, and practice of the Lord Jesus Christ," Williams challenged, confident that an appeal to Jesus' life and practice would render any insistence on religious compulsion unlawful by his moral precedent. In Williams's moral theology, the pattern of the incarnate Christ framed the moral obligations and expectations of Christian truth.

Besides a specific moral pattern for living, however, Williams also read the incarnate Christ as an endorsement of the moral enterprise in general, God's assurance that human beings possess the capacity for embarking on the endeavor to live an upright moral life. The incarnation is in part an indication that God considers the state of being human good, and thus fundamental aspects of being human are not to be rejected but embraced with gratitude. For Williams, the moral aspects of human living and the God-given moral faculties are among these good gifts of human existence. This incarnational approach allowed Williams to endorse moral capacities he observed at work in all human beings and to claim them as gifts of God, which in turn allowed him to expand the sources of insight to which his moral theology could appeal. As later chapters will show, Williams's Christian approach to moral living was based not only on direct revelation, but also in the inherent moral faculties of conscience and reason, and in these latter concepts lay the possibilities he envisioned for moral dialogue and cooperative projects with nonbelievers. Williams was able to claim these components of human morality as Christian resources through his theology of incarnation, in which God declared the "experiment" of human living—including the moral enterprise—to be good.

The incarnation is important to Williams's moral theology, therefore, because it provides a moral precedent for emulation (in the life of Christ) and because it endorses the normal human capacities for moral decision making and character building. In different ways, both of these contributions to Williams's moral theology stem from a focus on the person of Jesus of Nazareth. Yet his christology was thoroughly Chalcedonian in the sense that he acknowledged the implications of the Christ event as equally significant to Christian morality. In the event of the incarnation, God established the parameters and meaning of God's relationship with human beings, which led Williams to award the incarnation (and not the crucifixion or resurrection) principal attention in his moral theology. For Williams, the incarnation not only provided the standard for behavior expected of human beings in relationship with God, but also established the cosmic covenant in which human morality is understood and receives meaning.

As Jesper Rosenmeier has argued, Cotton and Williams debated one another from a common acceptance of incarnation as integral to understanding Christian morality, but their contrasting interpretations of the doctrine led to irreconcilable differences. According to Cotton, the incarnation of Christ was the most direct manifestation of the covenant of grace that God had established with God's chosen people from the beginning of history. In this sense, the relationship God had with the Israelites was ostensibly the same relationship God now confirmed with the church. Understanding the incarnation to confirm continuity in the divine relationship from Israel to the church through to the present, Cotton also interpreted the doctrine to endorse continuity in the details, using the social, political, and religious arrangements of the Old Testament as authoritative pretexts for similar arrangements in New England. He justified the Puritan conventions for church-state relations, for instance, by appealing to parallels in the stories of Israel, including the civil defense of religious purity. He was able to do so because he believed them to be details of a relationship between God and human beings that had remained the same since Israel's day. Just as God had ordained the symbiosis of religion and state authority in the covenant with Israel, so that arrangement remained ideal in the manifestation of the covenant under which the Puritans lived.

Cotton's conception of the incarnation allowed him to be cautiously optimistic about the prospects for a Christian society. He believed that the incarnation symbolized God's renewal and redemption of both the spiritual and earthly dimensions of human existence. The incarnate Christ was, in a sense, God's guarantee that human life once again had been made capable of goodness and that it was possible now to envision human beings, with God's help, striving toward a Christian society. Because human life had been renewed in the image of Christ's new humanity, through the institutions of religion and public law individuals could be led to participate constructively in the building of the kingdom of God.[10] This social goal was possible, however, only if citizens and civil practices were moved to increasing conformity with the dictates of Christian religion. Thus the possibilities to which the incarnation hinted became for Cotton a mandate to usher in the righteous kingdom, through the public standardization of Christian belief and practice. In fact, for Cotton the gospel of the incarnation not only promised the gradual redemption of the world, but also required faithful individuals and Christian society to labor for its completion.

Williams shared neither the sense of covenantal continuity nor the confidence that Cotton found in his understanding of the incarnation. To Williams, too, the incarnation represented God's graceful intervention to save humanity from its own sinfulness, but it also symbolized a radical break in the *way* God related to the world, the moment when God changed the nature of the relationship between God and human beings. God's covenant with the church was now of a completely different form than the one God had established with Israel. Formerly God had singled out one political entity with whom to hold covenant, endorsing an integration of earthly and spiritual methods and priorities to characterize and regulate that covenant. With the advent of Christ, however, the political manifestation of an elect people was replaced with a covenanted community that was spiritual in nature. Associated with no single nation or culture, the church regulated its membership by spiritual recourse only and relied on the persuasive powers of "scattered witnesses" or evangelists to propagate the Christian message. The disassociation of ecclesial and civil power that Williams believed characterized history after the incarnation reflected the fact that "the nature of Christian life until the millennium was implacable opposition between Christ and the world."[11]

For Williams, the incarnation set the ways of God and the habits of the world in radical opposition. In contrast to the violent manipulation of conventional political power, Christ, whom Williams called "the best Politician that ever the world saw," embodied the hope for a peaceful society insofar as he was "not delighted with the blood of men (but shed his owne for his bloodiest enemies)."[12] In his selfless disposition, nonviolent lifestyle, and sacrificial death, Christ established the dichotomy between his way and the world's and commissioned the church to separate itself from worldly convention and adhere to his spiritual vision. Where the world operated from violence, physical coercion, and restraint, the community of the incarnate Christ would employ only spiritual means of persuasion and discipline. The normal powers and means of civil government had no place in the preservation and propagation of the Christian religion, for "there is not a Title in the New Testament of Christ Jesus that commits the Forming or Reforming of his Spouse and Church to the civill and worldly Powers."[13] For Williams, the incarnate Christ embodied the radical opposition between worldly expectations and Christian values, in contrast to the collusion of civil and spiritual powers Cotton openly advocated.

The locus of their difference was in Williams's interpretation of the Old Testament covenant as only a foreshadowing of the new relationship between God and the church, a new covenant that was notably different from its precursor. Where the Hebrew covenant permitted violent maintenance and endorsed the cooperation of religious and political power, the new covenant established in Christ was characterized by peace and the avoidance of civil maintenance. In fact, Williams claimed that the New England churches, far from remaining faithful to the requirements of God's covenant as Cotton supposed them to be, were traitors to God's intentions for the New Testament covenant as expressed in the incarnation of Christ. By collapsing the distinction between the body and the spirit, the religious establishment of the colonies transgressed the new ecclesial dispensation embodied in Christ's incarnation.

This radical dualism between what Williams metaphorically referred to as the body and the spirit did not lead him to an otherworldly rejection of human life. After all, he taught that one important lesson of the incarnation was its endorsement of the created nature of human existence, including the moral life. What Williams did reject, however, was the assignment of soteriological value to this created dimension. Instead, Williams drew a sharp distinction between the Christian community and those persons and institutions normally outside the church. Where Cotton maintained that God had redeemed the whole of life in the incarnation and subsequently utilized different institutions of human society for the gradual realization of the kingdom of God, Williams denied that social and political structures were at all soteriologically useful.[14] To Williams, God equips civil life to restrain evil and to establish a morality suitable for cohabitation and mutual flourishing, but civil existence and its institutions do not act as means for the theological redemption of society. While the incarnation held together a respect for worldly existence with a dedication to the spiritual, it also refused to mix the two. This separation compelled Williams to resist involvement in the furtherance of religious goals by social institutions outside the church. God's covenant endowed the civil realm with no obligations or authority of spiritual significance, and thus his incarnational dualism became one of the important axes around which Williams's arguments for religious liberty and separation of church and state revolved.

Williams's understanding of the Christian life as incarnational piety directly influenced his approach to the relationship between church and state, for his radical Christian separatism also placed significant limits on the proper role of political institutions in religious issues. At the same time, the incarnation served to qualify Williams's separatism, for it constantly reminded him of the fundamental blessedness of human existence and the common identity as God's moral creatures that all human beings share. As a result, the incarnation allowed Williams to balance simultaneously a commitment to religious separatism and an acknowledgment of moral, social, and political commonality with non-Christians. As we shall see, this recognition of moral commonality allowed Williams to theologically justify his expectation that Christians would participate in public moral discourse and projects with persons outside the faith.

INCARNATION AND BIBLICAL TYPOLOGY

Perry Miller rightly observed (with characteristic exaggeration, of course) that the Bible was the most important source for Williams's moral theology, and in his emphasis on Scripture Williams was thoroughly Puritan. Appeals to Scripture reinforce most of his moral arguments, and in many moments of *The Bloody Tenent* it appears that Williams and John Cotton are arguing over little more than exegetical differences. But Williams's use of the Scriptures differed from that of the other Puritans in some fundamental ways, and in these differences Williams discovered possibilities for conceiving the relationship between religious faith and public interests in more liberating fashion than the Massachusetts authorities were able to entertain. The root of Williams's disagreement with the conventional Puritan appeal to the Bible was in the way his doctrine of the incarnation of the Word guided his interpretation of God's written word.

Typology was an interpretive method in Puritan biblical study in which certain stories, figures, and images in the Old Testament were taken to prefigure the New Testament gospel.[15] These Old Testament concepts serve as symbols, or types, that foreshadow events, people, and occasions to come in the New Testament, particularly in the story of Christ. While acknowledging the integrity of these Old Testament stories and figures in their own right, Puritan typologists located their supreme importance in the light Old Testament "shadows" cast on their New Testament referents. For Puritan typologists, Adam was a shadow of Christ, the attempted sacrifice of Isaac prefigured Christ's crucifixion, and the Davidic monarchy foreshadowed the reign of Christ as savior king and prince of peace. In the history of biblical exegesis, the typological meaning of a passage could coexist with other interpretive "levels," including the historical and moral meanings of a text. But while these other levels of meaning possessed integrity and importance for the Puritan exegete, the ultimate significance of certain Old Testament texts was in the theological illumination they provided for understanding the gospel of Christ.

Perry Miller rightly understood Williams to read the Old Testament typologically, and so he was correct to suggest that typology was important to understanding the differences between Williams's exegesis and Cotton's. But Miller misunderstood the prevalence of Puritan typology, and this caused him to mistake just what it was about Williams's typological interpretation that separated him from Cotton. Miller argued that the primary point of debate between the radical separatist and the New England establishment was that the former utilized typology while the latter did not. What Miller failed to recognize, however, was the extent to which typology was a *Puritan* strategy and not unique to Roger Williams.[16] Cotton also interpreted the Old Testament typologically, so that his complaint against Williams's interpretation of Scripture was not with his typological method, but with Williams's failure to read the Bible's typology *correctly*. Occasionally Cotton objected to some of Williams's typological conclusions because he believed that Williams was reading typologically a text that should not have required that method. The moral law, for example, was to Cotton's mind "of universal and perpetuall equitie, in all Nations, in all Ages."[17] It was not a "prefigure" for some other concept but was to be valued for its literal meaning. Williams was therefore incorrect to approach it typologically, as Cotton claimed he did. More often, though, Cotton objected not to Williams employing typology but to the conclusions his typological interpretations yielded.

According to Williams, the stories of the Israelites served primarily as "figures" that foreshadowed the story of the church, but whereas Israel was a national, ethnic, and visible community, the church that served as Israel's "antitype" was purely spiritual and invisible.[18] In other words, for Williams the earthly events and arrangements in the Old Testament simply foreshadowed the spiritual relationship between God and the church; the "physically embodied" manifestations of Old Testament religion and political order had only spiritual referents in the New Testament, and thus offered no direct precedents for New England's own social structures. By contrast, Cotton's typology was more complex: in Cotton's view Israel prefigured the church, but the antitype (the church) retained much of the religious and political interdependence characteristic of the type (Israel). Thus, Cotton believed that the collusion of civil and religious authority characteristic of the covenanted community Israel remained normative for contemporary Christian society, and he freely drew connections between Old Testament arrangements and the political and religious institutions of New England. Cotton could refer to Christian magistrates as "counted the light of Israel," justifying their regulation of faith as a political priority by rooting them in the Hebrew precedent of religio-political leaders.[19] His appeals to Israel and Judah sometimes identified Israelite monarchs as "types" of the church, but at least as often these Old Testament figures provided the pattern for Puritan conceptions of Christian society that assumed close cooperation between political and religious powers.[20]

In interpreting biblical typology this way, Cotton was, as on the issue of incarnation, thoroughly and consistently Calvinist.[21] Beyond the historical meaning of the Old Testament events, the stories of Israel represented for Cotton the unchanging covenant of grace between God and God's chosen people. This covenant remained the same from Adam to Christ, though it unfolds with increasing clarity as the biblical story progresses. The incarnation simply confirmed the arrangements of a divine-human relationship that had been in place since the beginning of history and hinted at in the "shadows" of Old Testament events. If the two biblical testaments witnessed to a single covenant, then it made sense to Cotton and most Puritans that many of the social and religious conventions for life under that covenant should also remain constant from the Old Testament to life after the incarnation of Christ. Therefore, the structures of Israel's religious and political life ought to have direct parallels or correspondents in the contemporary life of a society arranged in light of God's covenant. If God entrusted the defense of true religion to Israel's civil powers, for instance, then New England authorities were right to presume that God's covenant required them, too, to protect God's people against spiritual as well as bodily threats. As Miller explained, the New England Puritans

> founded their social and historical endeavor upon the reality of this temporal and organic development from Palestine to Boston, out of which came a solid system of interpreting the growth, the step-by-step unfolding of Christianity. Without this demonstrable continuity human history would be meaningless; without it the Christian community would dissolve into chaos.[22]

For Cotton and other New England divines, the incarnation of Christ served as confirmation of this historical covenant, and thus as the linchpin for the justified consistency between religious and political interdependence in the Old Testament and contemporary parallels.

As we have seen already, Williams's understanding of the incarnation differed radically from the conventional Puritan interpretation, and this difference also led to a variant use of typology in interpreting the relationship between the Testaments of the Bible. Unlike Cotton and most other New England exegetes, Williams denied a fundamental continuity between the covenant portrayed in the Old Testament and that declared in Christ's incarnation. Williams acknowledged that the stories and characters of the Old Testament were "shadows" or "types" of the divine relationship realized in Christ, but while foreshadowed in the stories of Israel, the covenant established in Christ's incarnation was fundamentally different in its actual nature from the relationship God established with the likes of Abraham and Moses. "He was a maverick among the intellectuals of New England," said Miller, "because he interpreted the relation of the Old Testament to the New not as an unfolding through time of an enduring covenant between God and man . . . but as a radical break."[23] For Williams, the advent of Christ was the beginning of a new covenant between God and God's people that terminated the arrangements of the old.

One difference between the old and new covenants lay in the fact that where the former had social, political, and religious dimensions, the divine covenant presented in Christ was only spiritual. Williams rejected Cotton's notion that the details of Israel's covenant with God stood as binding precedent for the New England churches. He did not believe that covenantal theology warranted the direct transfer of historical and political arrangements from the pattern of the Old Testament to contemporary life lived in light of the New, for the specifics of the covenants were not the same. To Cotton's invocation of the pattern of Moses and Israel to justify the political regulation of religious affairs, Williams responded that there was no basis on which to make the comparison. With the fall of Israel, God's particular covenant with that nation ended also, and since then God had not compacted with another civil state. Instead, with the advent of Christ, God established a spiritual covenant with God's people, the church. The Old Testament relationship between God and Israel produced a national church and an intermingling of civil and religious authorities, but God's covenant with the church was purely a spiritual one, meaning the conventional powers of civil authority had no place in defining and maintaining church order.

The distinct break between Testaments that Williams discerned in his reading of the Scriptures contrasted significantly with the basic continuity between covenants that Cotton and other Puritans read there, but Williams argued that his typological interpretation was supported by biblical evidence. Williams suggested that the prophet Isaiah referred to such a break between covenants when he foretold of a new era in which plowshares and pruning hooks would replace swords and spears as the typical instruments of God's people. At the moment of Christ's incarnation, "when the law of Moses (concerning Worship) should cease, and Christ's Kingdom be established," Jesus would usher in through his life an age when "the Weapons of his Warfare are not Carnall."[24] According to Williams, the prophet anticipated Christ's incarnation as the beginning of an age when true religion would no longer be defended by violence, but instead maintained by a spiritual covenant and by spiritual means.

Jesus himself confirmed this prophetic recognition of a new covenant, argued Williams, in his encounter with the Samaritan woman at the well in the fourth chapter of the Gospel of John. The woman refers to the collusion of political and religious identity characteristic of the old covenant when she refers to the separate holy places that divided Jews from Samaritans. But Jesus' response to the woman is to claim that the current circumstance is being replaced by a new arrangement. According to Williams, when Jesus promises the Samaritan woman that "the hour cometh when ye shall neither in this mountain, nor yet in Jerusalem, worship the Father,"[25] he describes for her the dawn of an age in which divine favor is no longer connected with political affiliation or power. Under the new testament between God and God's chosen ones, national covenants are abrogated in favor of a spiritual covenant, and God's people will no longer be known by their worship at particular holy places but by their spiritual relationships. "The hour cometh, and now is, when the true worshipers shall worship the Father in spirit and in truth"—Williams identified the commencement of this new covenant with the incarnation of Jesus Christ.[26]

Both Cotton and Williams, then, interpreted the Old Testament typologically, and by doing so Williams demonstrated that he was nothing but a conventional Puritan exegete, in general methodology at least. Despite the shared method, though, Williams arrived at a starkly different interpretation of the biblical mandate for religion's relationship to civil authority. The fundamental difference between Cotton and Williams lay in the theological motif at work within the typological method. What drove Williams's biblical exegesis to elicit moral conclusions that were significantly different from those of his Puritan counterparts was not typology itself, but the way Williams's understanding of the incarnation directed his typological interpretation. To Williams, Christ's incarnation marked a decisive new beginning to the relationship between God and God's people, and this new covenant shared none of the religio-political arrangements of the old. Hence, when Cotton justified New England intolerance on the basis of Old Testament precedents, he misused the Bible. Williams insisted that Christ's incarnation abrogated the earthly arrangements of Israel's covenant in favor of a spiritual relationship that was maintained by spiritual means and defended by spiritual weaponry only. By refuting the parallels between the Old Testament and the New, Williams undercut a substantial portion of the Puritan argument for the state's responsibility to compel religious observance.

SCRIPTURE AS SACRAMENTAL EXPERIENCE

Besides his exegetical method, other aspects of Williams's use of Scripture were influenced by the incarnational theology he brought to the text. Williams interpreted the very existence of Scripture as a continuation of Christ's incarnation. Just as the incarnation of Christ represented the intersection of the human and divine, giving tangible earthly presence to the divine and endorsing many dimensions of human living, so Williams seems to have regarded Scripture as a type of secondary incarnation, in which the words of God are manifest in tangible form and represent the real continuing presence of God in the midst of God's people.

As a seventeenth-century Puritan, Williams of course believed that the Bible's words were God's own in a more direct way than contemporary historical-critical appreciation allows, but for Williams Scripture was more than just God's words. Scripture was the Word, Jesus Christ; in a real sense the Bible represented the residual presence of Christ among his people and thus the continuation of the incarnation. The reading, preaching, and hearing

of God's Word, then, took on a sacramental nature, for in the faithful procla-
mation and hearing of the Word the assembled people of God would
encounter Christ, just as they would in the Lord's Supper and baptism. The
proclaiming and hearing of God's Word was an opportunity, instituted by
Christ, to encounter the incarnate Christ Himself, but like the sacraments an
opportunity one could not be compelled to experience.[27] Because the procla-
mation and hearing of the Word represented a quasi-sacramental moment,
Williams demanded the same purity for participation in it that the Puritans
insisted upon for the Lord's Supper. Faithful hearing and preaching of the
Word was a mark of true churches and an expression reserved for genuine
Christian piety; attending to the Word was not a matter to be compelled or
experienced in mixed company. On the contrary, Williams argued, against
the Massachusetts establishment, that true Christian responsibility required
that believers keep their worship free from the polluting presence of unregenerate participants, which was impossible if unbelievers were required to
attend. Stricter than most separatists on this point, Williams argued that the
purity of the Word's audience was so important that it was wrong for true
believers even to attend a service of worship at an unseparated church.[28]

Williams's sacramental approach to Scripture had the effect of under-
cutting one of the New England authorities' favorite defenses of religious
compulsion. The Massachusetts leadership believed that Christian responsibility required that they attend to both the pastoral and the evangelistic
needs of the colony. The church's ministers were responsible for the
spiritual care of their congregations, but the colony also had a religious
obligation to propagate the gospel to unbelievers. One of the Puritan establishment's strategies for fulfilling its evangelistic responsibilities was to
require all inhabitants of the colony to attend church services, which would
provide a captive audience for the preachers and, theoretically, the hope
that at least some of the unbelievers would be converted by the persuasive
power of the sermon. Compulsion of religious practice, the conventional
Puritans argued, was an evangelistic responsibility, because it placed
unbelievers in a position to be converted by the gospel as God directed.[29]

Williams rejected this strategy outright, on the basis of his sacramental
understanding of the preached and heard Word. For Williams, parish ministers had been given no such commission to be converting influences on
the unregenerate. Williams drew a sharp distinction between the offices of
"pastor" and "apostle" or "evangelist," and he believed that the evangelistic responsibilities of the apostolic office simply had not been passed on
to the ministers of New England's local congregations. Instead, the ministers of local parishes were called to be pastors only, caring for the spiritual
health of the Christian flock entrusted to them. To Williams, "the ordinarie
Ministers of the Gospels are Pastors, Teachers, Bishops, Overseers, [and]
Elders" whose "proper worke is to feed and govern a truly converted, holy,

and godly people, gathered into a flock or Church estate, and not properly preachers to convert, beget, [or] make disciples, which the Apostles and Evanglists professedly were."[30] According to Williams, the New England pastors had no obligation (nor authority, for that matter) to preach for the conversion of non-Christians, and thus they had no business preaching evangelistic sermons to unbelievers in their Lord's Day services. Their responsibility lay with the spiritual health of the regenerate church members entrusted to them, and part of that responsibility was to ensure the purity of the preaching experience. Therefore, not only was there no reason to seek the compulsory inclusion of unbelievers in Sunday services as a converting exercise, Williams believed that parish ministers had a responsibility to protect the integrity of Christian worship by *barring* from church attendance those who were not regenerate.

As a result, Williams's rejection of evangelistic preaching in the name of preserving the integrity of the scriptural experience dispensed with a popular Puritan justification for civil compulsion of religious practice. Cotton and others responded to Williams by warning him that the denial of the preacher's evangelistic responsibilities threatened the vitality of the church, to which Williams had little to say in return. His refusal to endorse the use of Lord's Day preaching as a converting ordinance derived from the sacramental respect he had for Scripture, a respect that stemmed from his interpretation of the relationship between the Word in Jesus Christ and the words of Scripture through the lens of the incarnation. In this way, the conflict between Williams and his Puritan colleagues over the reading, hearing, and interpretation of Scripture once again derived from deeper differences in how they understood the significance of the incarnation of Christ to moral theology.

INCARNATION AND RADICAL ECCLESIOLOGY

Whereas Perry Miller insisted that biblical method marked the key difference between Williams and his Puritan antagonists, historian Edmund Morgan demonstrated the important role that Williams's ecclesiology played in the development of his opinions on church and state.[31] According to Morgan, Williams's defense of religious freedom was inspired by his desire to maintain a high standard of purity among the congregation of Christian believers. In other words, Williams's radical ecclesiology motivated his defense of a separation of church and state. But Williams's ecclesiology, in turn, reflected his theological emphasis on the incarnation; both the moral pattern of Jesus of Nazareth and the distinctive identity wrought in the Christ event influenced what the church, in Williams's mind, was to be and become. At its most basic form, the church was for Williams the collection of persons who had been redeemed and gathered by the grace of God, and who through their conversion to faith in Christ were equipped to embark on a life of *imitatio Christi*.

As W. Clark Gilpin makes clear, Williams was conventionally Puritan in locating the commencement of the Christian experience in conversion.[32] He rejected the working Anglican assumption that citizenship in a so-called Christian nation made one a Christian, as well as the belief that baptism alone conveyed regeneration.[33] For Williams, the Christian life existentially began with personal conversion and required the experiential recognition of grace to be genuine. All Puritans would have agreed with Williams's emphasis on conversion, as well as his assumption that conversion ought to lead to a measurable change in lifestyle. According to William Ames, Christian assurance of grace comes in the discernible call to a change in behavior, to a life lived in grateful response to God's grace and molded after the pattern of Jesus Christ. "All who obey the call of God are completely turned from sin to grace and from the world to follow God in Christ." Because of this radical redirection, Ames described religious conversion as "the very beginning of a new life, a new creation, a new creature."[34] In *The Pilgrim's Progress,* John Bunyan's character Christian insists to Talkative that "the soul of religion is the practic part," meaning that genuine faith manifests itself necessarily in actions redirected by the disciplines of piety and service.[35] Williams shared this Puritan intimation that genuine religious experience must accompany a commitment to a Christ-centered life.

What distinguished his account of the converted life from that of his Puritan brethren was the extent to which he believed that conversion ought to set the Christian apart from the rest of the world. Williams minimized the distinction between the visible church and the invisible church; as strictly as possible, churches were to remain congregations of regenerate saints, tolerating no religious impurity and little moral diversity. In other words, Williams was a separatist. More than an association of purported believers, the church for Williams was properly the congregation of persons who definitively reflected, in distinctive worship and practice, the genuine experience of conversion to the pattern of Christ. What set a true church apart from the world, then, was the uncompromised integrity of its members' character, personal behavior, and corporate religious practices, all of which were now patterned after the example of the incarnate Christ. In fact, Williams accented the importance of distinctive behavior so much more than his nonseparating Puritan counterparts that John Cotton was compelled to charge him with commending an ecclesiology based on "works righteousness."[36] For Williams, however, purity in practice and character was not a means to salvation; it was evidence that a person had experienced the grace and heeded the call of the incarnate Christ.

But the incarnation meant more to Williams's ecclesiology than just prioritizing a pattern for institutional discipline and character. His theology of incarnation influenced his understanding of the church's origins and the factors that legitimized a church's formation and constitution. In this way his incarnational theology would distance him even from his fellow separatists (especially in Plymouth), but it also would substantially determine his teachings on the church's proper relationship with the civil powers. Conventional Puritan theology dictated that a church was essentially a self-created organization, based on the common agreement to religious association on the part of as few as two or three individuals.[37] Together they shared a covenant with each other and with God that provided the legitimacy of their constitution. Perry Miller's fascination with the covenant theology of the New England Puritans is well known and, despite its many detractors, offers a generally accurate look at the notion of covenant that underwrote much of Puritan self-understanding and organization.[38] According to Miller, the emergence of the covenantal scheme in Puritan theology was an attempt to make more digestible the confidence in God's sovereignty that Calvin simply posited. While not implying that God could be confined or constrained in any real sense, covenant theology taught that God related to human beings in a defined relationship in which God made clear the normal expectations for the relationship. The concept was made popular among Puritans by its exposition in the works of William Perkins and William Ames, the latter's *Marrow of Theology* quickly becoming the theological textbook of choice in New England. As they explored the concept of the covenant, the Puritans had a way of defining expectations for divine behavior in a manner that provided assurances to their congregations, while not violating the Puritan respect for God's sovereignty. As Perry Miller described it:

> The covenant of grace defines the conditions by which Heaven is obtained, and he who fulfills the conditions has an incontestable title to glorification, exactly as he who pays the advertised price owns his freehold. God may continue to choose the elect in the impenetrable fastness of His will, but according to the covenant He has agreed to give the individual descernible [*sic*] grounds for his decision.[39]

The intent of Puritan covenant soteriology was to provide believers with a basis of assurance, despite the unknowable nature of God's ways that conventional Calvinism celebrates so prominently. God was free to act as God wished, but through the covenant God had indicated that human beings could anticipate divine favor or disfavor according to discernible experiential indicators.

Another secondary result of this soteriological development, however, was that the covenant became a tool of Puritan morality, as it defined God's expectations for human beings. Besides providing a basis for talking about the motives for individual Christian morality, the covenant offered a structure for understanding the norms for social and political relations. God was a participant in political and religious covenants, setting the bounds and the obligations of human relations. In these social and political dimensions, the Puritan conception of covenant resembled other social compacts of the populist movement in seventeenth-century England. Contrary to King James's assertion of the divine right of kings, many Puritan thinkers (including Roger Williams) argued that God invested the power to determine social and political arrangements in the people. The people consented to endowing certain leaders with governing authority, and, as T. H. Breen has shown, the Puritans were quick to remind leaders and the public alike that citizens retained the right to evaluate and replace ineffective or unfaithful political leadership.[40]

The concept of covenant, then, not only described the relationship between God and individual believers in a way that provided some religious comfort and inspiration for good works, it also served to justify the Puritan understanding of the political arrangement of both state and church. As early as John Winthrop's sermon, the New England Puritans understood civil society and the church as organizations established through social compacts, each "a miniature edition," as Perry Miller describes them, of the divine covenant. These social compacts were, like the divine covenant, agreements between participants to form a relationship (or institutions) that would further the achievement of certain ends. Also as in the divine covenant, God was a participant in the agreement, providing through the divine law some of the ends and obligations that bound participants together in both civil society and the church. Thus, for the Puritans, both the society of the state and the society of the church were founded upon covenants, formal agreements shared among the human (and divine) participants, in which the members agreed to curtail their individual freedoms and be bound by the obligations of the institution.[41]

The Puritans, then, understood the church covenant as essentially a social compact, albeit a special form of compact. Though God's participation theologically limited the claim for human power, the decision to come together and form a religious association was, humanly speaking, voluntary. A church was formed when Christian individuals joined together and pledged to God and one another to be faithful in worship, ministry, mutual support, and admonition. And like its political counterpart, church leadership derived its authority from the precedent power of those who make up the institution. In the Puritan scheme, a church was formed, and then leaders were chosen. Churches commissioned ministers; ministers did not have the sole authority to form churches.

The biblical parallel to which the Puritans appealed to legitimate their conception of the church compact was the nation of Israel. As we have already seen, most Puritans interpreted the Old Testament references to Israel as typological references to the people of Christ. As was the case with Israel, the people of Christ (i.e., the church or churches) were constituted by a socioreligious covenant that bonded them to each other and to God. But also as in the Old Testament society, the boundaries between religious organization and obligations and civil membership and responsibility were imprecise. Israel was interpreted as typological symbol for both the church and the Puritan civil society, often simultaneously, and the New England Puritans likewise blurred the distinction between membership in the church and membership in civil society. Such confusion appeared in the restriction of the franchise (i.e., the privileges of citizenship) to male church members, a practice in place in the Massachusetts Bay Colony for several years during the mid-1600s.

In fact, the collusion of civil and ecclesial covenants, though incomplete and informal, was intentional. As Timothy Hall and others have observed, the New England Puritans increasingly depended on a view of history that understood the colonies to be at the center of "God's penultimate activity in sacred history." Refusing to distinguish between sacred and secular history, the Puritans believed that God was acting in history to fulfill God's purpose for the world, and the New England experiment was the focus of that divine activity. Even as England moved toward greater toleration after the middle of the seventeenth century, New England persisted in identifying itself as the "city on a hill," a beacon of religious purity and social stability that God was preparing to use as an example for the nations. That the civil and ecclesial covenants were intertwined in New England's self-understanding provided justification for the Puritan hierarchy to pursue religious conformity with the same zeal with which it demanded public order.[42]

Williams objected to the "city on a hill" mentality; the thought that God had bestowed "most favored nation" status on New England, or any other civil society, was to him repulsive. He criticized the confusion of boundaries between church and state and the idea of a divine covenant from which the confusion stemmed. In fact, Gilpin argues that sometime between his banishment from the Bay Colony and his first return to England (and thus the publication of *The Bloody Tenent*), Williams came to reject outright the whole notion of covenant as the primary metaphor for church legitimization. According to Williams, churches were not justifiably constituted by the shared agreement of two or three persons who invoke God's blessing on their compact, but instead were established only by apostolic succession. Churches were suitably formed when a fellowship of believers was converted and gathered by an apostle (or evangelist) who invited them to Christ by the authority of his apostolic commission, which was passed down from Christ through the succession of apostles. By arguing this way, Williams reversed the order of the relationship between congregational formation and ministerial calling that conventional Puritan ecclesiology implied. Whereas the Puritans had insisted that the church first constituted by covenant subsequently ordained ministers, Williams argued that no church was established legitimately except through the gathering authority of a minister of Christ, an apostle.[43]

Williams believed that true churches had to be established by an apostle in the direct succession of those commissioned by Christ himself. Apostolic evangelists were commissioned to preach a converting word to the people, and with this preaching to gather those converted to Christian faith in communities of simple fellowship. Not surprisingly, then, Williams believed authentic churches would look much like the pattern of the New Testament church, "built and framed according to the first most blessed line and rule of his holy institution and appointments."[44] An ecclesiastical primitivism, rooted in the commissioning authority of the incarnate Christ, was a key characteristic of Williams's conception of the genuine church.[45] The problem, according to Williams, was that apostolic succession and primitive purity had disappeared in the Middle Ages. The church, legitimately commissioned in its early centuries and purified through its constant endurance of persecution, had sacrificed the purity of its constitution and character when it surrendered to the hegemony of Constantinian legitimacy, having fallen "asleep" when it wandered into "the laps and bosomes of those Emperors professing the name of Christ."[46] Once "watchful" and faithful to its calling, the church since Constantine had polluted itself by becoming lax in its self-discipline and by constant flirtation with the institutions of political and cultural authority. Once it began to wander from the means and measures of its primitive institution, the "sleepy" church severed its connection to Christ's apostolic commission and sacrificed its legitimacy. "When Christianity began to be choked," wrote Williams, "it was not when Christians lodged in cold Prisons, but Downe beds of ease, and persecuted others."[47]

Thus Williams came to believe that the true church no longer existed in institutional or gathered form in the world. No single gathered community that maintained primitive purity or could boast of an apostolic connection survived. The church instead would have to wait for the second advent of Christ for apostolic appointment to begin again.[48] In the meantime, Christianity would live on in the "scattered witnesses" who preserved the purity of the faith in their individual piety and in the faithfulness of their small enclaves. The scattered but obedient witnesses of Christ (among whom Williams counted himself) were charged with the prophetic duty, not to institute churches, but to preach a negative word of witness, deconstructing those practices within and outside so-called churches that impeded the practice of godly religion and virtues. These were persons "immediately stirr'd up by Christ Jesus" and endowed with the commission and capacity to witness to the world's errors.[49] Railing against the "false Christs, false Faith, false love, false Joy, false Worship" of the world and unfaithful churches, these witnesses "prophecyed and mourned . . . for the routing [and] desolating of the Christian Church . . . and panted and labored after . . . [its] restoration," a restoration not to be expected until the millennial return of Christ.[50] Until then, the task of the witnesses was more to cry down old errors than to establish new truth, focusing more on the discontinuity between the present and the millennial glory than on any human strategies for substantial ecclesial reform.[51]

This is not to say, as some charge, that Williams's conception of the Christian life was simply individualistic. Despite his inability to locate in his age an example of a church that existed in genuine purity and incarnate legitimacy, Williams did nonetheless see value in the small enclaves of "scattered witnesses" that appeared in history from time to time. According to Williams, associations of these witnesses exist in "all ages," and he offered as examples the "Waldenses, Wicklivists, the Hussites, the Lutherans, [and] the Calvinists."[52] He commended religious association to the scattered faithful, suggesting that even in the church's wilderness condition Christian piety is exercised most suitably in a community of believers.[53]

Williams never could find a gathering of "scattered witnesses" that satisfied him enough for him to associate with it, but while his ecclesiology led to personal frustration it also directly influenced his powerful moral arguments on behalf of religious liberty. An ecclesiology that emphasized a dichotomy between the religious and the profane necessarily drove a hard division between the criteria for legitimacy of the state and that of the church. The church's constitution derived directly from divine power, while the extent and form of the state's power, as Williams would insist time and again, was based on the consent of the people ruled.[54] Williams's distinction undercut Puritan arguments that both state and church derived power from divine endorsement of consensual covenants, thus compromising Massachusetts's conventional conception of church and state as interdependent institutions for the pursuit of similar religious and political objectives. In rejecting the sociological, covenantal model for the church and removing its organization and government from the realm of popular consent and civil direction, Williams did not deny the possibility for cooperative measures between ecclesial and political institutions, but he did rule out the assumption that the two types were normatively codependent. Thus his argument for the separation of church and state was based in a radical ecclesiology that itself depended on Williams's particular brand of incarnational piety.

INCARNATION AND ESCHATOLOGY

As W. Clark Gilpin has demonstrated, Williams's radical ecclesiology was in turn inextricably bound to his eschatological views. According to Gilpin, during the years between 1636 and 1646 Williams gradually rethought the eschatology he inherited from his Puritan formation, a process of theological reimagination that eventually produced a millenarianism unique in his Puritan context.[55] While the historical evidence does not lend itself as certainly as Gilpin would like to pinpointing the chronology for the maturation of Williams's millenarian views, it is clear that by the time of his public writings, Williams subscribed to an eschatology that represented an unusual transformation of conventional Puritan convictions. Just as with his understanding of the Bible and the nature of the church, Williams's eschatology represented a unique reformulation of Reformed theological principles, indebted to his distinct interpretation of the incarnation.

The fact that Williams ascribed to a millennial interpretation of history was not unusual in itself. Millenarianism was a popular component of seventeenth-century Protestant religion, including Puritanism. The Puritans understood all of history to be moving toward a grand culmination, represented by eschatological texts of the Bible like Daniel and Revelation. In the life, death, and resurrection of Jesus Christ, God definitively disclosed a historical plan that included God's ultimate victory over evil and a time of rewards for the elect and eternal punishment for the wicked. According to the Puritan reading of the Bible, God's victory over evil declared in Christ's resurrection would be consummated in the second coming of Christ, toward which all of history was now heading. Technically the Puritans subscribed to a premillennial view, in that they believed Christ's advent and thousand-year reign on earth would precede the final moment of judgment to which all humanity would be subjected. Regardless of the precise chronology, however, the Puritans agreed that historical momentum was headed toward a *telos*, the victorious return of Christ as king and the definitive establishment of the kingdom of God on earth.

In the meantime, the Puritans believed that they were living in a decisive chapter in human history, during which God was sowing the seeds for the return of Christ and the flowering of the kingdom by turning both church and civil society toward reformation of religion and morals. At the heart of this final preparation for Christ's return, England was the locus for reformation and the symbolic center of importance in Puritan eschatology. God had established a covenant with the Christian people of England, argued many Puritans, and part of their responsibility in that covenant was to prepare the way for the second advent of Christ. Puritan calls for improvements in church worship and corrections in social morality were motivated by a belief that, in the reformation of English religion and culture, God was laying the foundation for the advent of Christ and his kingdom.

Because of the important role millenarianism played as motivation for their calls for ecclesial and social reform, eschatology is properly understood as central, and not peripheral, to Puritan notions of religion and piety. The interpretation of social events and personal obligations through biblical hints and images of the end times "provided a continuing impetus toward reform of the individual and society as well as a standard by which such reforms could be judged."[56] The vision of a projective narrative of history served not only as the foundation for the Puritans' demands for reformation in church and society, however, but also as their frame of meaning for understanding the world around them and their roles and responsibilities in it. In other words, millenarian eschatology provided a system of symbols for interpreting the meaning of one's existence in the larger narrative of history.[57]

Roger Williams was no different from his Puritan colleagues in his adoption of millenarian views of history, though his particular brand of millenarianism set him apart from the conventional Puritan interpretation. The standard Puritan eschatology presupposed continuity between present religious and social institutions and the kingdom Christ would establish at his return. Much of the motivation behind Puritan endeavors toward constructing a "holy commonwealth" lay in the belief that this commonwealth, completed and perfected by Christ, would serve as the foundation for the new kingdom. By contrast, Williams insisted that the kingdom Christ would establish at his return would be radically unlike the institutions now common in Puritan society. Like the distinct break he posited between the covenant of the Old Testament and that of the New, Williams also expected a radical difference between the experiences before and after the *eschaton.*

Part of this difference can be attributed to Williams's commitment to an ecclesiology that was also much different from the one subscribed to by his Puritan counterparts. As we have seen, Williams rejected an ecclesiology based on covenantal theology and based the authority of church formation in a theory of apostolic succession. Churches are formed not by a mutual agreement of prospective parishioners before God, but by the gathering authority of an evangelist in the direct spiritual lineage of Christ's apostles. According to Williams, the line of apostolic succession was broken in the Middle Ages, a victim of medieval corruption and the church's betrayal of its mission for political prestige and power. With the apostolic line severed, Williams believed that true churches—that is, those formed by true apostles—no longer exist in the world. When he returns, however, Christ will restore the apostolic office, commission and send out new evangelists, and reconstitute the church on earth. At Christ's advent, the church will recover its spiritual ministry and have its external offices (like evangelism and the sacraments) restored. Until that time, the best that Christians can hope for is to gather together in enclaves of "scattered witnesses," whose responsibility is not to form churches, but to exist as a negative witness against the corruption of the world. History for the Christian, then, is interim survival, a period of wandering in the spiritual desert, waiting for the return of Christ.

By interpreting the eschaton as the culmination and perfection of a combined religious and political community, conventional Puritans employed their millenarian views to justify the collusion of church and state interests. Church and state rightfully cooperated in the construction of a holy commonwealth, not just because God provided the pattern for a righteous society in the typology of the biblical past, but because similar collusion was the expectation of the eschatological future. The Puritans envisioned an eschatological kingdom in which civil and religious institutions and interests meshed in the ultimate cooperative endeavor of a righteous commonwealth. By contrast, Williams rejected the infusion of eschatological significance into civil structures. For Williams the eschaton was about the restoration and perfection of the church, the spiritual community of God's chosen, not about the perfection of any political arrangement. By rejecting a millennial interpretation of civil society, Williams weakened Puritan justification for the holy commonwealth, including the principle of religious uniformity that the Puritan political vision held so dear. For Williams, the eschaton will reestablish the true church, which will find its virtue not in its cooperation with political agents in the project of a religious state, but in its separation from all things profane, including the political realm. Civil society in the present, then, has no direct eschatological significance, but instead simply serves as the means by which human beings defend and preserve the lives of citizens so that they may live together peacefully and flourish in history. In other words, civil government has a negative social role (preventing violence, discord, and crime) and a positive social role (providing an atmosphere for human flourishing and harmonious cohabitation), but it does not have a *religious* role.

Williams's political theology, therefore, differed from that interpretation of civil society as the grand project of Christian righteousness so sufficiently symbolized by the Puritan "city on a hill" imagination. Williams preferred to think of civil society as the structure by which human beings exist in a "holding pattern" this side of the eschaton. Rejecting the standard Puritan political teleology, Williams also dispensed with the elevation of religious uniformity as the chief virtue of such an eschatologically important society. Instead he embraced a vision for civil arrangement that featured other values at its core. Civil society for Williams required the protection of civil order, but also the cultivation of freedom of conscience, freedom of expression, mutual respect, and social solidarity—values that supported the penultimate agenda of a "good society," the preservation of peace and an ethos in which its citizens might flourish. In other words, as we shall see, civility and not orthodoxy represented the chief virtue of Williams's good society.

The progressive impulse for Williams's political philosophy, then, originates in this alternative to the eschatological definition of the intentions for civil society. His noneschatological vision of the good society was nonetheless theologically justified, for it was rooted in his interpretation of the incarnation, and the separation of civil and religious identity and destinies that this interpretation required. In this way, Williams's millenarian piety was bound together with his ecclesiology and biblical hermeneutic to provide an incarnational foundation for his most important impulses regarding religious liberty and the separation of church and state. This has been the intent of this chapter, in fact, to demonstrate the effect of some fundamental Reformed doctrines—and Williams's innovations—on his teachings on church and state. Despite enduring misimpressions to the contrary, Williams did not arrive at his political ethics through an experiential pragmatism or commitment to theological relativism, but through a Calvinist preoccupation with ecclesiology, eschatology, and the authority of Scripture, themselves underwritten by a theological priority for the incarnation as interpretive lens. Williams understood himself to be a Reformed theologian, and his writings constantly betray this confessional orientation. His confessional self-understanding did not render him unwilling or unable to engage in moral conversation with persons outside his theological circles, however. As we shall see in the following chapters, Christian conviction and public ethics were not incompatible endeavors for Williams. By appeal to concepts and beliefs within Reformed theology, Williams envisioned broad possibilities for shared moral conversation between Christians and non-Christians alike, even as he protected the distinctiveness and integrity of the confessional perspective from which he wrote and thought.

PART II

ANTHROPOLOGY

So many stately Kingdoms and governments in the world have long and long enjoyed civil peace and quiet, notwithstanding their religion is so corrupt as that there is not the very name of Jesus Christ amongst them.

—*The Bloody Tenent of Persecution* (1644)

3

PLURALISM AND
NATURAL MORALITY

Cast into the New England wilderness by Massachusetts's General Court in 1636, Williams eventually made his way to Narragansett Bay, where he (and loyalists to follow) established the town of Providence as a haven for nonconformists. For his survival during that first winter of exile, though, and for the land on which the town itself would stand, Williams had the local Native Americans to thank. The relationship between Puritan colonists and Native Americans was always tentative. The English treated the Americans sometimes as targets of conversion, sometimes as obstacles to expansion, but seldom as persons with legitimate personal integrity and full moral worth. Unlike most of his fellow Englishmen, however, Williams enjoyed a very positive relationship with the Native Americans in the area, particularly the Narragansett tribe. While he was in Plymouth from 1631 to 1633, Williams had supported himself by trading with the Americans. His trading post provided him with extensive exposure to the Americans, so much so that he developed a deep respect and affection for many among them, feelings that were often reciprocated. This friendship turned out to be quite important, for the Narragansett Indians provided for Williams after his exile and sheltered him from the New England cold. When spring came, he was able to negotiate with them settlement rights for the location of Providence, and this new arrangement of neighbors, at least as far as the Narragansett chieftain and Williams were concerned, formalized their friendship. In fact, the arrangement Williams negotiated for use of their land for his new colony not only exhibited a fairness that exceeded similar "deals" struck between natives and colonists, it also articulated an intention to protect the Americans' property interests from erosion by colonial expansion. In the first dozen years or so of his life in Providence, Williams continued to operate his trading post, at which he dealt extensively (and fairly, by all accounts) with his American neighbors, and throughout the rest of his life in Rhode Island he served as ambassador between the native tribes and New England colonists.

As a result of his growing intimacy with the Americans during his time in Plymouth, Williams compiled a study of the Narragansett language titled *A Key into the Language of America*. More than simply a vocabulary guide, the *Key* is a detailed examination of Native American language, customs, and social standards. It also includes commentary on the behavioral patterns of both the Americans and Williams's colonial colleagues, in which the English frequently prove themselves to be morally inferior. When it was published during his first trip to London in 1644, the *Key* was quickly recognized as an important anthropological study and missionary tool. Noted less at the time was its witness to the moral capabilities (alas, frequent *superiority* in Williams's mind) of this "pagan" people. What made Williams's relationship with the Americans rare was the mutual respect he and the Americans demonstrated toward one another. Williams respected his American colleagues as equal moral agents, vehemently defending their personal and property rights and acknowledging in them a moral capacity that frequently outshined the hypocrisy of the so-called Christian English.

Williams's warm relationship with the Narragansetts would be put to the test again and again by the strained relations between them and the colonies. Despite the fact that they had kicked him out of the Bay Colony, John Winthrop and the other Massachusetts authorities continually called on Williams to act as a go-between for the colonies' relationship with neighboring tribes. The proximity of the English settlements to American communities, the growing native resentment of English occupation of their land, and the colonial governments' insistence on meddling in intertribal conflict all contributed to making the relationship between the English and the Americans tense and volatile. In 1645 the United Colonies interfered in a dispute between the Mohegans and the Narragansett, siding with the former in a declaration of war on the latter and provoking the threat of violence on all sides. Only the last-minute intervention of that friend of the Narragansetts, Roger Williams, averted all-out war, as he dutifully negotiated a compromise between the parties. Again in 1653 Massachusetts would call on Williams to arbitrate in the face of war between the colonies and the Narragansett, taking advantage of his unique relationship with his native friends. But continued provocation and the naive politics of the English never permitted their relationship with the Americans to mend, and in June 1675 the American tribes joined together to make a final bloody stand against the English invaders and to eradicate them from their land. With every tribal attack on colonial villages the English retaliated, and the brutality continued until August of the next year, when the American chieftain dubbed King Philip was slain. King Philip's War, as it was called, had been won by the English (so to speak), but in the process over half the towns in Puritan New England, including Providence, had been burned. The civility and friendship that Williams had shared with the Native Americans sadly failed to germinate.

Through to the end, however, Williams himself never wavered in his respect for his native friends, and the American casualties of King Philip's War grieved him as much as those the colonies suffered. To Williams there was no doubt that the "pagan" Americans were human beings of fundamental theological worth and admirable moral capacity. But how could Williams maintain both the intense confessional loyalty we have attributed to him and a willingness to converse with these non-Christians as moral equals? Hardly resembling the "irrepressible democrat" previous generations of scholars have tried to make of him, Roger Williams was a Christian theologian of the most peculiar sort—thoroughly Calvinist, dogmatically sectarian, and forever concerned with the effect of encroaching worldliness on the integrity of the church's faith and living. At the same time, Williams befriended the "heathen" Americans and is best known for views on conscience that still seem to "translate" equally well to both religious audiences and secular political culture. How are we to understand the relationship between Williams's confessional stringency and his public ethics?

Some have suggested that Williams's relationship with the Americans was a sign of his theological relativism, and that his views on religious liberty serve as evidence that he did not take religion very seriously. Such readings are possible, of course, only when a figure's reputation is passed down through history without anyone bothering to read his words. The real reason for Williams's ability to befriend Indians as moral partners and carve out a philosophy of tolerance capable of wide application is to be found in his theology itself. How Williams could subscribe to this kind of public ethics without transgressing his distinctive confessional commitment is the subject of the remainder of this book. That he took advantage of this type of broad conversation is incontrovertible, as his life story is a continuous narrative of moral exchanges with Catholics, Quakers, Native Americans, and others who did not share his religious views. This lifetime of public discourse was rooted in the conviction that religious and moral pluralism outside the church was an obstacle neither to the integrity of the church nor to the possibility of finding basic public agreement on moral norms and values. This forthright recognition of the reality of and possibilities within pluralism, in turn, was empowered by his utilization of the Christian conception of natural morality, which allowed him to negotiate fruitfully in a pluralistic environment without abdicating his theological commitments.

THE PROBLEM OF PLURALISM

From a separatist such as Williams we may expect to find a low degree of religious and moral tolerance, for the same dedication to purity of principle that drove him to separate from the Church of England ought to provoke him to seek distance from non-Christian beliefs he considered illegitimate. After all, the coincidence of religious separation and political intolerance continues to dominate the popular impression of New England Puritanism, of which we may expect Williams to provide extreme example. The desire for pure religion moved the Puritans of Massachusetts (though eschewing the complete break from the Church of England that Williams demanded) to practice a de facto separation from non-Puritan churches, as well as to place significant political restrictions within their own community on beliefs that differed from Puritan convention. The Puritans believed that their conception of religious and moral right was true, and that the proper use of their relative liberty in New England was to establish a community whose norms would reflect Puritan truth, an ambition that fostered a general atmosphere of religious, moral, and political intolerance.[1] In other words, the Massachusetts Puritans did not use their relative freedom to secure freedom for all thought, but to establish the one theology they considered correct. If separatism, then, breeds a spirit of intolerance, we might expect the extreme sectarian Williams to outdo his fellow Puritans in displaying this spirit.

Except that the relationship between tolerance and conviction is more complicated than our extrapolations from Puritan orthodoxy suggest. As David Little reminds us, tolerance (and, therefore, also intolerance) may take a number of different forms.[2] Tolerance may entail not only a respect for the right to hold differing beliefs, but also a respect for the beliefs themselves and an openness to conversation that bears the possibility of having our own beliefs changed. Yet this respect and openness is not a *necessary* component of tolerance. A person may respect the rights of others to hold different beliefs while at the same time believing that the beliefs of the other are false and that his or her own perception of truth is the only right understanding. Thus, an intractable commitment to a personal conception of truth is not necessarily incompatible with tolerance. At different moments in his writings, Williams exhibits both kinds of tolerance, the type that respects difference and the type that respects the *right* to difference while insisting that those differences are philosophically wrongheaded. Williams clearly recognized the predicament that religious and moral pluralism presents to civil society, to which in response he advocated a liberal spirit of tolerance. What is also clear, however, is that Williams managed to carve out a healthy relationship with both religious and moral pluralism while still maintaining his personal theological convictions.[3]

Williams insisted that religious and moral pluralism was not only a reality, but a necessary reality, an inevitable product of the human condition. As long as human beings operated with insufficient reason in an age in which the mysteries of God were not fully disclosed, they would continue to understand and answer the fundamental questions of belief in different ways. Because of this given fact, it was as important to Williams that the powers of religion not unjustifiably invade the realm of civil rights and responsibilities as it was that civil authority not impinge upon the freedoms and practices of religious communities.[4] For only in a civil sphere in which the political powers of religious bodies are checked could citizens live peaceably in the reality of pluralism. Only when civil rights and religious identity remained separate could the existence of religious and moral pluralism be negotiated without coercion or chaos.

What motivated Williams to draw serious boundaries of protection around individuals' core convictions was his understanding of the nature of belief. Williams maintained that the "problem" of pluralism could not be resolved through systematic coercion, because to try to compel religious and moral conviction is to transgress the very nature of belief itself. Personal belief, argued Williams, resides at the core of human identity; it is an inalienable dimension of who we are that cannot be externally compelled to become something different than it is.[5] The phenomenon of belief answers only to the personal pursuit of truth through search and examination, and its integrity requires voluntary assent.[6] Because of its peculiar nature, Williams insisted that genuine belief cannot be forced; it is a matter between God and the conscience that is susceptible only to persuasive argumentation, personal religious experience, and divine manipulation.[7] Not only does forceful intervention fail to change a person's core convictions, it may actually have the effect of hardening the subject's resolve and commitment to the beliefs in question.[8] Because of his understanding of the nature of true belief, Williams insisted that pluralism was a necessary part of human existence in history, a reality that must be confronted not with violent attempts to stamp it out but with toleration, patience, and dialogue.[9]

Most of Williams's references to respecting pluralism deal with *religious* pluralism, but Williams's understanding of the nature of conviction compelled him to respect the reality of moral pluralism as well. Williams has been read to have advocated religious freedom but moral uniformity, but it is a mistake to conclude that Williams was unconcerned with the protection of diverse moral beliefs.[10] Williams occasionally counted moral convictions, not just religious beliefs, among the matters of conscience that ought to be protected from coercion. For instance, in *The Examiner Defended* Williams explicitly takes up the question of *moral* deviance, wondering whether certain instances of moral disagreement warrant the same patience and toleration (rather than judgment and punishment) that he recommends in questions of religious dissent:

> I ask further, Whether or no some seeming Incivilities, which the Light of Nature more fairly may condemn, and hale before the Civil Tribunal, yet may not be such; and so Circumstantiated with Impressions from Heaven, that they ought not so suddenly and easily to be

condemned and punished, but with a more tender and observant Eye, be distinguished?[11]

Williams suggests that some moral beliefs and actions that seem to be "incivilities" by their apparent transgression of conventional codes of moral acceptability may in fact be morally licit from another point of view. Because uncertainty surrounds the judgment of many allegedly immoral acts, Williams suggests that apparent moral deviance need not always be met with communal punishment, and in fact in some circumstances it may not be morally right to do so. Perhaps moral pluralism warrants as much patience and toleration as it does zealous condemnation.

Williams was no relativist, however, for he believed in strong public protection of a social order with political and moral integrity. The question regarding which moral convictions the government may legitimately compromise, then, had less to do with whether the convictions are "religious" or "moral" than with whether they honestly threaten the public good. By definition, Williams believed that most matters of personal faith and piety do not constitute a threat to public safety, but many moral convictions are socially benign as well, so that a tolerant society can respect both religious and moral pluralism to a wide extent. Williams believed that some moral convictions and practices ventured into the jurisdiction of the magistrate, but only those that involve threats to public security or the transgression of moral norms that every human being can be expected to recognize (for instance, the wrong in killing an innocent person).[12] Williams concluded that, in the life of a civil community, a little respect for moral pluralism—as well as the cultivation of a spirit of patience and an "observant Eye" in cases of moral, as well as religious, difference—serves social health more than a proclivity to persecution. His respect for moral pluralism runs counter to the common interpretation that Williams disavowed religious establishment but actively sought moral uniformity in his Rhode Island colony.[13]

At the same time, Williams never abandoned his own definite convictions regarding moral truths and values, even while he simultaneously acknowledged the limits of human knowledge and the wisdom of exercising a degree of tolerance in the face of moral pluralism. In addition, moral tolerance was not without its limits, for a certain level of civil consensus on moral norms and values is necessary as a basis for social viability; a foundational respect for order fosters further moral conversation and consensus. Williams argued that social consensus on some basic moral norms and values is possible, even across religious and cultural boundaries, and his confidence in this potential for moral agreement came from his religious confession. For Williams, Christian theology confirmed that human beings could agree on basic moral norms and values, regardless of the religious and cultural particularities that separated them. The next chapter will examine Williams's understanding of conscience, perhaps the most vital component of Williams's moral theology to both his respect for pluralism and his optimism that basic moral conversation and consensus can take place across confessional lines. Chapter 5 will then explore his notion of "civility," his metaphor for how the society founded on basic moral respect and discourse should look. His development of both conscience and civility, however, depended on a moral anthropology that permitted the balance of theological particularity with hope for public conversation and moral agreement, a vision of the moral agent rooted in the Puritan understanding of reason and natural law.

REASON AS MORAL "FACULTY"

Despite his enormous effort to highlight the intellectual character of Puritan thought, Perry Miller's observation is nearly as true today as it was sixty years ago: "Neither the friends nor the foes of the Puritans have shown much interest in their intellects, for it has been assumed that the Puritan mind was too weighted down by the load of dogma to be worth considering in and for itself."[14] In contrast to this popular impression, however, the Puritans were far from anti-intellectual trumpets for a doctrine of total depravity that rendered all human moral faculties useless. The Puritans believed that there is an inherent "reasonableness" to God, a rationality that permeated not only the immediate practices and statutes of their religion but also their conception of the "profane" world beyond the church. God has invested in creation a rational ordering; creation itself originated as a product of God giving external form to the "rational scheme of ideas" already existent in God's mind. Having created in rationality, God endowed human beings with reason to honor them as the one species capable of reading and understanding the reasonableness of creation (including the moral order). Of course, the Puritans believed that sin had compromised the reliability of reason, but like Calvin before them they stopped short of declaring human reason totally inoperable. Human beings are rational beings, able to investigate, analyze, and understand (albeit with limited capacities) the rational truth of God's created ordering. No less of a Puritan divine than William Ames claimed that the powers of reason to invent, seek truth, and participate in rational discourse are all scaled-down reflections of the rational activity of God, and that these capacities have been partially retained represents the residual *imago Dei* in human beings.[15]

The Puritans inherited their understanding of the potential and limits of reason from John Calvin.[16] Calvin claimed that reason had been corrupted by sin, but that it had not been totally extinguished. He insisted that the exercise of reason continued to be an important part of the fundamental makeup of the human species; rationality is, in fact, one of the capacities that distinguishes us from "brute beasts."[17] God bestowed on human beings a "common grace" (as distinguished from the "special grace" of salvation) through which human beings, regenerate or otherwise, are endowed with certain knowledge and capacities, including effective gifts of rationality. Calvin acknowledged that sin constantly compromises the exercise of reason, a faculty that some persons, as a result of sin, seem less endowed with than others. Despite the qualitative diversity in natural gifts, however, human rationality signals "some remaining traces of the image of God, which distinguishes the entire human race from the other creatures."[18] In fact, in contrast to the stereotypical interpretation of the Calvinist doctrine of total depravity, Calvin argued, "when we so condemn human understanding for its perpetual blindness as to leave it no perception of any object whatever, we not only go against God's Word, but also run counter to the experience of common sense." Calvin was certain that the empirical evidence revealed "implanted in human nature some sort of desire to search out the truth to which man would not at all aspire if he had not already savored it."[19]

The truth to which Calvin referred included both religious and moral truth, for in his commentary on the Gospel of John, Calvin identified the "light which yet remains in corrupt nature" as the capacity in human reason to discern both "some seed of religion" and "the distinction between good and evil."[20] On both fronts, he immediately qualified his apparent optimism for the powers of reason, pointing out that, on its own, reason is prone to superstition in matters of religion and confusion in moral judgment. Indeed, while Calvin admitted his belief that some "seeds" of awareness of the divine are perceptible to reason, he was careful to clarify that nothing remotely resembling knowledge of salvation is possible by the powers of rationality alone. Following Augustine, Calvin stated that "the natural gifts were corrupted in man through sin, but that his supernatural gifts were stripped from him." The supernatural gifts are spiritual in object, including faith, love of God, interpersonal charity, holiness, and righteousness. Thus, while "some seeds of religion" remain with us to suggest to our reason the existence of God, reason is of no ultimate value in achieving salvation. The ability to truly know and love God and to exercise Christian virtue toward God and other persons has been stripped from human beings by sin, so that religious accomplishment is possible only by grace.

Calvin was more confident in a residual human capacity for moral discernment, however. In contrast to supernatural abilities, Calvin assured that the natural gifts are only partially corrupted by sin: "Since reason, therefore, by which man distinguishes between good and evil, and by which he understands and judges, is a natural gift, it could not be completely wiped out; but it was partly weakened and partly corrupted." Sin renders the moral faculties unreliable and distracted, but Calvin maintained that "in man's perverted and degenerate nature some sparks still gleam," and that this endowment of "reason and intelligence" allows us to "bear the distinction between right and wrong" and thus distinguishes us from "brute beasts."[21] This imperfect endowment is the gift of "common grace," and it explains the appearance of moral discernment among even those outside the body of saints.

Like Calvin, the Puritans drew a distinction between saving knowledge and "earthly" considerations like political coexistence and moral reasoning.[22] The former constituted the realm of grace, and no exercise of reason would merit salvation, for the "supernatural gifts" had been destroyed by the Fall and were restored only by divine grace. The natural gift of reason, however, remained operable, if corrupted, and provided human beings a common, universal capability for moral deliberation and cooperation.[23] Of course, the Puritans took the destructive effect of sin as seriously as Calvin did, believing that moral reason always performed better when supplemented, directed, and educated by Scripture and the disciplines of piety. Nonetheless, they recognized reason as a moral capacity that even the unregenerate possess, and their zeal to base moral arguments in reason nearly as much as appeal to Scripture indicates their confidence in reason as a common base for universal moral reflection.[24]

Williams reflected this characteristically Puritan confidence in reason as a basis for moral argumentation.[25] He frequently based his arguments for toleration in reason and experience in addition to Scripture, suggesting that the appeal to reason was as reliable a basis on which to demand toleration as revelation. At the commencement of *The Bloody Tenent of Persecution,* he signaled his intention to present arguments for religious liberty "from Religion, Reason, [and] Experience," and by the end of its sequel he was just as sure of the compatibility of these sources, insisting that he was "as humbly confident of Grace and Conscience, Reason, and Experience, yea, the God of all Grace . . . to be on his side."[26] Like his fellow Puritans, Williams believed that Christians relied on reason, scriptural appeal, and the disciplines of piety for moral deliberation; revealed sources supplement natural abilities with "an higher ground and principle." Christians may "see Gods wise" through a regenerate mind and a devotion to Scripture, but even in this acknowledgment of a "higher" level of Christian discourse, Williams recognized that the fundamental basis for moral conversation shared by Christians and "naturall men" alike are the "Rules of Reason and naturall wisedom."[27]

Williams insisted that his own arguments were themselves reasonable in addition to biblical, therein demonstrating a confidence in reason and rational argument as a basis for moral conversation that is not only compatible with overtly Christian sources but also accessible to non-Christians. Williams felt that appeals to reason were enough to sustain a basic level of moral conversation, as he demonstrated in his own initiation of public discourse on religious liberty. He sometimes made no appeal to religious sources in his arguments for toleration, choosing instead to rely entirely on rational argumentation. When John Cotton claimed that civil crimes and spiritual offenses were basically the same species and thus equally answerable to civil authority, Williams sometimes responded with alternative biblical exegesis, but other times he invoked only natural conscience and rational arguments.[28] His defense of toleration derived not only from biblical texts but also from a philosophical justification of popular consent as a limit on the nature and extent of governmental power. Much of Williams's political philosophy was a rational defense of the proposition that "Governments . . . have no more power, nor for no longer time, then the civill power or people consenting and agreeing shall betrust them with," a statement that Williams admitted has no direct basis in Scripture.[29] For Williams, reason was an important authority on which to carry on this broad moral conversation regarding toleration.

His confidence in reason was rooted in his Puritan belief that rationality is a gift of God. In the context of his verbal exchanges with the Quakers, Williams made clear that he attributed to the very "Spirit of God" a fundamental sense of rationality, and that he believed that God infused creation with an order (including the moral ordering) that is inherently reasonable.[30] Human reason, then, is a divine gift by which human beings become the one creature equipped to read and appreciate the rationality at the core of the created ordering. Though dulled by sin, even in the regenerate, reason remains an operable capacity for moral reflection.[31] This ability is a universal capacity, according to Williams, not simply an endowment of the Christians of New England. On this point Williams was quite clear, for among the remarkable observations regarding the Native Americans that Williams recorded in his *Key into the Language of America,* he indicated his recognition of sophisticated intellectual and moral capability in many of the natives he encountered. In his interactions with the Americans, Williams observed that they "are intelligent, many very ingenuous, plainehearted, inquisitive and . . . prepared with many convictions"—in other words, equipped with the moral faculty of reason.[32] Williams was superbly impressed with the Americans' moral development and considered them every bit as equipped morally as the Europeans. From his conversation and interaction with the natives, Williams concluded that in "the temper of the braine in quick apprehensions and accurate judgments . . . the most high and soveraign God and Creator hath not made them inferiour to Europeans."[33] In fact, Williams occasionally lamented that the Americans exhibited finer moral sensitivity than many of his English comrades.[34]

To Williams's mind, the Americans often exemplified the sharp potential for moral reasoning and cooperation that he believed all human beings possessed.

Thus Williams's clear confidence in the potential for moral cooperation, and even consensus on at least a basic level, between Christians and non-Christians originated in his recognition of a capacity for moral discernment and practical reasoning that all human beings hold in common. His belief in reason as this universal moral capacity, rather than setting him apart from his Puritan colleagues, simply represented his coherence with the Reformed tradition. Like Calvin, Perkins, and Ames before him, and his Puritan colleagues in old and New England, Williams exhibited a cautious trust in the human power to engage in practical reasoning and thus operate as moral agents, even without the regenerating wisdom of Christian faith. While sin and human finitude could compromise the efficacy of its performance, reason allowed human beings to live together as moral agents and provided a basis for cooperation and conversation, for it represented a common capability for considering moral dilemmas and identifying the norms and values that promote human flourishing and the common good. In addition, this rational capacity equipped Christian and "heathen" alike to access and understand the basic rules and requirements at the heart of God's moral ordering, the norms represented in the natural law.

THE NATURAL LAW

The true power of moral reasoning lay in its connection to the natural law. Belief in natural law frequently is considered a point of distinction between medieval Christian thinkers and the Reformers, but Calvin and his theological descendants never abandoned the catholic contention that there exists an eternal law by which God brought creation into existence and bound it together. Knitted into the very order of created existence, the natural law testifies to the rational order of God's creation and governance and includes the laws of science as well as the hierarchies of species and gender. The natural law also includes the moral law, and although it was articulated most thoroughly in Scripture (most notably in the Decalogue), like the rest of natural law human beings have fallible access to the moral law even without revelatory sources or regenerating grace. In the minds of Calvinist thinkers, the natural moral law rendered all sinners culpable before God; ignorance of God's moral requirements could not be invoked as excuse for sin. More positively, however, the natural law represented that level of moral understanding that every human being could be expected to attain, and upon which moral conversation and appeal could be founded.

Calvin taught that the Bible endorsed the idea of a natural moral law in his commentary on Romans 2:14–16. Specifically, in Paul's reference to the Gentiles being a "law unto themselves," Calvin interpreted the apostle to be acknowledging natural law, or "a certain natural knowledge of the law, which states that one action is good and worthy of being followed, while another is to be shunned with horror." To Calvin this "natural light of righteousness" to which all human beings have access provides human beings with an innate "knowledge of right and justice" that allows them to coexist in some semblance of social ordering.[35] He described the natural law similarly in the *Institutes,* writing that "there is nothing more common than for a man to be sufficiently instructed in a right standard of conduct by natural law."[36] The purpose of this natural law, according to Calvin, "is to render man inexcusable." In fact, he mused that it might be a satisfactory definition of natural law to consider it "that apprehension of the conscience which distinguishes sufficiently between just and unjust, and which deprives men of the excuse of ignorance, while it proves them guilty by their own testimony."[37] In conjunction with the conscience that ascertains it, this natural law serves as an "inner witness and monitor of what we owe God," presenting to us "the difference between good and evil and thus accusing us when we fail in our duty."[38]

Calvin did not discuss the moral content of the natural law systematically, but he associated it with the Decalogue. As he began his exposition of the Ten Commandments in the *Institutes,* Calvin noted that the "inward law . . . written, even engraved, upon the hearts of all, in a sense asserts the very same things that are to be learned from the two Tables."[39] Similarly, while outlining his political thought in the final chapter of the *Institutes,* Calvin argued that "the law of God which we call the moral law [or the Decalogue] is nothing else than a testimony of natural law and of that conscience which God has engraved upon the minds of men."[40] As suggested by this connection between natural law and both tables of the Decalogue, Calvin believed that natural law included the imperative to divine worship, though he was quick to remind that knowledge of or adherence to natural law is in no way sufficient for salvation.

Besides overtly religious references, though, the natural law includes certain general moral principles that every human being ought to recognize as right or good. Among these, according to Calvin, are "universal impressions" of what it means to share "civic fair dealing and order."[41] Indeed, he believed that human beings' sociality itself is a naturally determined characteristic, as are many of those virtues that allow this social animal to cohabit in communities and "to foster and preserve society." Social cooperation and assistance to the poor—"the sharing of tasks among members" of society—are obligations that the law of nature prescribes upon us.[42] Similarly, human laws that provide for social safety and order are rooted in natural law. Calvin recognized the disagreement within and between cultures over the appropriateness of specific political conceptions and structures of order, but he insisted that "while men dispute among themselves about individual sections of the law, they agree on the general conception of equity," that indeed "the fact remains that some seed of political order has been implanted in all men. And this is ample proof that in the arrangement of this life no man is without the light of reason."[43] It is the existence of this natural law that allows even those who do not know true faith to foster community, Calvin believed, for "it is beyond all doubt that they have certain ideas of justice and rectitude . . . which are implanted by nature in the hearts of men."[44]

Individuals within and between cultures certainly do disagree about how to interpret the general principles of natural law in particular circumstances, though, and Calvin argued that this is a sign and consequence of sin's effect on our ability to recognize, interpret, and live by the natural law. While the general norms of moral law are known to all human beings, they often are not understood clearly and seldom are applied accurately. Natural law certainly does not guarantee moral rectitude, said Calvin, for no person possesses an adequate command of the law for consistent moral virtuosity. Specifically, Calvin seemed to suggest that human beings' knowledge of natural law becomes less certain when it comes to applying its general principles to particular circumstances, because various loyalties and the complexities of specific cases make the application of natural-law principles a less dependable exercise than the knowledge of those principles in general.[45] Furthermore, he indicated that natural law provides knowledge of morality, but not the will to obey it.[46] It is because "man is so shrouded in the darkness of errors," despite the access to natural law, that "the Lord has provided us with a written law to give us a clearer witness of what was too obscure in the natural law, shake off our listlessness, and strike more vigorously our mind and memory."[47]

Despite his pessimism regarding its efficacy in particular cases, however, Calvin asserted that the natural law continues to function as a basic source for moral orientation and as a guide to human beings as they attempt to live together. Following Calvin, the Puritans maintained this role for natural law in the moral life, employing it with lasting consequence as a political argument against the extension of royal power designed to compromise Puritan spiritual freedoms. As William Haller described Puritan thought on this point, "the law of nature was said to consist of all those divine decrees which called creation into being and by which it moves. It is a law evident to reason, which is itself a work of God, and this law, though transcended, is by no means invalidated by grace."[48] Most importantly for the Puritans' political cause, "Law of man's making must conform to the law of nature or be of no force." Unfortunately for Charles I, the Puritans judged royal advances on their religious prerogatives to be against the law of nature and reacted accordingly, by removing his head.

Puritan preachers of prerevolutionary England argued vehemently against the king on the basis of natural law, and their appeal to natural law found camaraderie in the cause of gentry parliamentarians, who had taken to arguing for similar ends by employing Coke's notion of common law and the sense of natural right which it implied.[49] Yet the Puritan belief in natural law was more than a religious reformulation of common law theory. Natural law was very much at home in the Reformed confession of the Puritans as a theological argument based in the thinking of Calvin, Thomas, and Augustine. William Ames insisted that God directed all of creation by what he called "common government," which amounted to no more than "the law of nature common to all things" but which human beings have a unique capacity to ascertain.[50] The natural law "participates" in the divine will and command and governs all of God's creative ordering, as it has from the beginning. Natural law also serves as human beings' source of basic moral direction, informing the conscience and preventing persons from claiming ignorance in the fundamental distinctions between right and wrong.[51] Civil law, to the extent that it is morally justifiable, "is derived from the law of nature."[52] Ames's appeal to the moral role of natural law was equally at home in the work of his predecessor William Perkins, and similar invocations would be made by Puritans like John Cotton, Samuel Willard, and John Davenport after him.[53]

Roger Williams was quite comfortable in the natural law tradition. He testified to the existence of the "law of nature," or "natural wisdom," as "that Candle or Light" that remains in every person despite sin, providing moral direction and telling us the difference between right and wrong. It is the moral compass that differentiates human beings from other creatures and enables us to strive for that semblance of "Humanitie" in our moral lives and our cohabitation in community.[54] Natural law mediates God's will to human beings, and persuades us without appeal to external source "that some actions are naught, and against God's will."[55] In fact, natural law (especially as it is directed against us by conscience) serves as internal indictment when we do wrong; those who transgress the natural law are charged within themselves and thus "cannot but confess themselves sinners and justly punished."[56] While he taught that it could be "refined and elevated" by the effects of moral education and life experience, Williams was confident that the law of nature by itself was a moral power "common to all mankinde," upon which a basic level of moral performance and coexistence could be maintained and expected.[57]

Rhetorically less disciplined than Ames in many respects, Williams unsurprisingly offers no systematic account of the moral norms he considered part of the natural law. As is the case with many dimensions to his moral theology, the norms of natural law appear only in practice, only as he makes appeal to them in the process of arguing for toleration. Nonetheless his use of them gives us some sense of what Williams believed natural law to entail. Generally he believed that natural law was reflected in the second table of the Decalogue, in the prohibition of basic actions like murder, theft, lying, and adultery.[58] These were acts that, in Williams's view, any person regardless of culture or religion would consider wrong and "inconsistent to the converse of man with man."[59] Natural law provides moral ends and fundamental norms to both our interpersonal behavior and our civil existence. Without these ends, norms, and boundaries, social coexistence is impossible; for a civil society that is not governed by natural law, "it is impossible that men can live (as men, and nor as Beasts or worse) together."

Citing Tertullian, Williams argued that religious toleration follows from respect for this natural law.[60] Apart from biblical injunction, Williams believed even natural morality proscribes assault on other human beings as a product of their convictions. To persecute belief, argued Williams, violates the integrity of the person at a level natural morality seeks to protect. Religious persecution deprives persons of civil rights that are rooted in their natural rights, which the natural law gives no political institution or authority the power to compromise.[61] Indeed, natural law provided an important leg to Williams's grand argument for toleration, for it permitted him to make his argument relevant to Puritans and "papists," New England governors, Spanish "turks," English kings, and American sachems, not on the basis of particular revelation but on a foundation of moral principles that all human beings should be able to recognize as consonant with their own.

Toleration is just one of the norms of natural law that Williams thought that his Native American friends reflected admirably. The Americans proved the existence of natural law, because with no access to Christian teaching or Scripture, they nonetheless managed to order their communities on basic moral principles the Europeans also recognized. These included prohibitions against unjustified bodily harm, thievery, and dishonesty, as well as the cultivation of positive virtues like respect for the commitment of marriage, humility, and modesty. In the Americans Williams saw the confirmation of his belief in a natural law that could serve as common moral ground for conversation and cooperation across religious and cultural barriers.[62]

Moral cooperation was not as simple as an appeal to the natural law, as Williams's prolonged debate with the Massachusetts ministers made clear. Like Calvin, he believed that sin made knowledge of its norms unreliable and application of them tentative. Williams himself occasionally attributed questionable norms to the natural law. Against the Quakers, for instance,

Williams claimed that the socially deviant Friends violated natural law by their immodest behavior, a charge that occasionally appears as rooted in conservative Puritan social style as in any universal sense of moral right. More troubling, Williams insisted that the Quakers' habit of entrusting leadership and public-speaking roles to women violated the natural ordering by which God's creation and human society ought to be governed.[63] Like any other good Calvinist, Williams argued that the presence of sin made knowledge of the natural law a delicate exercise and one prone to error, and at times his appeal to natural law seems to demonstrate this negative potential. Despite the complications sin laid upon the endeavor to know and follow the moral law, however, Williams maintained that human beings' fallible awareness of the norms and values of natural law provided sufficient basis to make moral arguments, engage in moral conversation, and share cooperative ventures with persons of different religious and cultural backgrounds.

THE MORAL SIGNIFICANCE OF HISTORY AND EXPERIENCE

Although some of the language he used to describe how he thought human beings discern the laws of nature resembled the metaphysical intuitionism of medieval (and many Reformed) natural-law thinkers, Williams generally seemed to consider access to natural law to be the product of rational deliberation. Human beings discern the natural law by rationally considering the needs and ends of human flourishing and the common good and analyzing human experience, identifying those social practices that tend to further these ends. In particular, Williams frequently referred to current experiences, contemporary social practices, and historical events in order to extract values and principles that he would then claim represent both the fundamental human good and the requirements of natural law. In fact, Williams's appeals to human experience are at times so dominant in his arguments that he appears to have considered it a source of authority on par with rational argumentation itself and nearly as persuasive as appeal to religious sources. From the beginning of his greatest treatise on toleration, Williams constructed his moral arguments on the tripod of "Religion, Reason, Experience."[64] He believed that the moral principles commended by Christian faith and discernible by rational contemplation of the natural law manifested themselves in the practical existence of human beings in history and the present, and that the examination of the moral successes and failures of societies provided moral deliberators with evidence to interpret the norms that contributed to the common good.

Numerous times Williams pointed to instances in the historical record to demonstrate the civil advantage of the practice of religious liberty, as well as the moral detriment and social costs of intolerance and oppression.[65] He countered Cotton's desire to endow the magistrate with religious authority by pointing to what "histories and all experience demonstrate," that the injustices that so-called "Christian magistrates" routinely commit contradict the confidence that Cotton possessed in them. Human experience, argued Williams, indicates that Christian governors are equally capable of tyranny and non-Christian magistrates are just as prone to fairness and magnanimity.[66] He claimed that the principle of liberty (and, incidentally, democratic government) was plainly vindicated by "the experience of all commonweales," and that history also made abundantly clear that non-Christians make as peaceful and neighborly citizens as do Christians.[67] In short, Williams argued that toleration was not only reasonable and biblical, but also historically tested and empirically justified.

By his appeal to human experience, Williams implied that its testimony was fundamentally consistent with the moral direction of practical reasoning and religious sources. In fact, Williams tied his varied moral sources together during one of his most impassioned pleas for religious liberty, when he suggested that the commands of Christian religion and the lessons of human experience made similar demands, that toleration is not just a fundamental Christian imperative but a requirement for the expression of true humanity as well:

> Oh, will not the Authority of holy Scripture, the Commands and Declarations of the Sonne of God, therein produced by thee, together with all the lamentable experiences of former and present slaughters prevail with the Sons of Men (especially with the Sons of Peace) to depart from the dens of Lyons, and mountains of Leopards, and to put on the bowels (if not of Christianitie, yet) of Humanitie each to other![68]

Clearly Williams considered historical analysis of human experience to be an important tool for the practical deliberation of moral norms and values. When utilized in conjunction with the moral powers of reason and (among Christians) the testimony of religious sources, Williams believed the interpretation of human experience could contribute to the project of public moral discourse and discernment.

Williams's incorporation of human experience in the tasks of public moral discourse extended beyond the observation and analysis of moral values and vices in practice, however. To him the everyday experiences of human existence were also morally significant in the way that analogical connections could be drawn between morally certain experiences and more ambiguous scenarios, in order to seek clarity in the latter. Williams seems to have employed what David Tracy and William Spohn call "analogical imagination," an openness to reflection on a morally uncertain situation from the perspective of known experiences, values, and requirements.[69]

Tracy describes the power behind analogical imagination as the capacity "to note the profound similarities-in-difference in all reality."[70] In the frequent claims he made regarding the moral significance of historical and contemporary events, Williams exercised analogical imagination, drawing connections between events and experiences across historical and cultural lines and analyzing the moral values that this commonality infers. Sometimes his use of analogical thinking required him to identify the connections between two seemingly unrelated experiences, in order to show that the moral expectations we have in one situation inform what we should expect in the other. For instance, in *The Bloody Tenent* Williams drew an analogy between family dynamics and political arrangements in order to argue against compelled religious belief. He begins with the morally clear case of the family, in which he assumes that his readers will recognize both scriptural and rational prohibitions against a Christian husband compelling his non-Christian spouse to share his beliefs. From this clear case, Williams draws connections to the contested question of the appropriateness of political compulsion of belief. Arguing for the similarity-in-difference between the integrity of personal conscience on the familial and political levels, Williams uses analogical imagination to make moral arguments on the basis of appeal to experience.[71]

Sometimes his use of analogical imagination served not to draw connections between different experiences but to highlight the similarity in the experience of different persons or parties, as when Williams reminded John Cotton that the persecution New England dissenters suffered strongly resembled Cotton's own predicament in England.[72] In this way, Williams took advantage of another benefit of analogical thinking, its ability to link us to other moral agents by drawing connections between their experiences and our own.[73] Regardless of the specific form his analogical reflection takes, Williams's use of this method of incorporating human experience into moral argumentation reflects, as Spohn claims Christian analogical imagination must, a perspective guided by Scripture but nonetheless committed to the synthesis of religious authority with moral insight from other sources and experiences.[74] This allowed Williams to find in his appeals to human experience new interpretations of faithfulness to religious imperatives in his own circumstances, as well as moral connections with those for whom his religious imperatives may hold no moral weight.

In sum, experience served Williams's moral theology in two ways, by providing an arena in which moral clarity could be pursued through the analogical connection of related scenarios, and by itself inferring values and norms from the success and failures of certain experiences to contribute to human flourishing and the common good. As James Gustafson notes, "the possibility of inferring general values and principles from experience assumes that the continuities in human experience are greater than the discontinuities."[75] It was this assumption of similarity-in-difference that allowed Williams not only to utilize empirical reference and analogical thinking, but also to argue that the moral direction that experience (and reason) yields warrants a cautious optimism regarding the project of public moral discourse and cooperation.

RELIGIOUS CONVICTIONS AND COMMON MORALITY

We see in Williams's treatment of natural law, reason, and experience a theological recognition of basic moral capabilities among human beings qua human beings. Moreover, this same theological vocabulary allowed Williams to envision the possibility of wide public discourse on moral matters and, in fact, of commonly held moral norms and values. Natural law and moral reasoning represented for him an expansion of the range of ethics rooted in Christian believing, for they explain in religious terms the empirical fact that human beings share widespread agreement on basic moral values, despite differences in religion, ethnicity, or even culture. Natural law recognizes this moral common ground and explains it theologically by locating it within the creative dominion of God, as part of the ordering by which God has arranged and is arranging the physical and moral coexistence of all creatures. Williams's appeal to natural law assumed—and his dependence on moral reasoning made explicit—that human beings possess powers of rationality that play an important role in human moral performance. This capacity for practical reasoning allows human beings not only to recognize the distinction between moral goods and evils, but also to deliberate on the moral appropriateness of certain actions and to converse with others about basic moral norms. The cautious confidence in human moral reasoning that stands behind Williams's use of natural law, out of step with neither his own theology nor that of his Reformed brethren, provided him with a basis for moral appeal in his arguments for religious liberty, as well as a reasonable hope that those arguments might be persuasive to a broad public.

Williams's employment of natural law may appear to be of limited contemporary use in a philosophical climate in which metaphysical invocation of a law embedded in the nature of moral existence garners very little confidence. Indeed, as David Novak argues, traditional appeals to natural law, which tend to depend on an adaptation of Platonic-Stoic metaphysics, cannot work in a time when the epistemological claims underlying such appeals are no more universally accepted than the religious commitments such a turn to natural law seeks to transcend.[76] Insofar as his natural-law theory inherits these classical metaphysical underpinnings of Reformed theology, this intuitionism would seem to compromise the contemporary usefulness of Williams's moral theology. As his reference to natural law often suggests, Williams considered the natural moral law to consist of universal norms that were conceptually integrated into the very order of created and moral existence. Such a theological construal of natural law may correspond well with the conceptualization of the relationship between God, creation, and moral law that marks the distinctive perspective of Christian tradition, but its tie to specific metaphysical claims limits its usefulness when audience is extended beyond the religious community.

His appeals to natural law are more complex than an exclusive tie to metaphysical epistemological claims, however, for as often as he makes reference to innate moral law in the language of classical natural-law theory, more often he seems to establish the "universality" of certain moral norms not on the basis of intuition, but on observation. For Williams, the norms of natural law seem to be most clearly discerned by the empirical observation of their widespread confirmation in human history and experience. As a result, Williams's use of natural law appears to be as dependent on generalized observation of human coexistence as it is on metaphysical stipulations.[77] Understood this way, natural law serves as a theological explanation of the observed intersections between Christian moral reflection and the moral possibilities of persons outside the faith community. If the language of "universals" is perhaps too strong, then, natural law is essentially a theological argument for the existence of at least moral "generals"; it serves as an internal explanation of external observation, of the recognition of moral capacity and similar moral norms outside the borders of the faith community and the influence of its sources. The basis for its plausibility to an external audience, however, lies not exclusively in its conceptual commitment to a moral ordering inherent in the social and physical ordering of creation, but also in its being based on the observation of moral commonality among communities of different religions and cultures. As Novak describes his own preference for religious thinking grounded in natural law, when the religious community prepares to say something beyond its borders, it "will have to appeal to historically evident data rather than to . . . metaphysics," a shift Williams philosophically was equipped to make.[78]

Williams's appeals to experience in his moral arguments for toleration suggest that his confidence in the existence of moral norms that transcend the sources and pronouncements of particular religious communities rested in part on his observation of these general norms already at work in the world. The significant role that observation, history, and experience play in considering the general norms of natural law compelled Williams to coordinate his moral claims with sources beyond the overtly religious. In his works on toleration, Williams seeks coherence between "Religion, Reason, [and] Experience," and natural law is his primary tool for tying these various sources together. A theory of natural morality like Williams's seeks not only commonality with more "universally" accepted sources and facts, but also consistency with them. Its moral claims must be supported not just by revealed norms and values but by the other moral and non-moral facts available. Discontinuity between those facts and religious values not only calls the nonreligious facts into question but also opens religious principles and values to critical review and change. By his incorporation of historical events and personal experience in the epistemological foundation for his conception of natural law, Williams appears to have placed a high value on the need for coherence between his religiously generated moral values and sources and other relevant nonreligious sources of insight. His coordination of religious and nonreligious sources for moral reasoning resembles Robin Lovin's depiction of ethical naturalism, insofar as it "treats a very broad range of facts as relevant to moral assessments. Personal satisfactions, affective responses, and the cumulative experience of individuals and communities are among the elements around which a considered moral judgment must be built, along with other considerations susceptible to more objective determination."[79]

Williams's use of natural law and recognition of a general human capacity for moral reasoning allowed him to make the turn from an ethics of inner correspondence to one that cohered with and engaged possibilities and perspectives beyond its own internal story. Because the idea of natural law itself corresponded with the sources of his theological tradition, however, Williams was able to broaden his ethics without abandoning its confessional character. The result was an approach to public ethics that provided both internal theological justification and the prospect for drawing connections between Christian morality and other ethical perspectives in a philosophically legitimate way. Ultimately, Williams's theory of natural morality combined his commitment to the particular convictions of Reformed Christianity with his desire to extend moral cooperation beyond the faith community in a way that retained both theological and philosophical integrity.

4

CONSCIENCE

Without a doubt, any place Roger Williams enjoys in American lore he secured with his impassioned defense of the freedom of conscience. If he is known for anything, it is his apology for the integrity of conscientious conviction and the anathemas he pronounced on any attempts to coerce fundamental belief. Williams framed out his thoughts on freedom of conscience in his initial rejoinders to John Cotton, including *The Bloody Tenent of Persecution*, published during his first return to London in 1644. Williams's extended investigation of the question of conscience, however, was forced to wait for his second return to England, since no Boston publisher would touch his seditious blasphemy. In 1652 the citizens of Rhode Island asked Williams to return to London to defend their charter once again, this time against the sabotage of troublemakers within the colony. Upon his return to England, Williams sent to the printer his response to Cotton's response to *The Bloody Tenent*, along with several other political tracts and a devotional guide written for his wife. The sequel to his classic *Bloody Tenent*, imaginatively titled *The Bloody Tenent Yet More Bloody*, offered a more detailed portrait of the "faculty" of conscience, the phenomenon of conscientious conviction, and the principled reasons for protecting freedom of belief. By the time of its publication, John Cotton was already dead and Williams ostensibly had won their verbal contest, but *The Bloody Tenent Yet More Bloody* remains an important (though laboriously written) theological and philosophical exposition of freedom of conscience.

Williams was not the first representative of the Reformed tradition to explore the phenomenon of conscience. The early Reformers inherited their basic notions of conscience from medieval scholasticism, but their zeal to distance themselves from what they considered excessive scholastic legalism also stirred them to consider the concept in innovative ways. Especially in defense of a Protestant emphasis on Christian liberty, John Calvin developed a theory of conscience that both underwrote his rejection of papal regulation and provided boundaries to counter the libertarian temptations inherent in his doctrine of Christian freedom. Although he furthered the consideration of conscience conceptually and theologically, Calvin did little in the way of suggesting direct applications for his theoretical work to practical circumstances of human living. For the most part, the Puritans accomplished just the opposite, taking for granted the theoretical existence of conscience and dwelling instead on the extensive implications of this capacity for sometimes hundreds of specific moral scenarios. The "casebooks," as they were called, provided the Puritans with a demonstration of how moral reflection properly discerns norms and applies them to "cases of conscience."[1]

Williams's appeal to conscience in his moral theology characteristically offered little that immediately resembled the approaches of other Reformed thinkers. He neither took the time to outline an explicit theoretical understanding of conscience nor provided any long list of practical circumstances in which to trace its operation. Despite the apparent dissimilarity between Williams's utilization of conscience and the work of his Reformed brethren, however, a Calvinist interpretation of conscience plays a central role in Williams's moral theology, especially in his contribution to the question of the relationship between religious conviction and moral pluralism. His failure to develop a casebook on questions of conscience ought not to surprise us, for the pace of events in his life scarcely provided him sufficient time to compose the ad hoc pieces he did manage to publish. The exhaustive effort necessary for a casebook to be written lay beyond the capabilities of this already-pressed religious activist. In a sense, one might say, his life was preoccupied with one specific category of cases, circumstances in which the convictions of conscience put one at odds with the religious establishment of the state. Williams's entire corpus, in other words, could be considered one category in the casebooks of most Puritan moralists.[2]

Like the other elements to his moral anthropology, then, Williams's Reformed understanding of conscience is embedded in his application of it to the cause of liberty, requiring the reader to excavate from his polemics in order to reconstruct the conceptual assumptions with which he worked. Also like the rest of his moral theology, Williams's invocation of conscience was clearly theologically grounded. His disagreements with Cotton and the Quakers over freedom of conscience often revolved around differences in biblical exegesis.[3] He thought about conscience in the theological context of early English Puritanism, which provided him with the conceptual basis on which to contribute his revolutionary defense of conscientious freedom. In the face of repeated scholarly and popular attempts to read Williams through the lens of Thomas Jefferson, any successful interpretation of Williams on the question of conscience must first recognize him as the heir, and innovator, of the Reformed theological tradition.

CONSCIENCE AND THE REFORMED TRADITION

Williams's understanding of conscience was influenced by important thinkers in the Reformed tradition, but any consideration of the roots for his conception of conscience must begin with Thomas Aquinas (1224–1274), for both historical and philosophical reasons. The Reformed understanding of conscience to which Williams was introduced as a student at Cambridge was itself based, indirectly at least, in the theology of Thomas Aquinas. The two premier moralists of English Puritanism, Williams Perkins and William Ames, built on a conceptual foundation that they inherited from medieval scholasticism. Their work in turn served as the foundation for Puritan moral education and theological training for generations in old and New England, as their treatises became staples in the Puritan curricula. From his time at Cambridge and his lifelong association with the Puritan movement, Williams certainly would have been acquainted with the works of Perkins and Ames (as his occasional references to them confirm), and thus he was exposed to at least a modified Thomistic understanding of conscience. In addition to historical accuracy, another reason for reading Williams with Thomas in mind is the conceptual similarity between elements in Thomas's development of conscience and Williams's, in particular the appreciation for freedom of conscience. Williams's sympathy for conscientious freedom is remarkable for its liberality, and unique in this regard among the stalwarts of early Puritanism. He was unlike many of his Puritan colleagues in his unwillingness to compromise the freedom of conscience even in the name of doctrinal purity or religious conformity, but this facet of his thought represents one of his strongest affinities with Thomas.[4]

For Thomas, conscience consisted of two main parts, the *synderesis* and *conscientia*. The *synderesis* is a human being's intellectual capacity to be aware of first-order natural principles of morality. As Thomas understood it in his Aristotelian framework, the conscience is an intellectual habit, or the "natural disposition of the human mind by which it apprehends . . . the basic principles of behavior, which are the general principles of natural law."[5] These first principles of the natural law occur to the *synderesis* similar to how an idea strikes a person; they are received rather than actively acquired. Because these principles are not intuitively but necessarily or logically true, and since *synderesis* simply acts as a receiver for them, it cannot be wrong.[6] Thomas argued that the existence and availability of infallible moral principles made logical sense, since "in order that there can be some rightness in human deeds, there must be some enduring principle which has unchangeable rightness and by reference to which all deeds are tested."[7] *Synderesis* provides this enduring moral stability by making the first principles available to moral agents. Without the assurance that at least these first principles exist, Thomas argued, human beings' prospects for moral knowledge are tenuous:

> For there could be no stability or certainty in what results from the first principles, unless the first principles were solidly established. Anything which is variable goes back, accordingly, to some first fixed thing. So it is, also, that every particular apprehension comes from some absolutely certain apprehension about which there can be no mistake. This is apprehension of basic general principles, by reference to which all particular apprehensions are tested and in virtue of which everything true wins approval but everything false is rejected. If any mistake could occur about these, then there could be no certainty in the entire subsequent apprehension.[8]

Thus, for Thomas, "those unchangeable notions are the first practical principles, concerning which no one errs; and they are attributed to reason as to a power, and to *synderesis* as to a habit."[9] Because *synderesis* simply receives the first principles of natural morality, it, like its moral norms, cannot err.

Nor can it be extinguished, for the *synderesis* is a permanent and universal part of the human intellect. Thomas assigned to the *synderesis* that internal "murmur" that every moral agent ought to experience when he or she transgresses the moral law. Anticipating the objection that some people act as if they lack this capacity for self-indictment, Thomas insisted that the apparent absence of a gnawing conscience does not mean that a person lacks *synderesis*. According to Thomas, "it is just as impossible that *synderesis* should be extinguished as that the soul of a man should be deprived of the light of the active intellect, by which the primary premises [*sic*] of theoretical and practical reasoning are made known to us."[10] For Thomas, *synderesis* "belongs to the very nature of the soul"; it is what makes us moral agents and is part of being human. Therefore, Thomas argued, there is no such thing as a human being without *synderesis*.

Thomas was not as confident about the staying power of the second part of the conscience, the *conscientia*, which denoted the actual exercise of applying the norms ascertained by *synderesis* to particular moral circumstances. Illustrating its active character, Thomas described *conscientia* as the internal moral deliberation that "is said to witness, to bind, or incite, and also to accuse, to torment, or rebuke" us in the moments of moral decision making.[11] Thomas admitted that this active process of relating first principles to real-life moments is a complicated endeavor, as the norms of *synderesis* exist at a level of generality that does not make them immediately transferable to specific moral circumstances. *Conscientia* is capable of reflecting on those acts already committed as well as evaluating acts that are being considered, and when it operates in the latter manner, wrote Thomas, we say that conscience "binds" us to a certain course.

Whether evaluating acts antecedently or subsequently, the active exercise of conscience, unlike the passive *synderesis*, can make mistakes. Although the first principles themselves are without error, conscience can mistakenly draw false conclusions from the general principles or incorrectly apply first principles to specific circumstances. By locating moral error in *conscientia* and not the *synderesis*, Thomas preserved the infallibility of divine law while simultaneously acknowledging the existence of conscientious disagreement and error. Interestingly, Thomas also suggested that another way conscience is made to err is by being deprived of the free use of reason and choice it requires to operate with integrity.[12] The freedom of conscience is something to be respected, according to Thomas, even in the case of a conscience that appears to direct wrongly. This priority for the freedom of erroneous conscience marks a moment in which Williams seems to have shared more in common with the medieval scholastic than he did with his Reformed predecessors.

Unlike Thomas, John Calvin spent little time dissecting the inner capacities and processes of conscience.[13] In its most basic form, Calvin considered the conscience to be simply a power of moral "discrimination" or "judgment" by which moral agents know which acts are wrong and which are acceptable. More evocatively, Calvin described conscience as the experience of internal "arguments" by which an agent's actions are defended or indicted.[14] As with most of the Calvinists after him (in particular the Puritans), Calvin rooted his belief in a phenomenon called "conscience" both in the testimony of human experience and the witness of Scripture. Key among the biblical warrants for believing in the existence of conscience was the apparent reference to it in the beginning chapters of Paul's letter to the Romans. Paul claimed that even the Gentiles possessed a "law written in their hearts," or a "conscience bearing witness . . . accusing or else excusing them," and in the apostle's invocation of conscience Calvin read justification for developing his own theory of a universal faculty for shared morality.[15] He did so, however, not only as biblical exegesis but also as an attempt to incorporate into his soteriological and moral system what he took to be a universal human experience.

For Calvin, the internal argumentation of conscience is most notable for the negative experience it produces, the "pangs" of conscience suffered when the internal "awareness" or "witness" makes known to a moral agent the inappropriateness of a committed act. In this condemnation, said Calvin, the conscience delivers the equivalent of God's judgment on an agent's actions. Calvin called the conscience the "mean between God and man" that defies the human impulse to ignore or conceal one's sins; instead the conscience "arraigns" the moral actor "as guilty before the judgment seat." The conscience pronounces God's verdict, communicating "divine judgment" upon a particular moral act.[16] While Calvin emphasized its negative and judicial function, its subsequent condemnation of behavior that has transgressed moral "duty," occasionally he described conscience as capable of approving acts it judges to be appropriate. In his *Commentary on the Epistle to the Romans*, Calvin claimed that moral agents are "inwardly harassed and tormented when conscious of having done evil" but also "are sustained and comforted by their consciousness of good actions."[17] Clearly Calvin believed conscience to be capable of both positive and negative judgments. In addition, Calvin implied that the conscience is not only in the business of evaluating acts after they have occurred, but also of commending acts antecedently. Again in his discussion of Romans, he described the conscience as "a certain natural knowledge of the law, which states that one action is good and worthy of being followed, while another is to be shunned with horror."[18] The grammar in the recommendation that an act is "worthy of being followed" itself suggests that conscience has the capacity to make antecedent judgments, so that conscience serves not only as evaluator of past actions but as moral compass for considering present and future ones.

In both its antecedent and subsequent forms, the phenomenon of conscience is a universal capacity. In the *Institutes* Calvin insisted that a conscience is "engraved" by God on the minds of every human being, thus equipping them to know God's moral law and rendering them inexcusable before it.[19] In his commentary on Romans, he suggested that conscience provided even the unregenerate person with "knowledge of right and justice."[20] Through the internal pangs of conscience, every human person possesses "an inner witness and monitor of what we owe God," for in conscientious reflection this moral power holds before us "the difference between good and evil and thus accuses us when we fail in our duty."[21] It does so by appeal to the natural law, through that "inward law" written upon the conscience.[22]

Sin interferes with the conscience, however, compromising its ability to operate and rendering its witness "dimmed." Calvin neglected to explain clearly what he meant by a diminution in the powers of conscience—whether, like Thomas, he believed that the conscience perfectly understands the natural principles but errs in applying them, or that it struggles even to ascertain God's moral norms. Randall C. Zachman sees in Calvin's theology three levels on which sin could sabotage the operation of conscience. Sometimes sinners misidentify evil as good, or at least as too trivial to be of great moral consequence. Other times human beings are guilty of justifying a bad act by appeal to a larger good intention. In other words, we begin with an appropriate understanding of the general norms of conscience but erroneously use them to justify particular acts of questionable virtue. Finally, some persons explicitly override their consciences, committing an act the conscience insists is bad. This utter disregard for the dictates of conscience Calvin called "malice," and it was for him the highest order of moral wickedness.[23] Referring to it as "sinning against conscience," Puritans like John Cotton would invoke this blatant disregard for conscience to describe those who, after repeated attempts at correction, insisted on articulating beliefs contrary to what the Bible and their consciences insisted was true. The guard against those who "sinned against conscience" would be one of the chief platforms for Puritan enforcement of religious uniformity.

The Puritans inherited Calvin's presumption of the universality of conscience, the belief that God invests every moral agent with this capacity to make moral judgments and recognize moral norms. One of his most notable successors on the subject, William Perkins (1558–1602), combined Calvin's theological loyalties with a philosophical framework roughly indebted to medieval scholasticism. Like Calvin, Perkins was preoccupied more with the relationship between conscience, sin, and the regenerate life than he was in providing an in-depth moral anthropology or portrait of human ethical deliberation.[24] Nonetheless, Perkins's exploration of conscience provided him with a theoretical basis on which to build his moral casuistry. According to Perkins, the conscience is that part of human understanding that evaluates particular actions and draws conclusions regarding their moral appropriateness, that "naturall power, facultie, or created qualitie, from whence knowledge and judgement proceede as effects."[25] Conscience judges the moral appropriateness of particular acts, representing God's judgments on them. In language similar to Calvin's, Perkins suggested that the conscience operates "in the middle between man and God," as God's "gift" by which the moral agent may see his or her moral performance as God sees it.[26] The conscience is the "combination" of the divine and the human within a person's moral makeup, and thus conscience has a "divine nature," because it "is a thing placed of God in the middest betweene him and man, as an arbitratour to give sentence and to pronounce either with man or against man unto God."[27]

As a human faculty that pronounces God's verdict on particular acts, conscience makes both antecedent and subsequent judgments. Perkins was less clear, though, whether conscience has the power to recommend good actions or is limited to pronouncing judgment against wrong ones. As a result, conscience in Perkins's scheme takes on a predominantly negative, judicial role. Like Calvin, however, Perkins insisted that this faculty of divine judgment is a capacity all human beings share. He distinguished between "good" conscience and "evil" conscience, but what he generally meant by the latter was simply *natural* conscience, which he did not believe was completely incapacitated by sin. On the contrary, a natural faculty of conscience "is to be found in all men that come of Adam by ordinarie generation."[28] Perkins admitted that the natural conscience is corrupted insofar as sin weakens our ability to ascertain the moral principles of God, but at the same time conscience "hath in it some respects of generall goodnesse."[29] Conscience still understands goodness sufficiently to act as the executor of divine judgment, though it is not entirely clear what Perkins meant by this. Sometimes he seems to suggest that the natural conscience, though compromised by sin, still retains some diminished capacity to discern natural moral principles and apply them to cases of action, while at other times he appears to argue that original sin completely extinguishes our access to natural principles of goodness. When he argued for this more radical effect of sin, Perkins suggested that conscience retains only the hypothetical ability to operate, but depends on education (namely, through exposure to the norms of the Bible) in order to have a "storehouse" by which to judge. Of course, the regenerate conscience has much of its knowledge of divine moral principles restored by grace, and this fact, along with the effect of Christian moral education, made Perkins more optimistic about the ability of a regenerate conscience to guide a person in an upright life.

Whether regenerate or not, the human conscience survives in all human beings as the vicegerent of God, the human faculty "appointed of God to declare and put in execution his just judgement against sinners." Because the conscience participates in the divine as well as the human, Perkins believed that it was inextinguishable. Just as with the judgment of God, the testimony of conscience could never be wholly removed from a moral agent. Of course Perkins understood that many persons live as if they experience no pangs of conscience, which led him to explain that conscience could lie "dead" in a person without being completely extinguished. To be "dead" was for conscience to be present but virtually inoperable because of the negative effects of a "defect of reason or understanding in crased braines," strong affections or passions, or a pattern of erroneous judgment. Despite the possibilities for a dormant conscience, however, Perkins shared Calvin's belief that conscience is a universal capacity for morality.

In many ways William Ames (1576–1633), the most significant of Perkins's students, improved on his teacher's theory of conscience by exploring it in much more theological and conceptual detail. Ames wrote two important theological treatises, *The Marrow of Theology* and *Conscience, with the Power and Cases Thereof*, which soon became required reading for any divinity student in the Puritan colonies. In these works Ames provided a detailed analysis of the phenomenon of conscience, its operation, freedom, and limits. Like his predecessors in the Reformed tradition, Ames understood conscience to be the internalization of the moral judgment of God. He described conscience as "man's judgment of himself, according to the judgment of God in him."[30] By this description Ames seems to have shared Perkins's view that conscience is a "combination" of human and the divine, a human capacity that nonetheless draws its authority from divine association, from the norms of God's law that form its moral basis. Like Thomas before him, Ames taught that the conscience apprehends general principles of moral obligation through the *synderesis*, which he described as a habit of the reason.[31] Because, Ames argued, all human beings have consciences, the *synderesis* provides all rational agents with access to at least fundamental tenets of "natural" morality. Though he refused to provide an exhaustive definition of the principles that constitute natural morality, Ames believed that a basic moral foundation is accessible even to the most unregenerate conscience.[32] The *synderesis*, then, is a "habit" or disposition through which the human agent becomes aware of "the principles of moral actions, that is, such actions as are our duty."[33] In the *synderesis* "the knowledge of many things which we ought to do or shun" is stored until the operations of conscience require their access.

This natural morality is both a universal component of the human moral faculty and an autonomous authority, in that it does not depend on external sources of enlightenment or special revelation to operate. According to Ames, the human conscience acts as an "inner tribunal," evaluating the moral activity of an agent according to a standard Aristotelian syllogism, which consisted of three parts: the proposition, the assumption, and the conclusion.[34] In any specific moral scenario, the proposition represents the relevant principle of natural morality at stake, whereas the assumption or "witness" denotes the conscience's identification and evaluation of the particular act in question. The conclusion then consists of a conjunction of the proposition and the assumption, the application of the general norm to the particular case in order to determine whether the act in question violated the relevant norm. Ames awarded the general principles themselves high respect; because they are norms rooted in the divine law of nature, they do not err. The operation of conscience, however, could misunderstand these principles, the nature of the moral issue at hand, or which norms are relevant to the case. Since conscience could be wrong in its recommendations in a particular case, Ames advocated theological and social limits to the protection of a freedom of conscience.

WILLIAMS'S CONCEPTION OF CONSCIENCE

Though he seldom offered any systematic exposition on the subject, Williams's understanding of conscience reflected both his indebtedness to Reformed theology and the innovations he introduced to that tradition. In *The Bloody Tenent Yet More Bloody*, Williams offered his basic definition of conscience: "a persuasion fixed in the minde and heart of a man which enforceth him to judge (as Paul said of himself a persecutor) and to do so and so, with respect to God, his worship, &c."[35] Elsewhere he described it as "the secret checks and whisperings" that haunt all persons, regenerate or not, and which "take Gods part against mens selfe, in smiting, accusing, &c."[36] Like his Reformed predecessors and contemporaries, Williams sometimes identified conscience with the voice of God's judgment. For instance, as he argued in *The Bloody Tenent Yet More Bloody* for respect for conscientious freedom, he encouraged would-be persecutors to consider, as they "fought against many severall sorts of Consciences," whether it is "beyond all possibilities and hazard, that I have not fought against God, that I have not persecuted Jesus in some of them?" The implication of the self-questioning Williams proposed is that the convictions of conscience could be the equivalent of divine judgment or direction, a point Calvin made with his "mean" metaphor and Perkins with his attribution of divinity to the faculty. Williams made this point explicitly when he referred to the "internal convictions of Natural Conscience" as a means by which God "hath passed Sentence" on human beings.[37]

In his most vivid metaphor for conscience, Williams associated it with that spirit that exists as "the candle of the Lord, searching . . . within the bosome of all mankinde."[38] This "spirit," he claimed, resides in all persons, though it may be more refined in some by education, observation, experience, or simply "finer Animal Spirits." Two of Williams's favorite images for conscience, as "light" and as a "persuasion," both suggest in their context that Williams considered conscience to be part of the intellectual faculties. His suggestion that conscience is a "persuasion" in the mind and heart hearkens back to the "inner tribunal" metaphor of Calvin and others and implies a process of deliberation and argumentation, rather than simple enlightenment or discovery. Likewise, his fondness for describing conscience as "light," especially when he connects conscience to his insistence that matters of conviction require personal search and examination to be genuinely accepted, points to his belief that we experience the exercise of conscience as an intellectual operation. Though he never takes up the vocabulary of syllogistic reasoning so dominant in Thomas and Ames, Williams's metaphors reflect the deliberative nature of conscientious consideration that characterizes scholastic and Reformed notions of conscience. In other words, Williams adopted the conventional Puritan conception of conscience as internal courtroom, in which an agent's acts are tried, arguments for and against are offered, and a judgment about the moral appropriateness of the act is rendered. Within this internal courtroom an act is assessed, understood, and evaluated by moral norms with binding authority, and the agent is "persuaded" as to the rightness or error of an act. As it did for Thomas, Calvin, Perkins, and Ames, the evaluative function of conscience in Williams's thought depended on the natural law.[39]

For Williams, then, conscience was a forensic operation in which the actions and beliefs of an agent are evaluated according to the standards of natural morality. According to Williams, this operation was capable of both negative and positive judgments. He shared the traditional expectation that conscience produced "pangs" of condemnation in response to acts judged to be morally inappropriate. In *The Bloody Tenent*, for example, Williams presumed that the consciences of Constantine and other imperial rulers harassed them when their ambition caused them to persecute in the name of Christ, while in its sequel he described conscience explicitly as the "self-conviction" by which moral agents "smite and wound themselves."[40] According to Williams, however, conscience not only condemns transgressions of natural law, but also confirms acts and beliefs that are consistent with the law. This positive role for conscience is implied in the argument that persecution serves only to harden the convictions of conscience. The notion of a conscience hardened in its convictions, so vital to one aspect of Williams's argument for toleration, itself suggests a capacity for holding positive judgments. Presumably dedicated to not only what it thinks is wrong but also convictions regarding what is right, the conscience reifies its loyalty to these positive judgments in the face of what an agent may perceive as suffering for the cause. Thus, rather than simply remaining silent until triggered to produce the pangs of negative judgment, as some theological conceptions have assumed, Williams's sense of conscience was that it communicates affirmation as well as condemnation. In doing so, conscience represented for him not simply an internal source for self-correction, but also the inner strength that justified and buoyed fundamental convictions.

For Williams the authority of conscience was also bidirectional, in that it was able to evaluate acts before or after they had been committed. Again, Williams assumed the conventional expectation that conscience renders judgment on acts after the fact, what I have called subsequent evaluation. In addition, however, he seemed to adopt the less common belief that conscience can evaluate actions being considered, judging their appropriateness before they have been committed (what I have labeled antecedent evaluation). For instance, against Cotton's claim that dissenters who have been shown the error of their way are guilty of sinning against conscience, Williams insisted that following what one had determined to be a right course of action or belief is really "following one's conscience," not sinning against it.[41] Importantly, Williams did not describe it simply as following one's *convictions* (i.e., a set of fundamental beliefs), but as following one's *conscience,* that active inner voice or "persuasion" capable of testifying to the moral appropriateness of a course of action before it actually had been undertaken.

That the antecedent and subsequent functions of the conscience are interrelated Williams made clear in *The Bloody Tenent*. In the midst of a diatribe against the civil persecution of religious belief, Williams argued that persecution only strengthens the conscience's convictions concerning both the rightness of past action or belief and the appropriateness of persisting in its conviction or activity:

> Now all these consciences walke on confidently and constantly even to the suffering of death and torments, and are more strongly confirmed in their beleefe and conscience, because such bloudy and cruell courses of persecution are used toward them.[42]

An environment of civil coercion energizes conscience in its antecedent and subsequent activity. Persecution justifies the conscience in its judgments of past acts and beliefs, which simply encourages it to evaluate future circumstances in a consistent manner. The antecedent and subsequent operations of conscience require a certain consistency between them, which persecution only deepens. Williams believed that neither the dull interference of civil institutions nor the intense discomfort of persecution could sway a resolute conscience, for its headstrong ways come from confidence in its own deliberations, its recognition of authority only in the moral law, and its connection to God as its source of "light" and direction.

One of the most important features to Williams's progressive arguments for religious freedom was his assumption that this procedural, authoritative capacity known as conscience was a moral authority shared by all human beings: "This Conscience is found in all mankinde, more or lesse, in Jewes, Turkes, Papists, Protestants, Paganse, &c."[43] In fact, Williams insisted (in the harsh language characteristic of his time and place) that this "Conscience of good and evil" is something that even "every savage Indian in the world hath."[44] In fact, Williams was motivated to write the *Key into the Language of America* primarily by his observation of conscientious conviction in the character of his Native American friends. Under the pretense of constructing a guide to Native American languages, Williams instead provided a comparative analysis of Native American culture in relation to English customs and behavior. One fascinating observation he made was the prevalence of the experience of conscience among the Native Americans. Unusually for his day and culture, Williams recognized the Native Americans as sophisticated moral beings, endowed with the same natural conscience as the English colonists and, in fact, better than the English at the social nurture of this capacity.[45] According to his testimony in the *Key*, Williams believed that the Americans not only valued mature moral conscience more than the English, but they also showed far more respect for variations in conscience than he observed in his own society, certainly more than he himself experienced in the Massachusetts Bay Colony.[46]

CONSCIENCE AMONG THE MORAL FACULTIES

As Norman Fiering has explicated in some detail, the majority of seventeenth-century Protestant moralists were indebted to medieval intellectualism for their emphasis on the understanding as the dominant moral faculty. Human beings are capable of making moral decisions because the intellect reveals to the will what is to be accepted or rejected as the good. Thus moral error primarily amounts to an improper understanding of the good, not a deficiency of the will or a misdirected desire. Intellectualism enjoyed a strong following among the early Puritans, inspired by the Protestant theologian Theodore Beza.[47] William Ames represents a deviation from this intellectualism, as he reconceived moral psychology in a voluntarist mode, borrowing from Calvin and Augustine (as well as possibly the medieval theologian John Duns Scotus) to do so. For Ames, the will or "heart" was the seat of an agent's love; the appropriateness of a person's love determined moral correctness, just as corrupted loves betrayed sin's infection.[48] Ames's voluntarism led him to focus on the corruptibility of the will, for the will was invested with extensive freedom to disregard, infect, and sometimes overpower the more stable functions of the intellect, including the conscience.[49] In contrast to Ames's voluntarism, however, much of early Puritan moral psychology reflected a clear intellectualist bias.

Williams assigned both intellectual and conative capabilities to the conscience, defining it as "a persuasion fixed in the minde and heart" (where "mind" and "heart" are seventeenth-century shorthand for the understanding and the will respectively). In doing so, Williams was not unique; Ames, for instance, assumed that both the will and the intellect were involved in the operation of conscience, and that they generally cooperated in all moral deliberation or endeavors. In general Puritan moral anthropology avoided the abuses of an overly categorical psychology, the kind of compartmental approach that led John Locke to reject faculty language entirely. Rather than a question of complete location, the matter of debate between proponents of moral intellectualism and advocates of voluntarism was one of primacy. Assuming that moral capability resided neither solely in the intellect nor entirely in the will, Puritan intellectualists and voluntarists disagreed instead over which component of the moral agent was the *primary* director of moral deliberation and action. They agreed, however, that both "faculties" participated in moral activity, insofar as moral deliberation and action were activity of the reason, which consisted of both the intellect and the will.

Williams associated conscience with both the mind and the heart, but overall his conception reflected an intellectualist interpretation that resonated with that of early Puritan thinkers. In his diatribe against his Quaker opponents, for instance, Williams countered their theology of inner light with a discussion of his own interpretation of the "light of nature." His discussion involved a multilayered study of natural law, its relationship to human knowledge and morality, and the distinction between the natural and the supernatural assistance of grace. Within an otherwise belabored exploration of natural morality, however, Williams offered what appears to be a faculty psychology:

> All light, or truth natural, civil, or divine, it comes from without, and is received by the internal faculty according to the capacity, nature, and measure of it. All truth or falsehood, light or darkness, is first espied by the watch or sentinel, fancy or comprehension, &c. From thence it is conveyed to the Court of Guard, where Captain Reason or his Lieutenant, common Sense and Experience, taketh examination, and memory keeps a Record of proceedings which go on by degree to Actions, &c.[50]

What is clear by the context in *George Fox* is that this faculty psychology refers not just to the apprehension of saving knowledge but to the *natural* acquisition of *moral* knowledge. Interestingly, each component of this natural "internal faculty," as Williams describes it, is intellectual in nature. Truth is received by an agent through initial "comprehension," after which it is examined and evaluated by the intellectual reservoirs of reason and the knowledge yielded by "common Sense" and "Experience," and then it is cataloged by "memory" along with the "Actions" that follow from it. According to Williams, the task of moral deliberation, as a subset of the larger project of receiving and evaluating truth in general, is chiefly an exercise of the understanding. At no point in his portrayal of this "internal faculty" does Williams outline an independent role for the will.

Williams's preference for an intellectualist interpretation of human morality is reflected in his description of conscience as well, which he considered to be part of the faculty of understanding. Conscience was for him the internal source of divine principles; it provides knowledge of what is good and what is not, as well as the fundamental convictions by which a person with integrity lives and acts. In the relationship between the will and the conscience, the conscience always appears superior and more powerful. According to Williams, the conscience, though susceptible to error in its operation, is endowed with a certain degree of dependability by virtue of its direct association with the voice and moral law of God. It is also the most powerful dimension to the moral "faculty," capable not only of testifying against the actions of the will but also of influencing an agent's conative response. The will does not enjoy such influence over the conscience, for although it may quietly disregard or openly defy conscience, it cannot by simple force of will change or conceal the witness of conscience itself. While conscience may suffer the ill effects of a lack of education or moral development, it is relatively unsusceptible to direct manipulation by the will.

While a doctrine of the relative inviolability of conscience may not seem very radical, not all of Williams's Puritan colleagues shared this view, and the difference between him and other Puritans on this relationship between will and conscience contributed to his unique perspective on the question of freedom of conscience. John Cotton, for instance, suggested that the will was capable of interfering with conscience. Cotton justified his support for persecuting "conscientious objectors" by insisting that those who persist in deviant behavior do not follow conscience but instead "sin against conscience." What he implies by this assertion is that moral agents are capable of more than an intentional disregard for the witness of conscience. They are able instead to willfully change the dictates of conscience, so that their conscience appears to them to commend behavior that a "true" conscience should reject. Cotton suggested that this perversion of the conscience gave itself away by the "boysterous and arrogant spirit" with which deviant behavior is "seditiously and turbulently promoted."[51] In other words, headstrong conviction signaled that a dissenter was not simply ignoring his or her conscience, but instead had willfully manipulated conscience to cause it to advocate deviant behavior.

Williams, of course, dismissed Cotton's whole notion of punishing those who "sin against conscience," calling the doctrine a "Figleaf to hide the nakedness of that bloudie Tenent" of government-sponsored persecution.[52] What Cotton called sinning against conscience Williams claimed was conscientious conviction, and to undermine the trust in conscience was tantamount to "overturning and rooting up the very foundation and roots of all true Christianity."[53] One reason Williams rejected Cotton's argument was his belief in the relative inviolability of conscience as it related to the will. For Williams, the will is a secondary moral faculty; although it can disregard the conscience or blatantly violate it, it cannot impersonate it or change its testimony. Williams certainly believed that the conscience is not impervious to sin and is capable of error, but he believed this error to be usually a result of improper understanding, not willful manipulation. Erroneous or not, if a person believes conscience to dictate a certain course of action, he or she cannot be regarded as "sinning against conscience" to follow that course, for Williams found it inconceivable that an agent could willfully manipulate or obscure the judgment that conscience rendered.

THE PROBLEM OF ERRONEOUS CONSCIENCE

Though he refused to award volition power over the conscience, however, Williams did believe the conscience to be capable of error.[54] Oddly enough, despite his occasional use of the language of "erroneous" or "blind" conscience, John Cotton seemed at times to imply that persistently sinful so-called conscientious behavior was not a result of any inherent error in the conscience itself. In cases of "sinning against conscience," he suggested that the ultimate sin was *against* the conscience, not in it, so that those who violated orthodox religious convictions or time-tested social conventions in the name of following their consciences had in fact misunderstood or violated their own consciences. On its own, conscience could not possibly endorse dangerous dissension, because the conscience was tuned to the divine law of God. Instead, dissenters were guilty of either ignorance or malice. Perhaps they misunderstood the dictates of their consciences, in which case civil and religious authorities had an obligation to correct their ignorance, first privately and then, if necessary, by public admonishment. If dissenters persisted in the claim of "conscientious objection," even after being shown the error of their ways, then the conclusion was clear, argued Cotton: the perpetrators were engaged in a willful disregard or manipulation of the dictates of conscience, and thus the authorities acted properly in pursuing them. Implicit in the charge of "sinning against conscience" was a belief that conscience, at its core, could not err, so that the sin of a dissenter must be located not in the conscience but in the will.

Williams disagreed, insisting that the conscience itself can be wrong.[55] He believed that it was possible and even common for persons to conscientiously choose actions that may be judged inappropriate in retrospect or by objective standards. His appeals for freedom of conscience took for granted that the conscience is capable of making mistakes, of misunderstanding the circumstances of a particular dilemma or of misapplying a moral norm. At the same time, Williams insisted that the possibility for error did not diminish the binding authority of the conscience. In the standard Puritan discussions of conscience, something of a balancing act was required between associating it with the divine will and judgment and acknowledging that convictions of conscience could lead to error and bad actions. To identify the conscience with God's will implies infallibility, but the empirical evidence suggests that moral agents often claim as conscientious conviction beliefs that by other (sometimes more reliable) measures appear to be morally wrong. How to negotiate this apparent contradiction between the fallibility of conscience and its identification with divine judgment was a logical quandary that many Puritan thinkers failed to resolve satisfactorily.[56]

Williams largely avoided the contradiction by moving away from the metaphor of divine judgment when he argued against the violation of personal conscience. As fond of the metaphor as any other Puritan when he was describing the *experience* of conscience, Williams depended less on the association with divine direction when it came to the subject of coercion of conscience, centering his arguments instead on the inalienable nature of belief itself. He objected to the coercion of conscience not primarily because it usurped authority from God, but because it made no sense in light of the very nature of human belief. The convictions of conscience are an intellectual experience, not a volitional one, he argued, and therefore any attempt to *force* a change upon them was useless. Conscientious conviction is by definition an inalienable experience over which no third party can assume control. Williams believed it absurd to suggest that persons could "will or betrust such a Power to the civil Magistrate to compel their Souls and consciences" to conform to convention or a government mandate.[57] Conscientious conviction is subject only to the rules of understanding, which effect change on belief not by force of will but by persuasion, education, argumentation, and "Search and Examination."[58] As a result, to try to change matters of conscience by force was to Williams impractical and irrational.[59]

Williams avoided the contradiction between divine infallibility and erroneous conscience by arguing for the inviolability of conscience without identifying it with the voice of God. He could admit that the conscience sometimes errs and still insist that coercion of conscience is wrong, because the inviolability of conscience did not for him depend on identifying it with God's moral judgment. Still, in response to Cotton's belief that religious or civil leaders possess authority to compel conformity from individual conscience, Williams insisted that conscientious convictions should be considered binding on a moral agent by nature.[60] The integrity of conscience that Williams sought to protect from overextending human authorities had to do less with a metaphysical identification with the divine than with the nature of conscientious conviction itself.

Williams, therefore, advocated liberal protections for freedom of conscience, arguing for a presumption of freedom unless a strong case could be made, in the interest of the public, for restrictions on conscientious belief and practice. Williams at times has been understood as a pragmatic defender of conscience, and certainly his arguments include practical considerations. For instance, he often argued against compulsion of conscience on the empirical fact that coercion seldom works. Too often, insisted Williams, the attempt to forcibly change the conscience of an individual succeeds only in hardening that conscience.[61] In addition, persecution of conscience threatens civil peace: "Hence then I affirm, that there is no Doctrine, no Tenent so directly tending to break the Cities peace, as this Doctrine of persecuting or punishing each other for the cause of conscience or Religion."[62] In fact, Williams insisted that the quickest way to peace with moral integrity is not forced uniformity, but a liberal policy of toleration.

Behind these practical reasons, however, lay more principled arguments for protecting freedom of conscience. Williams argued that it is simply wrong to commit violence against persons by forcing them to speak or behave contrary to conscience, because of what the conscience is and how it behaves. To forcibly repress conscientious conviction risks the ruin of this moral faculty. The very survival of conscientious conviction as a moral foundation for civil society depends on the presumed honesty and freedom of its testimony, so that to compromise its independence or to force its conformity to social norms is to risk weakening it to the point of extinction:

> The straining of mens consciences by civil power, is so far from making men faithful to God or man, that it is the ready way to render a man false to both: my ground is this: civil and corporal punishment do usually cause men to play the hypocrite, and dissemble in their Religion, to turn and return with the tide, as all experience in the nations of the world doth testifie now. . . . This binding and rebinding of conscience, contrary or without its own persuasion, so weakens and defiles it, that it (as all other faculties) loseth its strength, and the very nature of a common honest conscience.[63]

Williams feared the systematic repression of conscience in part because he sensed that forced conformity trained and encouraged people to disregard their consciences, to transgress their moral faculties, to sever the moral cooperation between human intellect and will, and, in short, to choose irrationally and without conviction.[64] He greatly feared the prospect of moral bankruptcy threatened by a society whose moral agents have been taught or compelled to disregard the authority of their consciences.

Of course, Williams recognized that there are times when public safety might require that civil authorities compel people to act against their consciences (or at least to restrain them from acting on their consciences), but he believed it impossible to justify this coercion by appeal to conscience itself, as other Puritans attempted.[65] Rather than claiming by some linguistic or conceptual gymnastics, however, that such compulsion was not persecution (as Ames and Cotton both attempted), Williams admitted that even these instances are violations of conscience, but argued for their appropriateness by appeal to the common good. Williams insisted that the use of force against conscientious conviction *always* constitutes a violation of conscience; there was to him no getting around that fact. At the same time, he argued, it may be a justifiable violation and necessary to protect the common good of a society. The prima facie presumption for Williams, however, was that the restriction of conscientious conviction is wrong, a principle he derived from both practical observation and a philosophical understanding of the nature of conscience.

In the liberality of his doctrine on freedom of conscience, Williams represents one side of an ambiguity on the subject that is characteristic of the larger Reformed tradition. On the one hand, conscience in classical Reformed theology was often seen as the internal locus of God's moral judgment and direction, a divine association that compelled some Calvinist thinkers to afford wide latitude for conscientious conviction. If the conscience is the moral voice of God, argued some liberal interpreters of the freedom of conscience, then to interfere with the exercise of that voice was to antagonize the authority of God. "God alone is Lord of the conscience" was a sentiment acknowledged by Calvin and echoed by Reformed thinkers from Roger Williams to the present time. Even in light of a seemingly erroneous conscience, in matters that adversely affect the health and safety of no others, a moral agent's freedom to follow the dictates of conscience must be protected.

On the other hand, early Reformed theologians also emphasized the certainty of God's moral requirements in the revealed norms of the Bible. To allow the transgression of this clear moral code, even in the name of conscience, was to permit obvious disregard for God's scriptural mandates. Many Calvinist thinkers took for granted that the dictates of an erroneous conscience should be subject to correction by the more reliable and "objective" standards of revelation.[66] For some, in fact, the notion that God's voice in the conscience could contradict God's word in Scripture was itself absurd, so that in alleged cases of erroneous conscience what was in fact occurring was a willful disregard for the commands of conscience. Disobedience was a matter of the will, not of mistaken conviction, and so compulsion and punishment were both appropriate and necessary.

Thus the Calvinist tradition has never been of one voice on the question of respect for conscience, reflecting an ambiguity inherent in the thought of Calvin himself. Calvin tended to place priority on conformity to institutional authority over allegiance to individual conscientious conviction, considering the former itself a sign of a healthy conscience. In fact, Calvin's infamous relationship with Michael Servetus may be understood as a tragic consequence of the limits Calvin placed on freedom of conscience. At the same time, however, Calvin was not entirely consistent and sometimes suggested that there are occasions when following the dictates of conscience, even in defiance of institutional authority, is proper, and that the freedom to do so ought to be respected and protected.[67]

As a result, Calvin exhibited both a conservative streak and more liberal potential in his teachings on conscience. Ultimately he was unclear regarding how to negotiate between the two poles, and historically Calvin's own ambiguity encouraged two very different strands of thinking on the subject within the Reformed tradition. On the one hand, the Reformed tradition has produced conservative approaches to conscience, arguments for curtailing the free exercise of conscience and subjecting it to the higher end of public conformity in religion and morals. Richard Baxter's comments on religious liberty in his political treatise *Holy Commonwealth* typify this kind of perspective. Baxter admitted that liberty of conscience was an admirable goal for those who wished to practice "True Religion," but he was sickened by the prospect of granting similar liberty to those who would use it to counter a Christian establishment. He assumed that any Christian who realized the implications of such liberty would be similarly turned off:

> At least when a Christian that's now deluded with the specious name of "Religious Liberty" should see the practice, and hear his Savior reviled by the Jews, and the Mahometans, and the wicked heardened in their sinne, . . . it would make his heart to turn and tremble, and then he would say that this Liberty signifieth the Reign of Satan, and not of Christ. . . . Liberty in all matters of Worship and of Faith, is the open and apparent way to set up Popery in the Land: Therefore it is not the Good Cause.[68]

Representative, too, of the conservative strand of Calvinist thought on the freedom of conscience was the dominant spirit in the Massachusetts Bay Colony during Williams's lifetime. Massachusetts's religious and political leaders expended a great deal of energy attempting to subordinate the free exercise of conscience to the goal of producing a commonwealth that was highly uniform in religious practice and moral performance, and they justified their aspirations chiefly in terms of their Calvinist theological perspective.[69]

On the other hand, the Reformed tradition also gave birth to a left-wing Puritan movement that demanded, at least partly on Calvinist theological grounds, that the binding authority of conscience be shown extensive latitude. Chief among these radicals was, of course, Roger Williams. Williams represents the best the Reformed tradition has to offer on a liberal respect for the exercise of conscientious conviction, but it is important to emphasize that he is as representative of Reformed theology on this matter as the more conservative approaches of Baxter and the Massachusetts establishment. Williams developed his arguments for freedom of conscience from within his theological tradition—borrowing from Thomas Aquinas, Calvin, Perkins, and Ames—though he did so in a direction very few of his Calvinist predecessors and colleagues exploited to any depth. In doing so, Williams provided one of the earliest glimpses of a progressive theory of conscience in operation, not only suggesting theological means by which to negotiate pluralism within a religious community (i.e., Puritanism), but also providing a common authoritative appeal through which an entire civil society might encourage mutual respect and shared dialogue in the midst of clear differences of conviction. In the *Key*, Williams argued that no human being rightly considered, regardless of religious affiliation (or lack thereof), lacks a conscience, and this shared capacity for morality provides a common foundation to imagine public conversation and the possibilities for some agreement. Conscience is what makes human beings, even "natural man," capable of basic morality and sociability.[70] It is a theologically endorsed phenomenon that itself requires no participation in that theology in order to include, and in fact to be intelligent to, those outside the religious tradition. Williams's insistence on the universality of conscience serves as a basis for Reformed theology to articulate a respect for moral agents outside the faith community, as well as for the importance of dialogue with them.

PART III

ETHICS

We know that many excellent gifts wherewith it hath pleased God to furnish many, enabling them for public service to their Countries both in Peace and War (as all Ages and Experience testifies) on whose souls he hath not yet pleased to shine in the face of Jesus Christ: which Gifts and Talents must all lye buried in the Earth, unless such persons may lawfully be called and chosen to, and improved in public service, notwithstanding their different or contrary Conscience and Worship.
—*The Bloody Tenent of Persecution* (1644)

5

CIVILITY

For Roger Williams, conscience represented the heart of that capacity all human beings share: to live together in community, to cooperate in moral ventures and civil institutions, and thus to fulfill the social nature inherent to their species. Williams went a step further, however, insisting that human beings share not only this *capacity* for shared morality but also an actual *set of norms and values* that are generally acknowledged as right and good. He assumed that a skeletal set of general moral norms existed that all persons ought to recognize as advantageous for the common good and consistent with a safe and productive public society. Though agreement on this common morality sometimes requires considerable public deliberation and is often complicated by the ever-present effects of sin, a limited number of general moral rights and wrongs are in fact recognized by all human beings. This minimal agreement offers a basis for further moral dialogue concerning more specific norms and particular ethical cases, enabling citizens of different backgrounds to debate the relevance, refinement, and application of the norms they hold in common to specific circumstances. Williams referred to the respect for and cultivation of this common morality as the practice of *civility.*

COMMON MORALITY AND SOCIAL COHESION

Williams often appealed to the standards of "civility" in his demands for religious liberty, by which he meant a basic human agreement on a few moral norms necessary for coexistence. The "civil faithfulness, obedience, honesty, chastity, &c." that existed "even amongst such as own not God nor Christ" demonstrated the reality of civility.[1] Human beings are capable of civility through the exercise and education of the conscience, and they require it because without it there is no hope for the social cohesion human beings require as part of their very existence. The shared norms and values captured in civility, then, are the foundation for durable public society. Civility preserves public peace and maintains a semblance of order to civil cohabitation. It enables human beings to engage in the cooperative relationships necessary to live together. Civility equips persons to participate in the "Relations of government, marriage, service, notwithstanding that the grace of Christ had appeared to some and the rest . . . were . . . wholly ignorant of him."[2] In short, the shared moral norms of civility are, according to Williams, society's way of promoting the common good.

Importantly, Williams believed that all human beings share this moral knowledge, not just those who had been exposed to the teachings of Protestant Christianity. As David Little points out, Williams believed in the existence of "a common moral denominator based on certain shared notions of welfare and harm that do not require religious commitments in order to affirm."[3] In fact Williams judged John Cotton's assertion to the contrary "dangerously destructive to the very roots of all civil relations, converse, and dealing; yea, and any civil being of the world itself."[4] He wondered, for instance, "how Mr. Cotton could chaine up all Papists in an Impossibilitie of yielding civil obedience," when examples abounded of Catholics who respected the pope's religious authority without granting him power over their political loyalties.[5] Protestantism had no corner market on the moral ingredients necessary to make a person a trustworthy moral citizen; in fact, this basic morality was not even exclusive to Christianity. Williams's conviction that Catholics were capable of civility was alarming enough in the minds of many of his Protestant colleagues, but he extended the universality of civility further, arguing that even non-Christians share its fundamental moral values. Using the admittedly unattractive language of his day, Williams nonetheless insisted that "it is known by experience, that many thousands of Mahumetan, Popish and Pagan Priests are in their persons, both as civil and courteous and peaceable a nature, as any of the subjects in the state they live in."[6] Suggesting that Catholics and even non-Christians are capable of honoring civil peace and cooperation, Williams insisted that this capacity for civility ought to lead to respect for them as moral beings, and thus Catholics and non-Christians should remain unmolested until their actions threaten social stability. In this argument, Williams exceeded the toleration that even his philosophical successor John Locke was willing to grant.[7] Every human being is capable of discerning and agreeing to a basic set of moral values called civility, argued Williams, and the Bible not only acknowledged this fact but commanded that Christians cooperate in the cultivation of civility as well.[8]

The encouragement of this general moral consensus, according to Williams, belonged among the several responsibilities of civil government. Public leaders are charged with protecting the free space for civility to flourish, including the liberty of religion and conscience that Williams held so dear. Williams wrote that it was "the Duty of the Civill Magistrate to suppress all violences to the Bodies and Goods of men for their Souls beliefe, and to provide that not one person in the Land be Restrained from or Constrained to any Worship, Ministry, or Maintainence, but peaceably maintained in his Soul, as well as Corporall Freedom."[9] To Williams, maintaining the freedom to think, believe, practice piety, and even move about as an autonomous agent remained crucial to preserving an environment in which civility may flourish, and the responsibility for this public space lay chiefly with civil authorities. In addition, he charged public authorities with the obligation to promote civility themselves, encouraging moral values in their citizens and restraining persons who publicly violate civility's norms. Williams believed that "in all . . . cases wherein Civility is wronged, in the Bodies or goods of any, the Civil Sword is Gods Sword, as well as mans, for the suppressing of such Practices and Appearances, yea and the very Principles of them; and for the Incouragement and applause of the contrary, Chastity, Humanity, &c."[10] As clearly as he rejected the idea that government may use its authority to establish religious uniformity, he endorsed the notion that a society's public authorities are responsible for the preservation of the basic moral norms of civility.

This does not mean, as some have read Williams to believe, that establishing a moral code becomes an explicit function of civil government.[11] While he rejected any notion of religious establishment, Williams did believe that government held some responsibility for maintaining order and protecting the common good, and he even included an interest in public morality in this conception of the common good. Williams was far from advocating that government impose "a universal standard" of morality akin to the expectations of the Puritan establishment.[12] Unlike his Massachusetts contemporaries, Williams did not ask civil government to implement a moral code based on biblical principles, and he was in general much less ambitious than most other Puritans when it came to the moral authority he was willing to award the state. Williams envisioned the government's power in minimalist terms, allowing only those restrictions necessary to protect the common good, public peace, and social stability. He insisted that the state was equally responsible for nurturing the moral *freedom* necessary for moral agents to exercise their capacities to deliberate, agree on, and understand moral norms and values. Williams, therefore, never sought to implement a governmentally regulated moral code, but only expected public authorities to safeguard the public arena for the sake of common good and moral exercise.

CIVILITY AND CHRISTIAN RELIGION

Williams's social goal, then, was not the implementation of a strong, homogeneous, and largely Christian system of morality. He did not endorse the restriction of moral conscience any more than he did compulsion of religious conscience, except on a most fundamental level concerning only the minimal set of basic moral values he believed all human beings shared. The teachings of Christianity "are of another sphere and nature than civility is," and in the public realm Williams sought only the achievement of the latter.[13] While religious ethical commitments may coincidentally promote the same norms and values that civility upholds, to Williams's mind civility did not *require* religion to maintain public order and promote the common good. In fact Williams carefully suggested to his Puritan colleagues that, for the purpose of civil discussion, a sharp line ought to be drawn between religious beliefs (including religiously determined and motivated habits and character traits) and moral beliefs. Religious beliefs were a product of saving grace and the presence of the Holy Spirit. They were a sign of divine election, a distinctive mark of the true church, and a source of soteriological confidence. But they were the possession of the church and ought not to be forced on others who could not in true faith believe them.

Morality, on the other hand, was for Williams a set of norms and values encouraged and perfected by true religion but available outside of religious experience as well. Despite his sectarian desire for religious purity and his confidence that salvation was to be found only within the Christian faith, Williams nonetheless insisted that one did not need to be a *religious* person to be a good *moral* person. God's gift of moral conscience, invested in every human being, rendered each person capable of basic moral knowledge and performance, regardless of religious status. Thus "a Subject [or] a Magistrate may be a good Subject [or] a good Magistrate, in respect of civill or morall goodness" even though Christian "Godliness, which is infinitely more beautiful, be wanting" and only found among members of the true church.[14] The common good of civil society depended upon agreement on moral values like justice and "that civill honestie which makes a good citizen," not on a shared religious conception.[15] Williams's conception of civility did not require religion to succeed.

In fact, Williams believed that, in the interest of the common good, public society needed to take vested interest in cultivating civility, but it should avoid the direct endorsement of any religion. One reason he argued this way was his belief that established religion was unnecessary for social flourishing. Society does not need state-ordered religion, Christian or any other, argued Williams, in order to survive and prosper. The moral capacities with which every human being is endowed are a sufficient basis for public cooperation and cohabitation. Religion may help maintain a peaceable society, but sometimes it hinders public peace, and certainly it is not essential.[16] The health, or existence even, of religious communities is not crucial to the well-being of the state, as Williams made clear in this oft-quoted passage from *The Bloody Tenent*:

The Church or company of worshippers (whether true or false) is like unto a Body or Colledge of Physicians in a Citie; like unto a Corporation, Society, or Company of East Indie or Turlie-Merchants, or any other Societie or Company in London: which Companies may hold their Courts, keep their Records, hold disputations; and in matters concerning their Societie, may dissent, divide, break into Schismes and Factions, sue and implead each other at the Law, yea, wholly breake up and dissolve into pieces and nothing, and yet the peace of the Citie not be in the least measure impaired or disturbed; because the essence or being of the Citie, and so the well-being and peace thereof is essentially distinct from those particular Societies; the Citie-Courts, Citie-Lawes, Citie-punishments distinct from theirs. The Citie was before them, and stands absolute and intire, when such a Corporation or Societie is taken down.[17]

To Williams's mind, the stability of the social order, "notwithstanding . . . spiritual oppositions in point of Worship and Religion," would survive "if Men keep but the Bond of Civility." Indeed, to attempt a forced uniformity in matters of religion was "a breach of Civilitie it selfe."[18]

Some of his reasons for arguing this way were empirical. Williams referred to the historical record and observed that the success and stability of moral societies among people with no apparent ties to the Christian religion (or any religion, for that matter) proved that religion was not necessary to ensure political order. Williams observed that "so many stately Kingdomes and Governments in the World have long and long enjoyed civill peace and quiet," even though in their societies "there is not the very name of Jesus Christ amongst them."[19] Political leaders past and current proved that they did not need religion (or the right religion) to govern effectively and promote moral harmony. Neither external resistance to the church's witness nor unrest within it necessarily threatened a civil society's ability to cultivate a basic level of civility. Williams wrote that "therefore there may be . . . flourishing Commonweales and Societies of men where no Church of Christ abideth; and . . . the Commonweale may be in perfect peace and quiet, notwithstanding the Church . . . be in distractions, and spiritual oppositions both against their Religions, and sometimes amongst themselves."[20]

Adopting an argument surprisingly modern in tone, Williams noted that as often as not institutional religion not only failed to contribute to social stability, it compromised it, by insisting on propagating by conquest rather than dialogue. "Alas, too frequent experience tells us in all parts of the world," he declared, "that many thousands are far more peaceable subjects, more loving and helpful neighbors, and more true and fair dealers in civil conversation, than many who account themselves to be the only religious people in the world."[21] Williams did not argue that a propensity toward conflict *necessarily* accompanies religion, but he believed that in his time it was frequently true, especially among English Christians. The quest for religious conformity that preoccupied much of European Christianity threatened to rob civil communities of the benefits derived from having their most talented citizens serving in public leadership roles. Williams argued that religious requirements for political office—the insistence that political leaders pass religious litmus tests in order to serve—distracted attention from what truly made for effective leaders, for "a Christian Captaine, Christian Merchant, Physician, Lawyer, Pilot, Father, Master, and (so consequently) Magistrate, &c. is no more a Captaine, Merchant, Physician, Lawyer, Pilot, Father, Master, Magistrate, &c. then a Captaine, Merchant, &c. of any other Conscience or Religion."[22] To insist on religious qualifications for public leadership was to risk discouraging those most endowed with leadership skills from seeking office:

> we know that many excellent gifts wherewith it hath pleased God to furnish many, inabling them for publike service to their Countries both in Peace and War (as all Ages and Experience testifies) on whose soules hee hath not yet pleased to shine in the face of Jesus Christ: which Gifts and Talents must all lye buried in the Earth, unlesse such persons may lawfully be called and chosen to, and improved in publike service, notwithstanding their different or contrary Conscience and Worship.[23]

The common good of civil society depends more on the cultivation of civility and the utilization of leadership skills than it does on uniformity of religion.

In response to his Puritan agitators, Williams believed that he was able to establish empirically that religious practice or affiliation was not necessary to cultivate a spirit of civility among members of a public society. His argument was strengthened by his dependence on the concept of conscience and his theological refusal to locate moral capability solely within revealed religion. But while religion's primary focus is soteriological and unnecessary to civility's survival, religion can contribute to public morality, according to Williams, by cultivating a desire and capacity for civility. In particular the Christian religion provides unique motivation for Christians to be good moral citizens, to abide by the precepts of civility, and to encourage them in others. True Christian faith encourages basic civility, but it also defines and demands a moral life that surpasses civility.[24] "'Tis true," wrote Williams, "Christianity teacheth all these to act in their severall callings, to an higher ultimate end, from higher principles, in a more heavenly and spirituall manner, &c."[25] To Williams, therefore, religion can contribute to the common good both by the encouragement of civility it provides believers and by the insight into a higher brand of social cooperation it discloses to all. He nonetheless maintained that the preservation of religion was not *necessary* for maintaining a basic sense of social obligation and mutual respect, and thus should not be part of civil authority's responsibility.

CIVILITY AS PROCEDURAL NORMS

For Williams, civility was the union set of norms and values that human beings generally understood to be true or right or proper, accessible to all human beings independently of religious persuasion. But what did this set look like to him? First and foremost, he assumed that civility included certain expectations for the framework of moral discourse itself. Civility in part guided the spirit in which public conversation must take place in order to reach further substantive consensus on moral living. In other words, one aspect of civility for Williams was procedural, the rules of the moral game, the boundaries to the endeavor itself to establish moral consensus among a greater public. In his view, citizens may not agree on a complex set of moral norms, but among the basic values every citizen ought to honor is the appropriateness of common courtesy, truthfulness, and patience as parameters for the very act of engaging in public conversation on moral issues and norms.

Tolerance, the principle for which Williams is best known, can itself be understood in part as a procedural norm of civility, a guideline for safeguarding a public space for moral deliberation in a pluralistic society. In a letter that he wrote to his fellow citizens in Providence, Williams acknowledged that the familiar problems of pluralism were already beginning to show themselves in the early days of the Rhode Island colony:

> Worthy friends, That our selves and all men are apt and prone to differ it is no new Thing in all Former Ages in all parts of this World in these parts and in our deare native Countrey and mournfull state of England. That either part or partie is most right in his owne eye, his Cause Right, his Carriage Right, his Argument Right, his Answeres Right, is as wofully and constantly true as the former.[26]

The existence of differing but equally confident convictions is a staple of pluralistic society, suggested Williams, and could doom any attempts to reach a sense of common moral consensus and thus a stable public society, if not for the cohesive power of civility. Civility allows citizens to struggle for commonality and order in the midst of pluralism, for one of the most important aspects of civility is tolerance. Civility requires that citizens exhibit tolerance toward members of society who are different from them and toward the religious and political opinions they hold, as long as they or their opinions are not fundamentally destructive to the political project of a stable society itself.[27] In order for moral consensus to be possible, open moral discourse must take place, and that openness is protected only when all participants in public dialogue enjoy the freedom to articulate their most valued religious and moral convictions without threat of disqualification. Williams's principle of tolerance encouraged the freedom to hold, develop, change, and articulate beliefs in public forums, and this respect for the freedom to deliberate and to hold convictions was a procedural requirement upon which civility depended.

Williams believed that social stability and peace depended on the recognition of tolerance as a procedural norm of common civility, because without tolerance in the public sphere parties with differences are left to relate to one another only through power politics. Intolerance in public discourse short-circuits conversation, handicaps the powers of persuasion and genuine consent, and ultimately threatens violence and political chaos. Civil exchange disappears, and political interaction dissolves into dangerous wrestling for the loyalty of whatever political machinery will allow one to "win," defined as the enforcement of one's own position on all dissenters. Thus, those who successfully obtain the allegiance of political institutions employ them as the "executioners" of their own intolerance, while those without such friends in high places are led to believe that violent disruption of power imbalances is the only way for them to achieve moral freedom.[28] From both directions intolerance brings civil conversation to an end and threatens a society's political viability.

By contrast, tolerance acts as a boundary condition by which both public discourse and (more broadly) social stability may be maintained. Williams believed strongly that tolerance, as a way of constructing the parameters of public interaction, begets peace, social solidarity, and cooperation.[29] While he assumed that this procedural norm was completely consistent with Christianity (calling it a "great and Christian policy"), he also insisted that toleration was recognized as a valuable moral norm by citizens outside the Christian faith.[30] Christians, Jews, Muslims, and pagans were all capable of honoring tolerance as a condition of public discourse, whether they understood it in the context of a religious worldview or not.[31] In fact, Williams responded to John Cotton's concern that some politicians' tolerance may be motivated by beliefs that "will not stand with Christianity" by arguing that tolerance alone is capable of moral defense regardless of its philosophical context. Tolerance enables public discourse and cooperation, allows "for the peace of the State and preventing of Rivers of civill Blood," and thus "will be found to agree most punctually with the Rules of the best Politician that ever the World saw" in spite of the unchristian belief system that accompanies it.[32] Tolerance is a procedural norm of civility that ought to be recognized by all as morally valuable.

As important as toleration was to Williams's theological opus, the procedural dimensions to his conception of civility went beyond this principle to include the more specific courtesies of conversation and dialogue. Listening with integrity and genuineness, showing respect for one's opponent, and refraining from personal insults were also among the procedural boundaries Williams believed civility placed on civil moral discourse.

Williams was unafraid of arrogant opinions or erroneous beliefs; to his mind they were no threat to society themselves and their holders should be given the freedom to voice them. But he sincerely believed that civil peace and the prospects for moral consensus were compromised when opinions were offensive or threatening *in the way they were offered* in public discourse, or in his words, in "the way and manner of holding forth."[33] Williams remained deeply concerned with public debates that were highly argumentative or that contained personal attacks or threats, for he feared that such disrespect for others in public discourse transgressed the civility on which such conversation depended.

In fact, one of the reasons Williams was so exasperated with the Quakers was their alleged violation of civility, specifically the need to conduct public conversation respectfully. In between and after his ventures to London on behalf of the colony, Williams's attention was often preoccupied with leading Rhode Island through the rough and uncharted waters of becoming a haven of tolerance. When he returned from England in 1644, Williams was quickly elected "chief officer" of Providence, and during his three-year term he labored to bring the four towns together into some semblance of a unified colony, both to conform with the charter he had been granted in London and to provide a common defense against external enemies. This was not an easy task, for communities founded by zealots for individual liberty do not necessarily and immediately discern the importance of the common good. The conspiracy of intolerance outside his fledgling colony, as well as instances of land greed and excessive individualism within it, made Williams's task a daunting one.

In the early 1670s, with the tragedy of King Philip's War still on the horizon, Williams found himself dealing with another disturbance in his quest for civil harmony in Rhode Island: the Quakers. The Quakers were one of several religious groups that sought asylum early and often in Rhode Island, and no dissenters were persecuted more passionately in Massachusetts than they. Though he would not refuse them religious freedom, Williams shared the Bay Colony's distaste for the Quakers' antinomian theology and anti-institutional lifestyle. Far from the genteel characters of subsequent generations (best represented by William Penn), the Quakers of the early seventeenth century were a disruptive lot, frequently inciting public spectacles and behavior that ranged from disruption of public forums to open displays of nudity. Such deviant behavior was intentional; as James F. Childress observes, "Quakers waging the 'Lamb's War' engaged in numerous nonviolent acts that violated social expectations, custom, and law in order to point to critical issues such as social inequality and to convert others to their religious perspective." In other words, they pressed for the disruption of convention for the transformative effects they believed it would have on their society.[34]

Transformative or not, Williams feared that the Quakers' behavior threatened the stability of public society itself. He was neither subtle nor succinct in voicing his distaste for the Quakers and all for which they stood, protest that culminated with his long-winded public debates in 1672 with three Quaker representatives, John Burnet, John Stubbs, and William Edmondson. *George Fox Digg'd from His Burroughs,* the last of Williams's works to be published, was his personal transcript (with extensive commentary, of course) of these debates.[35] Throughout this volume, Williams refuted the serious doctrinal errors of which he believed Quaker theology to be guilty, but he also was genuinely troubled by the lack of civility in the debate itself. He was taken aback by his opponents' boisterous behavior and abandonment of common courtesy during the debate, so much so that it incited him to vehement and verbose protestations. He accused them of interrupting his arguments, shouting him down, attempting to humiliate him personally with name-calling and ridicule, misrepresenting his convictions, and displaying a noted lack of truthfulness in their own arguments. In short, Williams charged that his three antagonists disregarded accepted rules for decorous conversation and deliberation, and to do so, he said, was "against the sober rules of Civility and Humanity."[36] In other words, one of the major reasons Williams wrote *George Fox* was his disdain for the very manner in which the Quaker representatives behaved themselves in public discourse, for in his view they violated the accepted procedures for having civilized conversation. To do so was not, as the Quakers insisted, an acceptable exercise of free conscience. Instead it was a moral violation of the basic requirements of civility, a transgression of the procedural rules for public deliberation that Williams held with such esteem that he was willing to imagine "a due and moderate restraint and punishing" of those types of "incivilities" and considered it "a Duty and Command of God unto . . . all mankinde Societies" to do so.[37]

THE PRINCIPLES OF CIVILITY

Civility provided a procedural framework for conducting public moral conversation, but there was more to it, according to Williams, than simply rules of deliberation. Not only did he believe that civility guided the spirit of moral dialogue, he also suggested that as a result of public deliberation human beings could discover a *substantive* set of moral norms they held in common.[38] Moral dialogue is possible in the public arena, Williams implied, because at the root of the various moral and religious conceptions that make up the pluralistic ethos is a minimal set of values and norms that all persons should defend as right or good. Civility includes this basic set of norms whose "universal" acceptance provides the foundation for a common morality and marks a starting point for public moral conversation. All human beings could assent to the protection and encouragement of the norms of civility, whether they took the form of principle-based action guides for individual moral choices or the commendation of certain virtues of character that ought to be cultivated.

Williams seems to have envisioned civility at times as the minimal set of "rules" for human coexistence that all human beings could recognize as moral boundaries on behavior. Among these rules Williams included prohibitions against murder, adultery, theft, and lying. Williams believed that there was never any generation, "but by the dark light of nature," that would disagree that these prohibitions were necessary for social stability and interaction.[39] Despite the obvious parallels with the second table of Mosaic law, the universality of these moral principles stemmed not from their appearance in Scripture but from their origin in natural law. Williams believed that "the second Table contains the Law of Nature," or more precisely, that the second half of Mosaic law summarizes the natural law to which every human being has access through reason and conscience and that enables human beings to live together as moral agents. Human beings naturally know that murder, the betrayal of spousal trust, thievery, and lying are morally wrong. These are moral rules, vested in the natural law, to which all human beings have access, with which all human beings ought to be familiar, and to which all persons could be expected to give assent.

Besides these four rules, Williams also understood justice as a general principle of natural law, a basic standard of Golden-Rule self-consistency, or desiring for another what you would want granted to you in similar circumstances. He believed that all human beings shared this inherent knowledge of the "Principles of common Justice," which could be used to evaluate particular actions and which he himself invoked to argue that religious persecution offends some of the most basic moral norms human beings share.[40] Indeed, this was one of Williams's favorite appeals in his written duel with Cotton, accusing Cotton of violating this spirit of self-consistency known as justice. Several times in their exchanges, Williams reminded his elder colleague that in England Cotton had been on the other side of religious persecution. Under the oppressive eye of the Church of England, Cotton had wished and argued for the Puritans' freedom to practice their religion freely, but on reaching a position of acceptance and authority in New England, he denied that same freedom to those who disagreed with his conception of piety. To refuse to extend to others the same opportunities Cotton had wished for himself, argued Williams, was to transgress the rule of justice.[41]

Understood this way, the natural-law principle of justice begets as corollary the principle of toleration. We have seen already how tolerance operates as a procedural norm in Williams's theology, setting the parameters for morally acceptable public conversation. Toleration also served as a substantive rule, governing the limits to appropriate behavior between moral agents, establishing bounds to legitimate governmental intervention into the life of the citizen, and providing more specific content to Williams's development of justice as a principle of fairness. In the case cited above and others like it, Williams argued that toleration was an imperative because it embodied a public disposition that those in power would want to have extended to themselves if social roles were reversed.[42] In other words, Williams understood toleration as a regulative principle of his definition of justice. Endorsed by Christian faith but established on non-Christian grounds as well, toleration served Williams as a political principle of justice that negotiated the tension between genuinely held conviction and religious and moral pluralism. It did so by restricting governmental interference in the realm of conscientious convictions that did not tangibly threaten the stability of the social ordering, as well as by demanding that those in power extend to the powerless the same freedoms of thought, belief, and practice that they valued themselves.[43]

Williams's principle of toleration resembles what Henry S. Richardson has called *specification* of moral principles, in this case the general principle of justice as fairness. Williams was well aware that an appeal to the principle of justice, as well as to its corollary toleration, would require that the principle be specified, for in its generality the demands of justice conflicted with the requirements of other social needs and moral norms. Richardson describes the practice of specifying moral norms in conflict as the revision of "one's normative commitments so as to make at least one of them more specific." This higher level of specificity is reached by adding clauses to a general norm that indicate more precisely "where, when, why, how, by what means, by whom, or to whom" the action in question is to be done or avoided. Specification relates an action, which the principle takes up in general form, to the particulars of a moral scenario, in a way that remains true to the original content of the general principle while making clearer what ought to be done in the particular scenario. Specification "helps us imagine how our ethical precepts, many of which are very general and abstract, can reach concrete cases without generating unacceptable implications."[44]

In his attempts to relate the principle of tolerance to the events and circumstances in New England, Williams demonstrated an approach that was roughly analogous to Richardson's understanding of specification. By tolerance Williams never meant to advocate complete social acceptance of any beliefs and practices. He acknowledged the possibility of conflict between the requirements of toleration and the demands of other principles of social stability and common good. His response to this likely conflict was to suggest that neither the principle of toleration nor the rules with which it may conflict could be applied directly and in all cases. Nor did he propose that "balance" be sought between the norms by intuitive and arbitrary assignments of weight that "therefore lack discursively expressible justifications."[45] Instead Williams offered qualifications and specifications of the norms in question that remained true to the content of the original general principle yet were tailored to the specific moral scenarios and provided a clear rationale for prioritizing one above another.[46]

For example, in his response to the refusal of some Rhode Island citizens to participate in a colonial militia, Williams was forced to negotiate between several of the moral principles he held to be important. As he did so, Williams demonstrated that specifying the content of moral norms helped him to develop priorities and resolve moral conflicts. In response to claims of conscientious objection, Williams specified his understanding of toleration, from a general principle that protected acts originating from considered religious convictions to a rule that protected liberty of conscience only insofar as its exercise did not interfere with a citizen's responsibilities to the common defense and maintenance of the community.[47] In addition, Williams's willingness to entertain the existence of a militia at all represented a specification of his generally nonviolent principles. Williams specified his aversion to violence by admitting its necessity "in Execution of Justice upon malefactors at home, or preserving of Life and lives in defensive warr."[48] He recognized the danger in applying even so-called universal norms without negotiating the conflict with other norms that their generality often produced. At the same time, he insisted that the adaptation of general norms to a greater degree of specificity and applicability be justified rationally whenever possible.

Williams's practice of specifying his moral norms resembled a strategy that was common among other Puritan moralists. To the Puritans, the concept of *equity* represented the need for general moral norms to be adapted to particular circumstances. Equity, a rule of moderation that the Puritans inherited from Calvin, was a principle that underlay the natural law and governed the application of all other moral (and civil) rules.[49] To Calvin the principle of equity demanded that any attempt to apply moral norms and values take into consideration the particular circumstances surrounding the moral act in question. He contrasted equity, or what John T. McNeill identifies as the Calvinist principle of "discerning justice," with the application of the letter of the law; equity often requires a more subtle negotiation between the intent of a general rule and the specific circumstances to which it may be applied.[50] Calvin's interpretation of the Ten Commandments, for example, may be seen as an extensive exercise in reading moral rules with the eyes of "natural equity," as his interpretation of the

Decalogue expands and restricts the scope of each general norm with creative, but justified, specificity.[51] Calvin argued that it was completely appropriate to take into consideration the "condition of times, place, and nation" in order to determine the relative weight and specific meaning of moral rules or the appropriate severity of punishment. He took for granted that these particular circumstances would affect the specific application of moral rules and even alter them to a degree, but he insisted that such "adaptations" were "necessary and expedient" in order "to maintain the observance of God's law" in changing times and places.[52] The principle of equity acknowledged the need to specify moral norms rationally in a way that resolved conflict between norms without threatening the integrity of the general rules themselves.

E. Clinton Gardner has demonstrated how Puritan moral reasoning after Calvin incorporated a consideration of equity, in particular in the work of William Perkins. Perkins taught that public equity was concerned with "the right and convenient, and the moderate and discreet execution of the laws of men," in which moral and civil laws are applied in specific situations with regard to particular circumstances. Though the initial presumption when applying the law is its literal meaning, argued Perkins, equity requires that mitigating circumstances be considered when they are present. In addition to the influence of particular circumstances, the application of moral law is also affected by the relevance of other rules of natural or moral law that might also factor into the situation, conflicting with or qualifying the application of the strict sense of the original principle. Perkins did not share Calvin's argument that equity was a "natural" principle (basing his claim instead chiefly on Scripture), but he did agree with his predecessor that the application of general principles of moral law to particular circumstances requires the specification and balancing that equity encourages.[53]

Although Williams did not explicitly invoke the term *equity* that Calvin and Perkins used, his consideration of moral principles reflects a similar understanding of the need to adapt general norms to particular circumstances. The requirements of civility include general principles of obligation that nonetheless cannot be universally binding in every circumstance. The principles of civility sometimes conflict with one another, and so the challenge is to negotiate, both privately and as a society, the resolution of that conflict in particular instances. Moral reasoning on both levels requires a commitment to fleshing out the often conflicting relationship between norms like tolerance, public order, and justice. The general principles of civility are universally recognized as morally binding, Williams insisted, but he acknowledged that their application is a much less certain process. For this reason, Williams's twin foci of toleration and public discourse are all the more important.[54]

CIVILITY AS PUBLIC VIRTUE

Much of Williams's commentary on civility appears to regard the concept as a set of rules, but while moral law was important to him, Williams also described civility as the cultivation and exhibition of certain shared virtues. Civility was agreement not only on the general principles that governed the moral life but also on the kind of character that furthers public cooperation and conversation and that all human beings ought to recognize as good. The opposite of barbarism, civility represented human traits of "sociableness" that allowed human beings to live in relations "soberly and justly among their neighbors."[55] At the heart of this dimension of civility was Williams's belief that there are certain character traits and ways of living that all human beings recognize and encourage as good for human coexistence and flourishing, a "civil righteousness" of which all human agents are capable. He assumed, for instance, that the extension of common courtesy and the display of "gentleness" in human interaction were marks of civility.[56] So were social and political loyalty and dependability, respect for civil authority, honesty, and chastity.[57] Williams insisted that a whole set of civil virtues like these existed and was known to be necessary for social stability and cooperation even by those "wholly ignorant" of Christian faith.

One virtue of civility that Williams pursued to some depth was a spirit of gratitude. Williams assumed that human beings with character and integrity would exhibit a spirit of thankfulness toward those persons to whom they were indebted. He reminded the Rhode Island citizens of this virtue in a letter he wrote to them in 1666. John Clarke had made a trip to England to act as ambassador for the colony, lobbying for a royal charter in the face of enemies from both Massachusetts and Rhode Island who disputed the colony's legitimacy. But the town of Warwick had failed to raise the money needed to finance Clarke's trip, forcing Clarke to absorb much of the expense personally (as Williams had been forced to do on both of his trips to England on the colony's behalf). Cajoling the people of Warwick to remit their share, Williams did not appeal to moral law or some civil rule of obligation. Instead, he encouraged them to see the act of raising the necessary funds as a reflection of "Common Gratitude," the display of admirable virtue or true character. To reimburse their ambassador would demonstrate the town's appreciation for one who had interceded heroically on its behalf. This type of gratitude, argued Williams, was a virtue of civility that was common "among all Mankind, yea, amongst Brute Beasts even the Wildest and Fiercest, for Kindness received" and thus ought to be displayed among the people of Warwick as well.[58]

Williams believed that all human beings were capable of virtues of civility like gratitude, not just the "civilized" societies of Europe. What he observed in the Native Americans only confirmed to him that human beings universally value certain character traits for their positive contributions to social flourishing. He experienced firsthand the virtue of common courtesy "among these wild Americans," who deliberately cultivated the virtue in their children and extended it "both amongst themselves and toward strangers."[59] In fact the personal courtesy that the Americans displayed served as an indictment on the English, argued Williams, who were not nearly as dedicated to cultivating this trait among themselves, despite their claim to being a "Christianized" people. The moral superiority of the Americans, to which their courtesy attested, exposed the Europeans' failure to live up to the requirements of civility that both they and the Americans recognized as moral goods:

> 1. The Courteous Pagan shall condemne
>   Uncourteous Englishmen,
> Who live like Foxes, Beares and Wolves,
>   Or Lyon in his Den.
> 2. Let none sing blessings to their soules,
>   For that they Courteous are:
> The wild Barbarians with no more
>   Then Nature, goe so farre:
> 3. If Natures Sons both wild and tame,
>   Humane and Courteous be:
> How ill becomes it Sonnes of God
>   To want Humanity?[60]

Williams also considered friendship an important virtue of civility at which the Americans excelled. The cooperation and "friendly joyning" with which the Americans went about their labors confirmed to Williams that it was "true with them as in all the World in the Affaires of Earth or Heaven: By concord little things grow great, by discord the greatest come to nothing."[61] The Americans' capacity for loyalty and productive camaraderie confirmed for Williams that this virtue, too, was a universally accepted norm of human civility. In fact, its prevalence among the natives aggravated the relationship between the Americans and the English colonists, for the Americans were troubled by the colonists' inferior sensitivity for friendship. The Narragansett sachem, though willing to live alongside the English, evidently shared serious misgivings with Williams regarding the trustworthiness of any friendship with the colonists. After reporting his attempts to satisfy the sachem's unease, Williams suggested that there was a moral lesson to learn in the irony of these so-called barbarians questioning the dependability of the "civilized" English. Their questions had merit, Williams implied, because they stemmed from an appreciation for the "universal" virtues of friendship and faithfulness that the Americans valued and cultivated more consistently than the Europeans.[62]

Also among the virtues of civility Williams observed in the Native Americans was a spirit of helpfulness, a willingness to come to the aid of another human being, and not only members of their own communities but also strangers from even the English settlements. Williams testified that he and other colonists had benefited personally from this virtue, for when they had been lost in the wilderness "my selfe and others have often been found, and succoured by the Indians."[63] As we have seen, gratitude also served as an important component to Williams's understanding of civil virtue, and he recognized this trait as well in the life and labor of the Americans more honestly than in the culture of his European readers.[64] In short, the *Key into the Language of America* became Williams's testimony to certain universal virtues of civility recognized by humans generally and on display in particular among the Americans. Despite stark differences in culture and religion, the natives valued some of the same basic norms of moral character that anchored English society. Williams's discovery of basic virtues of civility among the Americans confirmed his belief that certain character traits were valued by all human beings and all societies as good, and that this fundamental level of morality provided a foundation for human cohabitation and flourishing, even across religious and cultural boundaries.

In fact, Williams sparred with the Quakers so vehemently not just because of the theological error he perceived in their teaching and their transgressions against decorous conversation, but because he feared that the practices they commended threatened the cultivation of some of civility's important virtues. He argued that their habit of permitting long hair on men and the reputation of a few women in their group for parading naked in public violated the virtue of modesty on which human society depended.[65] He objected to their habit of publicly ridiculing and interrupting their opponents because he saw in such behavior disrespect for common courtesy and friendliness.[66] In the end, what Williams feared so much about the Quakers was not their theology, which he countered confidently in debate, but the practices among them that threatened both the procedural and substantive norms of common civility. He worried about their irreverence for civility because he believed that respect for its virtues and imperatives was essential to developing citizens with the character to contribute to the common good of society.

CIVILITY AND THE COMMON GOOD

Popularly remembered as a patron saint of individual liberty, Williams in reality sought to balance his advocacy for freedom of belief and conscience with an appropriate attention to public interest. The notion of the "common good" appears frequently in Williams's writings, both as grounds for arguing for toleration and as a boundary condition on the individual free-doms that toleration protects.[67] Williams observed that human beings as a species need to socialize, to live together productively, but he also observed that sin complicates the species' attempts at social organization and cohab-itation by pitting self-interests against the common good. Because of this conflict of ends, Williams believed that every human society needed to be regulated, making the resources of government a necessary part of human social organization. One aspect of government's responsibility is to ensure that the private interests of the citizens do not lead them to compromise the needs and interests of the common body. The common good of society was an important priority for Williams, a priority he believed civility fostered.

Williams's attention to the common good was far from unique among the Puritans and other early Calvinists. The Puritan doctrine of vocation dealt in part with the nature of an individual's responsibility to the com-mon good. William Perkins, for instance, taught that God ordains every per-son with a vocation or calling to be used "for the common good."[68] To use one's gifts and calling to further private ends was to abuse the calling. Instead an individual ought to understand himself or herself to be endowed with specific skills or knowledge in order to contribute to the social mission of the community and the good of all its citizens. Ideally every citizen would be trained in an understanding of "how great a part of their duty lieth in caring for the common good, and how sinful and damnable it is to live only to themselves."[69] Clinton Gardner draws a connection between this priority for the common good and the Calvinist emphasis on covenant, specifically as the latter idea is expressed in the image of a "holy common-wealth." The good of the elect society was the responsibility not only of its government and leadership, but of the citizens who resided in it. Brought together by their shared goal of serving God, the citizens of the chosen nation were entrusted with the responsibility for ensuring peace and pro-ductivity in its future. In the minds of the Puritans, this responsibility often demanded that public good receive priority over private interest.

Williams had little appetite for the social uses to which the Puritans put covenantal language, but he did share their interest in the common good. The common good, specifically the "bodies and goods" of citizens, is the proper responsibility of civil government, argued Williams, and a neces-sary focus for human beings to live safely and peacefully.[70] With his Puri-tan colleagues, Williams agreed that "not to study and not to endeavor the common good . . . is a treacherous Baseness, a selfish Monopoly, a kinde of Tyranny, and tendeth to the destruction both . . . of private and publike safety."[71] He insisted, in fact, that the priority on "a common good of the whole" was one reason for advocating religious toleration. Appealing to the parable of the Wheat and the Tares, Williams argued that God warns against trying to root out heathens and heretics from civil society precisely because such persecution would do more harm than good to civil order.[72] The common good, in other words, was clearly more threatened by persecution and intolerance than by liberty of conscience.

Using his famous metaphor, the "Ship of the Commonwealth," Williams argued that the stability of civil society required civil cooperation and mutual obligation.[73] According to Williams, a political community is like a ship whose safety and survival depend on the good work of its crew and whose sailors are therefore limited to a certain degree in their options and freedoms by agreeing to be part of the crew. If the sailors pursue their own interests with no regard to mutual responsibility, the ship wanders dangerously and eventually sinks. The sailors' agreement to sail signals their acceptance of certain social obligations and their tacit consent to some restrictions on their freedoms; each sailor's responsibility to his role ensures the ship's safe passage.

Likewise, he argued, by their participation in a particular society citizens give tacit consent to certain basic obligations and restrictions on their freedoms. Williams argued, for instance, that the men of Rhode Island had no prerogative to opt out of participating in a volunteer militia, for their settlement in Rhode Island implied their agreement to take partial responsibility for the common needs of the colony, including its physical preservation. Similarly he supported colonial taxation to finance the acquisition of a royal charter, because the objective of the tax was to secure the colony's safety from the ambition of its neighbors. Williams was even willing to entertain the notion of public restrictions on certain religious practices when those practices incited civil rebellion and the persecution of other citizens (Williams used this argument to call for some regulation of the Quakers).[74] But Williams would not endorse the restriction of religious acts that threatened no clear and tangible social danger, nor would he support taxes to pay for the salaries of clergy. In these cases, infringement on individual freedoms benefited not the common good but the interests of a private, voluntary association—namely, a church. Williams insisted that the responsibility for supporting the private interests of a religious body or similar association lay with its constituents, while all citizens were obligated to support the common good of the society as a whole.[75]

Part of this common obligation, as Williams understood it, involved an adherence to the basic virtues and moral principles of society. Service to the common good meant more than the literal and physical protection of "bodies and goods"; it also required dedication to moral norms that served to stabilize the community and ensured peace and public order.[76] These moral norms identified behavior that endangered public order and which should be avoided as a result, but they outlined positive contributions that citizens were encouraged to make to society as well.[77] Williams was less ambitious and intrusive than his Massachusetts colleagues in defining basic moral requirements to the common good, insisting that respect for pluralism and freedom of conscience were important dimensions to, and not enemies of, the pursuit of stable society. Civility was never more than a minimal set of shared morality, but it represented Williams's desire to balance the moral integrity of individual conscience with the importance of social cohesion to human flourishing. In his moral theology, citizens were responsible simultaneously for both the protection of moral pluralism and the cultivation of the common good.

Because Williams carefully considered responsibility to the common good by way of his concept of civility, Robert Bellah betrays an unfamiliarity with Williams's theology when he blames Williams for the current disregard for social cohesion and mutual benefit in American culture. Bellah claims that the abandonment of the common good in American culture is rooted in an increasingly excessive individualism that itself originates in the doctrine of conscientious freedom that Williams first espoused. "Roger Williams was a moral genius," Bellah admits, but he was "a sociological catastrophe," because he shifted the center of "sacredness" so completely and naively to individual conscience that his moral philosophy left little room to cultivate a concern for the common good.[78] According to Bellah, this inattention to public identity and solidarity created a void in Williams's own colony that economic individualism quickly filled, establishing a marriage between moral and economic atomism that threatened Rhode Island's political stability and ever since has eroded appreciation for collective destiny and interdependence in American society. (Amazingly, Bellah claims that this pattern began in Rhode Island because "Williams ignored secular society," despite the historical evidence which demonstrates that Williams was actually *obsessed* with civic affairs.) Referring to the periods of political upheaval in the colony's first years, Bellah insists that "Rhode Island under Williams gives us an early and local example of what happens when the sacredness of the individual is not balanced by any sense of the whole or concern for the common good."

Bellah's caricature is grossly mistaken, however, for civility as Williams describes it *demands* civic cooperation and mutual respect and places boundaries on the free exercise of conscience. Williams most certainly would have agreed with Bellah's judgment that "without a minimal degree of solidarity, the project of ever greater recognition of individual dignity will collapse in on itself." In Williams's view, the social requirements of civility provided this balance to the protection of individual dignity. He recognized that many of the citizens of his young colony had "long drunk of the cup of as great liberties," an indulgence that "rendered many of us wanton and too active" in demanding personal liberty.[79] As Timothy Hall points out, Williams realized that the success of the colony depended on his ability to convince its citizens that there is a difference between liberty and license, the former properly bridled by the greater context of social solidarity and common good.[80] Only by shared commitment to the common good can respect for conscience be located in the healthy sociality necessary to human flourishing. But Williams also emphasized that no pursuit of solidarity can sustain its moral integrity as long as it allows systematic violation of individual conscience, and this qualification on the pursuit of the common good is what distinguishes him from the Massachusetts Puritans and secures his place in American political history.[81] Williams sought a balance between freedom of conscience and social cohesion, and for this reason the purported demise of a sense of common good in contemporary American culture is not (contra Bellah) because we have adopted Williams's moral vision too enthusiastically, but perhaps because we have failed to truly understand it at all.

FAITH IN CIVILITY: PROBLEMS AND POSSIBILITIES

Williams's conception lends itself to the theological justification of moral dialogue between Christians and partners from a broad range of philosophical and religious perspectives, for it posits the existence of a basic minimal set of moral norms concerning which all of the participants in public moral conversation can expect to agree, regardless of their creedal or philosophical orientation. He defended his belief in this fundamental common morality while remaining loyal to the particular convictions of his Christian belief, for the theological framework he employed included a deference to moral conscience and a belief in natural law, the conceptual building blocks for claiming the existence of a "universal" moral capacity that nonetheless is consistent with the particularity of Christian theology. Williams's development of civility has its problems, of course. Chief among them is the fact that when he invokes civility, Williams occasionally refers to norms that most people today would not consider to be universal. In other words, not everything Williams included among the norms of civility strikes the modern reader as a universal human value. It is one thing, then, to endorse his theory of civility as perhaps instructive for contemporary Christian ethics engaged in public conversation, and a somewhat different task to evaluate his version of the specific norms he believed civility to include. Sometimes Williams appears to have cast the net of civility too wide, including in its minimal set norms that seem neither fundamental nor universal to modern readers.

Some of the moral norms Williams claimed for civility present few problems. For instance, Williams cited as principles of civility veracity and a prohibition against harming the innocent, two values that current human-rights arguments also often endorse. Some contemporary defenders of human-rights initiatives would agree with Williams that the principles of truth-telling and the protection of the innocent from bodily harm should be considered intuitions that are universally recognized as moral goods. By contrast, Williams also argued that modesty was a universally shared moral value, a claim that seems less rooted in common sense than, say, the prohibition against taking innocent human life, especially as Williams invoked modesty against the Quakers. Modesty may be difficult to demonstrate as a virtue that all human beings generally value above and beyond cultural and religious association, principally since the very definition of modest and immodest behavior seems to be culturally determined. In fact, we need look no further than Williams's own application of the virtue for an example of the problem of modesty's cultural dependency, for his condemnation of the Quakers' long hair and unusual patterns of dress would seem rather uncivil and illiberal to many now.

Clearly some of the moral norms Williams included with civility no longer resemble universal values. Williams seems on safest ground when he stays close to his claim that civility represents only a minimalist conception of common morality, for the more specificity Williams tries to invest in civility, the greater the occasion for disagreement with him. What he demonstrates in his occasionally objectionable attribution of excessively specific norms to civility, however, is the complexity of the task of specifying and applying moral norms in particular cases, even when there is agreement on the general moral guides. Even if we agree with Williams that modesty is generally recognized as a moral good, we might still object to his specific use of it in the case of the Quakers. Williams errs in application, we might say, but in doing so he demonstrates the larger moral project that civility requires.

In fact, one of the real strengths of Williams's ethics is his assumption that civility itself, as well as its use in specific moral scenarios, depends on a complex relationship between the norms that individual exercise of practical reasoning elicits and a society's intentional moral deliberation. The development of civility in this manner portrays the moral life more realistically and accurately than proposals that excessively rely on elaborate moral intuitions on the one hand or oversimplified appeals to pragmatism or, worse yet, community conventions on the other. Contrary to more simplistic models for moral decision making, Williams believed in intuitively and "universally" recognized moral norms, but he also assumed that our use of these shared norms required engagement in public moral deliberation and attention to how norms are embedded in social and institutional conventions. Civility requires both the individual reasoning of conscience and the rational deliberations of public moral discourse. Far from consisting of immediately applicable action guides, civility requires moral dialogue between the practical reasoning of moral agents and the deliberations of historically situated communities in order to provide some hope for consensus on the specific norms of civility for a time and place. Sometimes Williams's deliberation resulted in norms that contemporary citizens would hardly recognize as universally affirmed moral values, but in his occasional "illiberal" invocation of civility, Williams simply demonstrates the moral endeavor that civility places before us all.

6

CHRISTIAN INTEGRITY, PUBLIC DISCOURSE, AND THE LEGACY OF ROGER WILLIAMS

Much of this book has been dedicated to demonstrating the coexistence of two priorities in the writings of Roger Williams. On the one hand, Williams's thought was intensely confessional, rooted in a Reformed theology that emphasized a commitment to a christocentric piety and the integrity of religious identity. On the other hand, Williams made his greatest philosophical contributions in his arguments for religious toleration, arguments that were intended for both fellow church leaders and a wider public audience and that continue to have significance to the political foundations of American democracy. As a result, Williams offers both an important historical defense of Christian conviction and a social ethics that meaningfully responds to the reality of religious and moral pluralism. My aim has been to demonstrate that Williams held these two priorities together without fatal compromise of either commitment. He maintained loyalty to his theological roots despite his call for wide religious and moral toleration, and, in fact, his advocacy of freedom of conscience grew out of his confessional beliefs. At the same time, his Christian convictions did not qualify his advocacy of freedom of conscience, but instead compelled him to expand the call for freedom to include peoples previously (and subsequently, for that matter) refused protection by the broadest conceptions of religious liberty. In the moral theology of Roger Williams, Reformed theological values and a respect for religious and moral pluralism worked hand in hand to yield one of the great apologies for conscientious freedom in American political and theological history.

In this final chapter I want to suggest ways in which Williams's moral theology might inform contemporary reflection, not on the usual questions of religious freedom, but on the broader issue of the relationship between Christian conviction and public ethics. How (or whether) the preservation of distinctive Christian identity is compatible with participating in public moral discourse is an extremely important debate in recent American theological ethics. To this issue in particular, I want to relate Williams by considering him in light of two sets of questions. The first concerns the level of loyalty Christian ethics ought to reflect to the special sources and narratives of Christian tradition. How distinctive ought Christian ethics be among the other moral proposals nascent in the environment of American pluralism? What exactly do we mean when we say that Christian ethics should be distinctive? How does Williams suggest we might keep together a commitment to the distinctiveness of Christian ethics without abdicating a meaningful contribution to public discourse in the process? This is an enormous debate among Christian ethicists today, and anything resembling an exhaustive address of the terms and personalities it involves is beyond the scope of this book. Asking this series of questions on an introductory level, however, may help us to understand how Williams's approach to the relationship between Christian particularity and public responsibility improves upon both the universalizing tendency in much of Christian liberalism and the selective historical memory of liberalism's communitarian critics. Williams's work suggests a way to understand Christian distinctiveness while accurately retaining the "public-oriented" dimension to the church's moral tradition.

If our first set of questions asks how we may preserve the religious integrity of Christian ethics as it seeks to do public ethics, a second important series of questions represents in some ways the reverse concern: how may Christian ethics maintain its public integrity as long as it insists on doing ethics from a distinctively religious perspective? This second set wonders whether it is possible for a confessional stance to make a meaningful contribution to public moral discourse and decision making. How should we understand the role of the Christian ethicist in public moral discourse? Can a religious perspective make a meaningful contribution to civil consideration of moral issues without leaving its religiosity at the door? This, too, is a hefty issue for religionists and secular ethicists alike, but again I want only to introduce the issue of the role of the Christian ethicist in public moral discourse in order to sketch some contributions that Williams's approach to public ethics may make to the ongoing debate.

Though the parting words of a book on a Puritan dissident may not be the place for an exhaustive study of any of these questions, I at least want to suggest that the moral theology of Roger Williams can illumine certain dimensions of this current debate, perhaps suggesting new ways of thinking about the easily employed but frequently imprecise language of "distinctiveness" and "public ethics." Williams reminds us that there is historical precedent in Reformed theology for thinking about Christian public ethics in more creative ways than the universalist's tendency toward theological dissolve and the communitarian's threat of public withdrawal. In this way, I actually believe a seventeenth-century Puritan may be able to contribute to our exploration of this odd relationship between confessional commitment and public participation.

THE DISTINCTIVENESS OF CHRISTIAN ETHICS

The central characteristic of the particularist turn in Christian ethics is the insistence that Christian ethics derives its identity from the uniqueness of its sources and its origination in a community of belief and practice that embodies this uniqueness. Rather than a timeless collection of universally recognized moral truths, Christian ethics done from a particularist point of view recognizes the foundational role that the religious community and its tradition play in forming Christian norms and values. Christian ethics is rooted in the story of the community of faith centered on Jesus Christ, and it protects its identity as Christian ethics only as long as it takes seriously its connection with that community's history and tradition. Christian particularism recognizes that Christian ethics cannot be done without reference to its location within the community of faith.

Of course, how one interprets the specific effect of the community's narrative and identity on Christian ethics varies greatly among ethicists generally sympathetic with the particularist emphasis on historically bound moral tradition. More radical interpreters insist that Christian belief, practice, and community ought to sharply distinguish Christian ethics from other moral perspectives. They argue that Christian ethics by its very nature is unique insofar as the specific commitments to discipleship and the church yield moral direction unlike that available from other moral perspectives.[1] Thus a radical particularist has great reason to reject any effort to transform the particular beliefs and practices of a specific historical community into a system of belief universally accessible to persons outside the community of faith. Such efforts to reinvent Christian ethics, they charge, usually entail the identification of a moral "essence" to Christian thought that can be offered to a wider public apart from the historical and ritualistic context of church tradition. The purely historical components of religious believing are rejected altogether, or are subjected to "translation" into language and concepts more easily digested by modern sensibilities. Conversely, the radical Christian particularist insists that Christian ethics protects its integrity only when the distinctive and historically grounded elements play a formative role in the development of ethical practice and perspective.

Perhaps no contemporary American theologian more ardently articulates the call for Christian ethics to return to its distinctive roots and meaning than Stanley Hauerwas. Hauerwas rejects the whole endeavor of trying to find some universal core in Christian morality, yet he believes that the overwhelming majority of Christian moralists since the Enlightenment have envisioned their task in precisely this way. At least since the Enlightenment, says Hauerwas, Christian ethicists have sought "not revision but accommodation," writing and teaching as if Christian religion, in order to warrant continued allegiance, must be translatable into universally accessible moral norms and values.[2] As a result, Christian moralists have "attempted to deny the inherent historical and community-dependent nature of our moral convictions in the hopes that our 'ethics' might be universally persuasive."[3] According to Hauerwas, however, the attempt to translate the particular moral vision of the Christian community out of its historical basis and into a "nontheological idiom" only legitimates the question regarding why a theological idiom should be necessary at all.[4]

By contrast, Hauerwas imagines Christian ethics to be "the kind of practices that shape the way Christians must live if we are to embody in our lives the confession that Jesus Christ is Lord."[5] He remains suspicious of attempts to translate the specific requirements of Christian practice into universally recognized norms and values, because he suspects that the effort to do so insufficiently respects the way Christian norms (and the language in which they are articulated) are embedded in a community of story and practice. In other words, to divide moral norms and practices from the community, stories, and language in which they are rooted is to sever them from their sources of meaning and to radically transform the nature of the norms and values themselves. Apart from the language of a particular community's story and tradition, these values become, in a real sense, something different, no longer Christian norms and requirements. Hauerwas admits that a commitment to the integrity of such distinctive language "may make it difficult, perhaps even impossible, for Christians to 'fit in'" among other moral perspectives.[6] Ultimately, however, he believes the Christian should be unconcerned with fitting in, for the central theological question of Christian morality is not how to make Christianity intelligible to the modern world, but how to "make sense of the world, given the way we Christians are taught to speak in and through our worship of God."[7]

Yet there may be other, more subtle ways to envision the distinctive effect of piety and Christian belonging on religious ethics. To James M. Gustafson, the distinctive nature of Christian ethics does not require a radically disjunctive relationship with the norms and language of other ethical perspectives. Instead, specifically Christian sources and values may nuance one's orientation without requiring uniqueness. The language of Christian morality signals a fundamental commitment and perspective from which moral value is estimated. Representing the experience of every moral moment in light of "the reality of God and of life before God," Christian belief can add distinctive character to Christian ethics in three areas: the reasons for being moral, the character of the moral agent, and the points of reference used to determine conduct.[8] In addition, Gustafson argues that religious language often helps to illuminate the morally significant features of a particular scenario, revealing significance where not immediately apparent and suggesting "what values are at stake, what attitudes are fitting, what principles ought to govern action in particular associations, and what means of action are appropriate."[9] This theological perspective may then help clarify the moral moment by interpreting the problems and values at issue and by suggesting appropriate motives, character, and norms to employ. In these four areas—motive, character, situational analysis, and sources for moral reference—religious experience and belief may qualify the moral agency of the Christian.

From this less extreme definition of "distinctiveness," the theological character of Christian ethics nonetheless tempers the human predisposition to restrict moral concern locally, encouraging agents to understand moral cases as part of the greater whole of human existence. Gustafson claims that this is one of the great contributions of a theocentric perspective, that it reminds us of the complicated interdependence of creatures and forces us to understand ourselves and our moral predicaments in as wide a context as possible.[10] Similarly, in his study of Christian realism Robin Lovin suggests that a theological perspective may disclose "something about the character of reality as a whole, something congruent with the part of it which we directly experience, but extending beyond that to encompass a unity that we have not experienced and cannot reduce to a completely rational formulation."[11] By way of its theological commitments, Christian ethics often reminds us that our moral obligations transcend immediate interests, because reference to God "provides a reality in which a comprehensive unity of moral meanings is conceivable." By providing this larger moral context, Christian ethics "impels those who apprehend it in faith to seek forms of justice that go beyond present expectations, even when that search involves considerable risk to themselves."[12] By enlarging our moral perspective, theology leaves its distinctive mark on the motives, character, and interpretive mind-set of ethics.

Adopting this more moderate interpretation of the distinctive nature of Christian ethics, we discover that it is unnecessary and unreasonable to claim that Christian ethics is altogether unique. That this is the case follows in part from the empirical recognition that the modifying effect of language and experience goes both ways; just as Christian ethics is interpreting and contrasting with the dominant cultural milieu, it is itself interpreted and altered with respect to other cultural perspectives. While Christian concepts and symbols often disclose to us a significant aspect of the moral scenario that remains hidden without the interpretive insight of Christian belief, nonreligious knowledge and experience may shed light on our understanding of Christian belief and practice. Gustafson insists that theological concepts and symbols "always have a double reference" because they denote simultaneously how religious experience illuminates lived events and circumstances and how lived experiences affect the articulation of the understanding of God.[13] Likewise, Lovin argues that religious traditions and symbols "identify attitudes, values, and virtues that are relevant to more comprehensive assessment of present choices, but those present choices also give substance to the tradition."[14]

Because the interpretive assistance of lived experience and "natural" knowledge cooperates with the particular insight of Christian piety, a more realistic and faithful approach to the distinctiveness of theological ethics will affirm that Christian ethics may be *distinctive* in a number of ways without being entirely *unique* in the norms, values, and direction it produces. Gustafson in particular draws a clear difference between the terms "distinctive" and "unique," where the former respects the particular sources, motivations, and points of view of Christian morality without insisting that Christian ethics therefore differs qualitatively from every other moral perspective on every issue.[15] The "points of reference" that faith offers Christian morality provide "clarity" to the issues and norms at stake in moral scenarios, but they do not represent a system of morality that is inherently superior at every level to the norms and values knowable from other ethical perspectives.[16] Christian faith may have a distinctive effect on ethics, then, without producing an ethics that is totally unique. As a consequence of this limit on uniqueness, Christian ethics has room for greater optimism regarding the prospects for Christian participation in public moral discourse and the level of transferability in Christian moral norms and values than some particularists suggest.

To be sure, Hauerwas rejects Christian liberalism's strong impulse to "translate" theology into secular discourse, but he equally rejects the notion that his ethics is sectarian, arguing instead that claims to universality must proceed *from* particular theological accounts. Too much of modern theological ethics "stands outside the tradition and seeks to show that selected aspects of the tradition can no longer pass muster from the perspective of the outside."[17] The universality of Christian morality cannot rest on the rescue of certain "reasonable" convictions from an otherwise hopelessly dated tradition, nor on the identification of "inherent human qualities" for which Christian rhetoric is nothing more than appropriate symbolism. Instead, Hauerwas insists that "the basis of our universalism comes by first being initiated into a particular story and community." Genuine Christian universalism begins in faith in the God of Jesus, but it recognizes in the commonalities between specific religious beliefs of the Christian community and the best humanistic alternatives nothing more than the confirmation that the lordship of Christ transcends the community of those who "know him by his right name."[18] From Hauerwas's perspective, Christian ethics starts with the acknowledgment of its particularity, "from a frank . . . recognition that, methodologically, ethics and theology can only be carried out relative to a particular community's convictions."[19] From there it can move out to universal claims about God's true intentions for human existence without giving up its particular identity, and without letting pluralism itself dictate what is an acceptable "translation" of Christian ethics or what universal values Christian language appropriately symbolizes.

Despite this important reminder of the primary importance of particularity to Christian ethics, however, Hauerwas often does not seem to move very successfully from this particularity to more universal claims. Having insisted that Christians ought to approach public discourse and the prospect of universal moral claims from within the particularity of the church's story and tradition, he claims that this location will allow Christians to "negotiate and make positive contributions" to the society in which they find themselves. Precisely what kind of contribution Hauerwas envisions is hard to say, though, for he seldom offers any portrait of the Christian engaged meaningfully in such discourse. Instead the picture he paints is of Christian people standing on the sideline of public moral discourse, objecting to the rules of the debate and the arrangement of the chairs, instead of participating meaningfully, as Christians and citizens, in a manner that may be comprehensible and thus helpful to others in the conversation. In fact, Hauerwas insists that the church is not in the business of recommending moral guidelines generally acceptable to a pluralistic society, and furthermore that tension between the church and public institutional existence is to be accepted as a given, with no attempts to resolve it:

> Christians are called first and foremost not to resolve the tension between church and state, but to acknowledge the kingship of Christ in their lives, which means leaving church-state relations profoundly unresolved, until the day when He comes again in glory.[20]

This lack of commitment to addressing the resolution of public moral issues seems to justify the difficulty many of Hauerwas's critics admit regarding how his ethics may actually be practiced in genuine cultural engagement.

Particularists, then, often fail to demonstrate a meaningful role for the church in public moral conversation, if by "meaningful" role we expect more than the simple assertion of stance and identity. The hope for public moral conversation depends on mutual exchange, openness to the criticism and interpretation of the other, and an effort at sharedness that may include the approximate "translation" of certain norms and values into a language that conversation partners may understand, if not adopt. Particularists resist such efforts out of fear that such exchanges will lead inevitably to the dilution of Christian identity and meaning. By contrast, Gustafson imagines the church participating in public moral conversation from a perspective that protects and honors its particular story while still pursuing exchange with those outside that story. The beliefs and practices of the church distinctly inform the moral perspective of Christians without rendering it incapable of conversing with those outside, and in fact, participation in moral dialogue is a way for the church to avoid collapsing in on its own history and identity:

> Moral discourse, governed by the affirmations of the faith, enables the church to keep its identity without isolating itself; it moves from the center of its faith and life, Jesus Christ, outward to its community, its world, its culture.[21]

Gustafson believes that this interest in inclusive moral discourse is an important part of Christian identity, and that the commitment to moral conversation is one of the church's greatest gifts to the world around it. The church exists as a community that cultivates character from a theocentric perspective, but that also serves as a "community of moral discourse" that can "provide a continuity of deliberation that is much needed in our society."[22] In other words, the church contributes to public moral discourse in part by *patterning* healthy discourse.[23]

Their different emphases lead Gustafson and Hauerwas to much different notions of what it means for the church to participate in public moral discourse. To Hauerwas, Christian participation entails witnessing to the "different way" of the church, while Gustafson expects the church to have substantive conversation with other members of the public based in both the distinctive insight garnered from a theocentric perspective and the commonality shared among all human beings. The difference, then, between a radical notion of Christian particularity and a more moderate conception of the same seems to originate partially in different expectations of what constitutes "meaningful" participation in public conversation. For Hauerwas, the preservation of its distinctive identity is the church's most significant contribution to public moral conversation:

> Theologians, therefore, have something significant to say about ethics, but they will not say it significantly if they try to disguise the fact that they think, write, and speak out of and to a distinctive community. Their first task is not, as has been assumed by many working in Christian ethics and still under the spell of Christendom, to write as though Christian commitments make no difference in the sense that they only underwrite what everyone already in principle can know, but rather to show the difference those commitments make. At least by doing that, philosophers may have some idea how the attempt to avoid presuming any tradition or community may distort their account of the moral life as well as moral rationality. Our task as theologians remains what it has always been—namely, to exploit the considerable resources embodied in particular Christian convictions which sustain our ability to be a community faithful to our belief that we are creatures of a graceful God. If we do that we may well discover that we are speaking to more than just our

fellow Christians, for others as a result may well find we have something interesting to say.[24]

This may very well be the case, and the importance Hauerwas places on theological integrity is a needed corrective for much of modern Christian ethics, yet if the Christian contribution to public ethics amounts to no more than this, it sells short both the richness of Christian tradition and reasonable expectations for open dialogue. With Hauerwas's cautions duly noted and respected, then, a more faithful rendering of the Christian tradition's relationship with moral pluralism will take advantage of the significant resources in that tradition for an ethical perspective from which religious persons can engage meaningfully other members of pluralistic society.

WILLIAMS AND THE QUESTION OF DISTINCTIVENESS

What does this rehearsal of the debate over religious identity and public discourse in contemporary Christian ethics have to do with Roger Williams? A principal motivation for this book lies in my belief that Williams's writing and public activity offer a subtler understanding of the relationship between religious identity and public participation than we see in much of the current debate. Williams faithfully balanced his zealous protection of the church's identity as the distinct body of Christ with his sense of responsibility to participate in the consideration of moral issues that preoccupied the larger civil community, by identifying within his Reformed tradition ideas that articulated a theological connection between the beliefs and practices of the church and the common moral agency shared by all human beings. Williams's theological ethics begins with the life of Christian faith, the particular beliefs, commitments, and practices that derive from confessing Jesus Christ as Lord. Of more than rhetorical usefulness, the overtly theological language and reference of his work represents Williams's belief that religious commitment necessarily ought to manifest itself in clear and distinctive ways in the thought, beliefs, and practices of members of the church. His dedication to the integrity of the distinctive nature of Christian thought and practice informs his ethical discourse as well, though, for he reaches the "universal" norms and values to which he appeals in his arguments for toleration only by locating himself first solidly in the context of Christian confession. In the tradition of early Christian apologists, Williams began his reference to generally recognizable moral norms from the context of Christian believing, arguing that certain norms and values at the heart of Christian morality are in fact values that other reasonable moral agents will identify as conducive for human flourishing as well.

Williams did insist, though, that these values inspired by Reformed theology were compatible with a wider audience and with the context of religious and moral pluralism. From his commitment to the distinctive character of Christian belief and living, Williams could identify a capacity in Christian ethics for speaking to persons outside the faith. This can be done from a Christian perspective, suggested Williams, because Christianity entails faith in the God who orders, sustains, and governs the world—including the moral world—by a natural law accessible to every moral agent. Williams's deity is the God of biblical tradition, who reigns not only in matters of redemption but over creation as well.[25] This theological conviction gave Williams the courage to engage in moral conversation with non-Christians, and even to formulate some of his theologically grounded moral norms and values in language with minimal theological import, without the fear of abandoning his theological identity, for his motivation and justification are themselves embedded in that identity.

Williams's insistence on the necessity of balancing a distinctive commitment to religious identity and language with an effort to take that same piety into true conversation with others in his pluralistic world found theological root in his Reformed sense of the economic unity of the triune God. In other words, Williams began with his belief in a God who governs not only over matters of salvation but over creation as well. God in Christ is Lord of the regenerate but also the ultimate foundation of all reality, the Logos from which all created existence stems. From this belief in a God who claims authority and responsibility for both creation and redemption, Williams ordered his conception of Christian existence, which included both an emphasis on a religious community whose allegiance to God renders it unique in many ways among the other religious and moral alternatives in this pluralistic world, and a responsibility to moral cooperation with the other components of that pluralistic creation.

It is important to note that Williams's characteristically Reformed starting point with the economic unity of the Trinity gave form and meaning to his ecclesiology, an order that may explain some of the differences between his embrace of public conversation and the more limited expectations of a perspective like Hauerwas's. Although both Williams and Hauerwas exhibit strong resemblances to Anabaptist sectarianism, Williams's separatist urges occurred in the larger context of this Reformed trinitarianism, a fact that prevented him from ever envisioning the gulf between church and world so great as to eliminate the moral commonality that all human beings—in and outside the church—share. Thus, despite his obsession with the religious purity of the church, Williams insisted that Christians and non-Christians shared enough of an anthropological foundation as moral agents to cooperate meaningfully in political, social, and moral community. Williams's ability to hold his separatist understanding of the church in balance with a sophisticated public ethics stems from the doctrine of God with which his moral theology begins.[26]

Like his theological forefather Calvin, Williams subscribed to a theological vision in which "nearly all the wisdom we possess, that is to say, true and sound wisdom, consists of two parts: the knowledge of God and of ourselves," with the assumption that human existence is unified in common subsistence in the one God.[27] Calvin's discourse of God the Creator immediately discloses its dependence on christological revelation, because for Calvin genuine Christian knowledge of the Creator is impossible apart from the divine expression in Jesus Christ. Williams's theology follows this Calvinist pattern, insisting that the distinctive Christian claims about the Creator are expressed in Christology and manifested in human living in his ecclesiological vision of a separated community. While he attributes true religious understanding to the Christian faith, however, Williams (also like Calvin) insists that the Christian God is also the governor of all human beings; creation is God's dominion, and our common role as moral agents in that dominion binds all human beings together on at least some fundamental social and moral level. By beginning with this acknowledgment of divine lordship over all created reality—in a sense, balancing the differences of the covenanted community with the sameness shared by all creation—Williams's Reformed theology permanently reserves a place of importance for this sameness. Our shared identity as moral agents in God's ordering provides a foundation of commonality upon which we may understand Christians as participants with the rest of humanity in the common tasks (social, political, and moral) of being human, rather than always as a unique alternative.

Just as Christians and non-Christians qua human beings share a common ability to be (and relate to each other as) moral agents, so Williams argued that a limited number of moral values exist that are generally recognizable among all human beings, an assumption specifically rooted in his theological conception of natural law. Williams recognized that much in the human condition—namely, sin—complicates prospects for moral cooperation, but the existence of natural law and the inherent rationality of human beings provide hope that some of the moral values that Christian believing commends may also be attractive to non-Christian moral agents. In other words, Williams did not imagine the "unregenerate" human moral life and Christian life to be so disjunctive as to preclude the shared recognition of some basic moral needs, norms, and values. Despite his theological sectarianism, he was able to envision moral commonality between the church and its neighbors. This commonality allowed Williams to hope that Christians could do more than "witness" to their fellow moral agents; he believed that they could engage them (and be engaged) in moral conversation and share a common (if very basic) vocabulary of norms and values. For Williams, the distinctive nature of Christian belief and living did not eliminate the fact that part of that lifestyle involved the norms of "civility," standards of moral performance recognizable to agents beyond Christian confession. He would have agreed with Gustafson that "'Christian' ethics then is highly distinctive, though not unique in all respects, and to be a Christian is to be obliged to follow the distinctive as well as the ordinary morality that is part of a Christian way of life."[28]

The relationship between the "distinctive" and the "ordinary" is important to understanding how Williams commits to a sectarian ecclesiology while maintaining his desire to participate in public moral discourse. Williams did not lose sight of the fact that Christian piety consists of more than widely recognized moral norms. Christian discipleship involves a more stringent lifestyle that contributes to the radically distinctive appearance that Christian association and living should take. Some of the peculiar lifestyle commitments that Christian piety requires are moral in nature, and these special moral obligations of Christian faith are distinctive; they may even be unique in the stringency of their claims, in the character they develop, and in the motives they provide for Christian morality. Although they are not recognized as norms outside the specific commitments and context of the Christian community, upon the members of the Christian community they are not supererogatory. Christians are obliged to live by the requirements of the "special ethics" of Christian believing even while they are also bound by the "ordinary" norms for human flourishing and cohabitation that Christian ethics includes. At the same time, these "ordinary" norms are also a part of the Christian vision of virtue and moral obligation, and it is the existence of this category of moral values that binds all human beings (Christian or not) and provides a shared basis for conversation with those outside the faith.[29] Williams's recognition of the sameness-in-difference between Christians and non-Christians allowed him to identify alongside the more stringent claims of Christian living certain moral norms and values that human beings in general may recognize as contributing to human flourishing, and which consequently provide a basis for Christian participation in public moral discourse.

THE UNIVERSALITY OF CONSCIENCE

Williams's confidence in the existence of these basic moral norms and values accessible to all human beings depended on his conviction that conscience is a *universal* human phenomenon. Through the conscience, human beings have the capability to be rational moral deliberators, and thus partners in public moral strategies. Obviously the universality of conscience was as vital to Williams's appeal for religious freedom as was his defense of its inviolability. He claimed not only that persecution was a violation of the integrity of the conscience, but that religious uniformity was unnecessary to guarantee a stable civil society. Civil harmony is properly established not on coerced religiosity, argued Williams, but by appeal to the conscientious convictions of society's citizens. The universality of conscience, of human access to basic norms and values crucial to stable coexistence, represented for Williams the proper moral foundation for peaceful and productive construction of civil society. Conscience made religious enforcement unnecessary and actually unwise, and served as the anthropological seat of his optimism regarding the public values of civility.

The existence of something called "conscience" is a belief that today enjoys extensive popular support. Though the concept received its most intensive development in classical Western theological and philosophical traditions, contemporary human-rights dialogue seems to indicate that other belief systems possess analogs to the experience connoted by the term.[30] Certainly in popular American culture, the idea of an internal moral compass called "conscience" and found in every human being is extremely prevalent. Intuitively at least, we seem to know what we are referring to when we invoke the concept of conscience, and we consider people abnormal, inhuman almost, if their actions suggest that they operate without one. We routinely expect a "good conscience" from our neighbors, our doctors, and our political leaders.

Despite the popular recognition of such a phenomenon, conscience enjoys uneven support within modern Reformed theology. Influenced by the theology of Karl Barth, some thinkers reject the universality of conscience in the same breath with which they dismiss appeals to natural law, suspecting that appeals to conscience betray a desire to avoid claims to authority of particular Christian sources. Though Barth himself did not discard the language of conscience entirely, he was careful to "reject all more primitive ideas of conscience, the idea of a voice of truth immanent in man by nature, or that of a voice of humanity which sums up supposedly individual voices of conscience."[31] Properly understood, wrote Barth, conscience is neither an innate capacity of the human condition nor a product of social education; it depends on neither universal principles nor the internalization of human standards. Instead, Barth co-opted the language of conscience for his portrayal of Christian ethics as adherence to the command of God.

According to Barth, Christian moral responsibility originates in the obligation that bears on us from our transcendent God, and which God expresses to the Christian in a specific personal event, or command. Conscience, then, represents that relationship with the Triune God from which comes direct awareness, not of timeless general principles, but of this personal and particular command of God. Conscience is our "co-knowledge" with God of that which God commands us to do in the present, so that our acts might align with Christ's kingdom to come.[32] To commit to a universal capacity called conscience without christological foundation is to substitute static human principles for the dynamic command of God, to attempt to elevate universal human constructs to a level of superiority over the Word.[33] "If there is concrete fellowship with God the Redeemer, then and only then there is such a thing called conscience. . . . To have a conscience is no more and no less than to have the Holy Spirit."[34] Rather than a starting place for drawing rational commonality between Christians and non-Christians, conscience for Barth only made sense when understood in the prior and superior theological context of the command of God, and certainly the idea should not be used to imply universal access to natural-law principles.[35]

Although it is enjoying a light renaissance in philosophical literature, the concept of conscience as a universal capacity is not as highly regarded among contemporary philosophers either as it is in the lay public.[36] C. D. Broad utilized the concept of conscience but rejected both exclusively theological interpretations of the phenomenon and the implication that conscience must rely on absolute deontological principles. For Broad and others, conscience, if it "exists" at all, is a subjective process of reflection rather than access to objective norms, which evidence suggests are not universally agreed upon anyway.[37] J. F. M. Hunter argues that there is no literal meaning at all behind the word "conscience." Citing numerous logical problems with trying to argue for its existence from inference or deduction, Hunter also claims that conscience cannot be identified by the vocabulary of psychology or located in certain neurological functions. His conclusion is that whether considered philosophically, psychologically, or biologically, we cannot prove the existence of some faculty or phenomenon that we can identify with confidence as "the conscience." Thus, "in using the word 'conscience' we are using a fancy idea, the literal truth of which is irrelevant, to convey a plain meaning."[38]

Hunter's dismissal of any logical, psychological, or physiological identification of some discrete power or faculty called "conscience" leaves him with limited options for responding to the term:

> Our conclusions concerning the [doubtful] existence of conscience [as a literal entity] suggest the following problem: in view of the doubtfulness of its existence on the one hand, and the apparent confidence in its existence presupposed by so many of our uses, on the other, ought we to purify our speech by ceasing to use the term, thereby eradicating the confusions and false or doubtful beliefs which its use engenders, or is there some way of understanding the logical machinery involved, which will have the same effect while allowing us to carry on using the same term?[39]

Hunter concludes that the prevalence of the language of conscientiousness requires that we retain it, but he prefers that we reformulate popular appeals to conscience to understand them as shorthand for other moral processes.

Thomas Nagel rejects psychophysical reductionism like Hunter's as a pretense for judging the validity of a conception like conscience. Nagel acknowledges the impossibility of being able to describe "the *objective* character of an experience, apart from the particular point of view from which its subject apprehends it."[40] But he immediately argues that it makes no sense to deny the final existence of an experience simply because it is impossible to describe the experience in objective terms. Nagel takes this to be common sense, that the legitimacy of a subjective experience like conscience would resist the objectification that psychophysical reductionism demands. Nagel prods us to wonder "whether any sense can be made of experience's having an objective character at all. Does it make sense, in other words, to ask what my experiences are really like, as opposed to how they appear to me?"[41] Thus, from his point of view the ultimate legitimacy of a concept like "conscience," the subjective experience of which is widely acknowledged but which resists the reductionism of current physicalist preoccupations, does not depend on our ability to locate or objectify it.

Even some philosophers who reject the notion that there is an identifiable faculty or operation in the human moral makeup that can be labeled "conscience" agree that the reference to conscience itself is universal. Despite his suggestion of logical problems involved in any attempt to identify a specific location or substantive meaning for conscience, Hunter himself admits that the concept has staying power. Conscience is a firmly rooted moral concept because it is universally used, people mean something when they say it, and they generally know what others mean when they invoke it. Though he thinks the literal idea of the conscience a "fancy idea" and recommends "the abandonment of any belief or suspicion anyone might have about the 'existence' of conscience," Hunter does not push for the avoidance of the term. For as he is forced to acknowledge, "there are many things we want to say which are very aptly conveyed by this terminology, and often only awkwardly by any alternative way of speaking."[42]

Therefore, even one who doubts the literal existence of such a thing is compelled to admit that the concept of conscience is indispensable. Whether or not we agree with his claim that conscience is a "fancy idea" with no promise of logical, neurological, or psychological "location," we must with Hunter acknowledge that the referent *experience* of something called "conscience" is widely shared and recognizable. Even if we avoid using the term "conscience" to "assert or presuppose the existence of things of its description," as Hunter desires, we may by its use acknowledge "that the description is well known, and that working from this description people will understand what we mean, what we are trying to say."[43] The experience of some internal moral compass that dictates to a person the difference between right and wrong action is a generally accepted phenomenon. As a result, the idea of conscience may serve as a shared moral conception and provide a beginning point for common moral conversation.

The universality of conscience is important, for the very idea posits that human beings within and outside the church hold in common a capacity to converse and potentially concur on at least basic elements of a shared sense of morality. In centering his call for mutual respect and shared moral dialogue on the concept of conscience, Williams suggested a basis for envisioning ethical conversation that transcends creedal boundaries. But Williams reached this basis not by abdicating his own theological framework; instead he developed a concept that his religious tradition already recognized as *theologically* legitimate. In other words, conscience for Williams was a theological concept that simultaneously serves as a more widely accepted starting point for envisioning a society of respect and dialogue. A religious orientation that incorporates this appeal to conscience already includes a theological foundation for envisioning public moral cooperation, because the idea itself implies the possibility of members of the larger community of human beings sharing basic standards for moral dialogue and consensus, regardless of religious confession. Williams' devotion to conscience provides theological rationale for considering members of the wider social community potential partners in moral dialogue and decision making, and it cautions Christians against constraining divine possibility by confining Christian moral authority to revealed language and sources, thereby neglecting the more universal experience of general morality that the tradition recognizes. The universality of conscience reminds us that the Reformed tradition, Barth's objections aside, includes vocabulary to recognize the integrity of moral agents and ethical insight outside the faith community. In other words, with the distinct language of Reformed theology, Williams reminds us that it is not only the particular but also the universal that Christian faith utilizes and values.

CIVILITY, THEN AND NOW

The concept of conscience, then, provides theological language for taking non-Christians seriously as moral partners, and this moral commonality contributed to Williams's endorsement of Christian participation in public moral discourse. That he assumed that Christians could participate as religious persons in this wider conversation there is no doubt. He lived and wrote from a specific expectation that the religious voice has a seat at the table of public discourse, contributing to this conversation in meaningful ways. From both his writings and his own public participation, we can perhaps glean a couple of important convictions for understanding the role of the religious voice in public moral discourse. The first belief that reverberates clearly throughout Williams's theology is that this public participation is possible and justifiable from a *Christian* point of view. Christians can participate in public moral endeavors without abandoning particular convictions by appealing to dimensions within their own theological tradition, and by embodying Christianity's relative optimism that what is best for human flourishing and recognizable to a certain degree by the natural rational capacities of moral agents will also find rough parallel among the values and obligations of Christian living. For the Reformed tradition, as with most of Christian theology, the ideals of Christian living represent in fact true *human* living, and although those outside the Christian faith may not possess adequate theological knowledge, they are capable of knowing something of the moral foundations of human coexistence.

A second conviction on which Williams's work depends is that Christian participation in public discourse is possible from a *public* point of view. This is a much different point than the first, but it is related insofar as a positive response to Christian publicity depends upon the ability of Christian ethics to avoid the dual traps of irrelevancy and redundancy. Christian ethics risks irrelevancy by refusing to formulate its contributions to public discourse in language and concepts that have some entry point for persons outside the faith community. Alternatively, Christian ethics risks redundancy when reformulation overextends into translation, and Christian vocabulary becomes simply rhetorical flourish for values and insight entirely available by means independent of Christian piety. Williams symbolized, in both his life-service and his thought, that Christian ethics may contribute to public discourse and avoid both pitfalls. Of course, the danger of irrelevancy perhaps loomed less in a preliberal society like New England, where an institutionalized Christianity characterized the cultural and political landscape, but Williams's understanding of his role as public participant did not depend on this assumed hegemony. In fact, he rejected the presumed institutionalization of Christian belief—Christendom—as strongly as contemporary communitarians. Instead of depending on a latent Christianized culture, Williams appealed to Christian norms and values that resonated with rational human deliberation on the purposes of social coexistence and the requirements of human flourishing. He set out to demonstrate that his contributions to public moral discourse and endeavors, made from a confessional standpoint, were compatible with the deeper philosophical norms and values that every moral agent, cultural Christian or not, ought to recognize as essential to human cohabitation. Christians can participate in public moral endeavors when they are able to articulate those dimensions of the religious tradition that appeal to deeper meanings, needs, and capacities we associate with genuine human living.

Invited to the table, then, what specific contributions can the Christian make to public moral discourse? First, the theological point of view can bring public deliberation back in touch with the fundamental values of the common good, reminding us of some of the basic ideals and expectations that are at the heart of moral agency and social cooperation. Ultimately, Williams's advocacy of civility is aimed precisely at this end. Civility is all about regaining a sense of common agreement on those norms and values that allow us to coexist and even to cooperate in the larger task of public living. It seeks the maintenance of those boundaries that allow us to live, talk, and work together in the pursuit of moral agreement and common accomplishment. The theological voice can refreshingly call our attention to those values that bind us together.

Religion, Williams demonstrated, can also serve as a critical voice, deconstructing widespread assumptions, demonstrating how conventionally accepted institutions and practices are in fact morally problematic and detrimental to the task of living together civilly and seeking moral clarity on public issues. Certainly Williams's particular conception of Christian identity and piety permitted him to serve this critical function in his society. Against long-held assumptions of the danger of religious pluralism and toleration, Williams insisted that even Catholics and Muslims could be good citizens, a revolutionary suggestion in his time. His critique of political intolerance was rooted in a theological vision that was able to focus on and emphasize the human identity and moral capacities of persons who, religiously speaking, were the sectarian Protestant's lifelong adversary. Williams demonstrated in word and practice that religious conceptions can bring this kind of critical vision to public discourse, shedding evaluative light not only on commonly held civil values and norms but on the values of other religious and philosophical perspectives involved in the conversation.

Furthermore, if we understand Williams's debates with Cotton as both public conversation and ecclesial debate, we might see in Williams's work a glimpse of how the religious community may become a pattern for moral discourse. The procedural norms for civility that Williams commended in general he especially expected to govern theological conversation in the church, though to his disadvantage he was frequently alone in that expectation. Williams seldom enjoyed the benefit of a theological community in which diverse perspectives were respected and entertained, yet he never retreated from his expectation that such conversation, if no place else, ought to take place among Christians. His vision of the church as an ideal for moral (and religious) discourse resonates with Gustafson's similar suggestion that churches may "serve the temporal good" by providing "a continuity of deliberation that is much needed in our society."[44] A religious community that conducts its own theological and moral conversation in a manner similar to Williams's vision allows itself to serve as a pattern for civilized and compassionate discourse in a wider civil sense.

Christian religion contributes to public discourse in these ways, then, while still assuming that non-Christian dialogue partners do not always need theology for effective moral conversation and cooperation to take place. This optimism regarding public moral discourse, symbolized in Williams's idea of "civility," seems as pertinent now as it was in his day. Obviously, though, this view of the relationship between religion and moral citizenry was not the dominant perspective in seventeenth-century New England, and it still is not shared by all voices in contemporary religion and politics. Representatives of the organized Religious Right, for instance, maintain an essential link between successful moral citizenry and religious (usually Christian) convictions. Despite his acknowledgment that "we are, by design, a pluralistic society" and that it is beyond the purpose of politics to "promulgate a doctrine of faith," Pat Robertson has insisted that the successful cultivation of common morality requires a return to "ethical systems derived from (and strengthened by) Judeo-Christian values." With an admiring bow to former Latin American leader Augusto Pinochet, Robertson lifts up Chile as an example of the improvements in social behavior and moral consensus that the United States could expect if it simply recognized the vital connection between Christian belief and moral living. "[A] high percentage of dedicated Christian believers will normally translate into stable families, law-abiding children, hard working honest workers, a bias toward education and responsible participation in government. . . . Common sense tells us that a government should foster the religious values that produce such attributes among its citizens—and General Pinochet clearly fostered the growth of Christianity in Chile."[45]

By contrast, Williams argued that common morality can exist without the establishment (institutionally or otherwise) of Christianity, and that the reasonableness of civility provides a basic set of norms and values which empower public moral debate. Again, Williams's confidence in the existence of civility was theologically based, even as he argued that the viability of civility did not require religion's establishment. Instead, civility depended on a complex relationship between the human moral faculties, the product of practical reasoning on moral values discernible through conscience and deliberated in civil discourse. This realistic complexity is one reason that Williams's classical moral theology may provide a helpful corrective for contemporary proposals like Stephen L. Carter's use of similar language. In his book *Civility: Manners, Morals, and the Etiquette of Democracy*, Carter attempts to rejuvenate the language of civility in order to provide a basis for restoring a degree of moral cohesion to American society. Like Williams, Carter argues that the term "civility" may stand for a conception of basic moral norms that citizens hold in common, the denial of which constitutes a threat to the fundamental cohesion, and therefore to the integrity, of society itself. Also similar to Williams's moral theology, Carter insists that respect for civility furthers the common good of all citizens, and, in fact, civility for Carter is largely the exercise of self-restraint that encourages citizens to prioritize the common good of the neighbor and society over individual prerogative. Finally, Carter, like Williams, includes in civility a respect for the etiquette of moral dialogue itself, for the ability to converse intelligently and respectfully, insisting that the protection of constructive and polite public discourse is essential to public morality and the common good.

Carter's understanding of civility differs from Williams's, though, in that for Carter the norms of civility are chiefly grounded and justified in social convention. By contrast to the foundation Williams provided in natural law and practical reasoning, Carter insists that the norms of common morality are found usually in the traditional conventions of American society, and thus civility normally entails an obligation to abide by societal norms. Carter argues that civility's goal "to live a common moral life" requires that "we should try to follow the norms of the community if the norms are not actually immoral."[46] Thus, the cultivation of civility partially involves teaching children "to follow rules rather than instinct unless there is a good reason to make a different choice."[47]

Carter's excessive dependence on social convention for the rules of civility presents several problems, however. Most obviously, as a reflection of custom Carter's conception of civility provides too little room for civility to critically evaluate social norms and conventions. If civility essentially requires that we "follow the norms of the community" and adhere to "rules rather than instinct," what resources does civility possess to call communal norms and rules into question, to evaluate the moral appropriateness of society's current conventions? Certainly one of the most important functions of civility in Williams's moral theology is the critical role it plays against the Puritan "conventions" of religious uniformity and persecution. Carter's reliance on social custom for cues to the content of civility robs his moral project of this important power.[48]

Occasionally Carter confuses his definition of civility by stating that "civility values diversity, disagreement, and the possibility of resistance," a characterization of public dialogue that seems ill at ease with his emphasis on conformity with social rules. Further contradicting his heavy endorsement of social moral conventions, he concludes from this oddly out-of-place appeal to diversity that "the state must not use education to try to standardize our children."[49] The political agenda behind his critique of public education is obvious enough, but the moral justification for his stance is less clear. If civility amounts to an adherence to communal rules and conventions, why would we not want to standardize our children to these rules? Carter's resistance to educational standardization appears to contradict his allegiance to cultural norms, unless one concludes that he is drawing a distinction between "community" and "the state," but if such a distinction is operating behind the scenes here then Carter's conception of civility ultimately accomplishes nothing at all. For with a distinction between community and state in place, civility amounts to little more than a communitarian appeal to the particular conventions of a specific society or segment of society that can never serve as common moral ground for citizens of different political subcommunities. In the end, Carter's civility does not engage moral pluralism with integrity and thus offers very little new insight to the Christian seeking to participate in moral dialogue with citizens who do not share the same religious background.

Civility as Williams envisioned it, though historically dated to be sure, offers a corrective to inconsistencies in a contemporary proposal like Carter's. Williams offered the conceptual resources for imagining a minimalist common moral ground that rose beyond the conventions of current social arrangements by rooting his understanding of civility in natural law, the conscience, and a complex partnership between public deliberation and individual practical reasoning. As a result, civility in Williams's moral theology sometimes reflected cultural custom, but at least as often it exhibited freedom to critically evaluate social institutions and established norms. On the grounds of civility, for instance, Williams defended the conventional Puritan expectation that citizens would support the state's defense, but at the same time he criticized a social convention just as longstanding in Puritan polity, religious uniformity. Because civility was based in the rational deliberations of conscience, the standards of natural law, and the product of public discourse, it maintained its critical edge in a way no simple appeal to convention or tradition is able. And while civility as Williams portrayed it was clearly consistent with his Christian theology, he could offer it as a foundation for public dialogue without the direct ties to religion that jeopardize Carter's project.

Certainly this is what makes Williams's account of civility such an important contribution to the question of Christian participation in public moral discourse, that he is able to demonstrate how the Christian might go about considering a basis for these conversations in theological terms. Civility as Williams understood it assumed that human beings, especially those tied together in social communities, shared a basic consensus on certain fundamental moral norms, and that this common morality could provide a foundation not only for stable society but for further public moral deliberation. Despite contemporary denials, it is difficult to argue with the reality of common morality at the heart of Williams's notion of civility.[50] To claim, as some theologians and philosophers do, that we share no basic set of norms and vocabulary for moral discourse makes little empirical sense, for in the very act of debating the existence or nature of this common morality we demonstrate a minimal moral language, without which our claims would be unintelligible to those with whom we debate. Williams began with a recognition of this minimal foundation for moral dialogue, and then proceeded to explore its substantive potential for public cooperation through the concept of civility.

To engage in such a cooperative project, however, need not threaten the theological quality of Christian ethics; to Williams, the shared values of civility and the distinctive nature of religious morality need not be at odds. Williams seemed to think that meaningful public participation was possible for the Christian without abandoning the particular convictions of Christian piety, as he demonstrated with his writing and life work. In fact, his own lifelong service as a citizen of Rhode Island and his correspondence with fellow members of that colony suggest that he viewed public participation not only as a possibility but also as an imperative of civil life—and of the Christian conception of civil life in particular. From Williams's point of view, meaningful Christian participation in the ethical debates and endeavors of the civil community is an obligation not only of social belonging, but of Christian identity as well. Few individuals in either the history of American democracy or the story of the church fulfilled this duty more thoroughly.

ROGER WILLIAMS, REFORMED THEOLOGIAN

Peace: We have now (deare Truth) through the gracious hand of God clambered up to the top of this our tedious discourse.

Truth: O 'tis mercy unexpressible that either Thou or I have had so long a breathing time, and that together![51]

Many pages ago, this book set out to present Roger Williams as a moral theologian of pivotal importance to Reformed theology in America. Throughout I have argued that in order to understand his contributions to the issues of church-state relations and religious freedom for which he is better known, Williams must first be read as a sophisticated theological thinker standing in the tradition of Reformed Christianity. During the last half century or so, scholarship on Roger Williams has profited from the resurgence of interest in Puritanism more generally, but this scholarship has been almost exclusively the domain of historians, who generally have viewed this outcast Puritan simply as one American patriarch of the political doctrine of religious freedom. Many have assumed that there was in fact little theological foundation to Williams's pronouncements on religious liberty and church-state relations, and indeed some have read him not as a theologian but as an agnostic seeker whose teachings on tolerance stemmed from an efficient pragmatism formed by the experience of intolerance in both old and New England. Stalwart expositors of American history like Vernon Louis Parrington and James E. Ernst proclaimed Roger Williams a prophet of "individual liberty," a value that he allegedly elevated above all other religious and political claims.[52] According to Ernst, Williams was the "Tom Paine of the seventeenth century," in that his interest in international affairs and his defense of a principle of liberty were grounded in a political individualism that developed independently of Williams's various religious convictions. The interpretation of Roger Williams as an "irrepressible democrat" dominated much of modern scholarship until relatively recently, and even now Williams fails to be mentioned among the important theologians of American Christianity.

Even when recognized as a thinker dependent upon some theological framework, more often than not Williams is interpreted as a Seeker or a Baptist, but never as a Reformed theologian.[53] Because of these consistent errors in interpretation, Williams remains a mythical character in national lore and the honorary father of Baptists in America, but he is often regarded as irrelevant to the Reformed theological tradition. By contrast, this book has made a different claim, namely that Williams is properly understood as a Reformed theologian, for he was doing and using Reformed theology when he argued for religious liberty and the separation of church and state. His arguments for tolerance, as well as his career in public politics, were grounded in Reformed notions of natural law, human reason, a robust understanding of conscience, and the moral significance of the incarnation. From these standard doctrines of the Reformed tradition, Williams was able to develop his concept of civility, upon which he set his relative optimism that civil society could engage in moral discourse on the basis of certain shared values but without the need for a shared theological conception or an established religious institution. From the riches of Reformed theology grew a vision of fruitful public discourse and cooperation.

That Williams believed that Christians could be a part of that public moral cooperation has been another important discovery, for when we faithfully reconsider his writings as theology, we quickly realize that Williams lends valuable insight to the contemporary debates over religion in public life. He offers important contributions to this contemporary debate by exemplifying that dimension of the Christian tradition that has balanced public participation and confessional commitment in ways more subtle than some of the prominent options currently before us. He demonstrates how the Christian moral thinker might appeal to concepts and language in Christian tradition in order to understand the engagement of non-Christians in public discourse as not only a possibility but also a Christian responsibility. In addition, he witnesses to a theological basis on which the Christian may optimistically seek at least some common foundation for moral conversation and moral agreement with those outside the faith community, without abandoning Christian confession. By illustrating his affinity with the Puritan Calvinism of which he was an heir, then, I hope to encourage the recovery of Williams as an important contributor to the Reformed tradition of Christian ethics. I also hope to have demonstrated the sophistication of his thought and its continual relevance to issues that perplex (and divide) us. To rediscover the moral theology of Roger Williams permits us not only to better understand him as a representative of American Puritanism and an ancestor of that great national doctrine of religious liberty, but also to discover in him an untapped historical resource for contemporary Reformed theology and ethics.

NOTES

INTRODUCTION

1. I have borrowed the description of Williams as a "deviant" Calvinist from David Little; see, for instance, his "Reformed Faith and Religious Liberty," *Church and Society* 76 (May/June 1986): 18.

2. Gene Outka, "The Particularist Turn in Theological and Philosophical Ethics," in *Christian Ethics: Problems and Prospects*, ed. Lisa Sowle Cahill and James F. Childress (Cleveland: Pilgrim Press, 1996), 96–99.

3. James M. Gustafson, *Christ and the Moral Life* (New York: Harper and Row, 1968), 5. As H. Richard Niebuhr explained, "A type is always something of a construct. . . . When one returns from the hypothetical scheme to the rich complexity of individual events, it is evident at once that no person or group ever conforms completely to a type. . . . The method of typology, however, though historically inadequate, has the advantage of calling to attention the continuity and significance of the great motifs that appear and reappear in the long wrestling of Christians with their enduring problem." H. Richard Niebuhr, *Christ and Culture* (New York: Harper and Row, 1951), 43–44.

4. New York: Russell and Russell, 1963.

5. Stanley Hauerwas, *Wilderness Wanderings: Probing Twentieth-Century Theology and Philosophy* (Boulder, Colo.: Westview Press, 1997), 3–4.

1. WILLIAMS AND THE REFORMED TRADITION

1. Ola Winslow fancies that Williams may have been exposed to Puritans and separatists firsthand in his childhood neighborhood in *Master Roger Williams: A Biography* (New York: Octagon Books, 1973), 32. My own biographical narrative is indebted to Winslow's fine book, as well as to the wonderful story of Williams's life and controversies Edwin S. Gaustad tells in *Liberty of Conscience: Roger Williams in America* (Grand Rapids: Wm. B. Eerdmans, 1991).

2. Winslow, 28.

3. Gaustad, 6.

4. Winslow, 70–71.

5. Winslow, 74–76. Henry Chupack also suggests that Williams's decision to leave the university for Essex was an indication that "his Separatist sentiments may have hardened into a firm conviction." See *Roger Williams* (New York: Twayne Publishers, 1969), 35.

6. Winslow, 75.

7. Winslow, 90. See also W. Clark Gilpin, *The Millenarian Piety of Roger Williams* (Chicago: University of Chicago Press, 1979), 31. In *Roger Williams and Puritan Radicalism in the English Separatist Tradition* (Lewiston, N.Y.: Edwin Mellen Press, 1989), Hugh Spurgin resists this interpretation by Winslow and Gilpin. Spurgin insists that Williams's gradual turn toward (and later beyond) separatism did not begin until the 1630s, but his argument does not deal sufficiently with the evidence that Williams was influenced by separatists from his youth. Williams himself refers to this meeting in *The Bloody Tenent Yet More Bloody* in *The Complete Writings of Roger Williams*, vol. 4, 65–66 (hereafter to be abbreviated *YMB*).

8. *The Journal of John Winthrop, 1630–1649*, ed. Richard S. Dunn and Laetitia Yeandle (Cambridge, Mass.: Harvard University Press, Belknap Press, 1996), 34.

9. William Bradford, *Of Plymouth Plantation 1620–1647* (New York: Random House, 1981), 286.

10. Winslow, 119–20.

11. As quoted in Gaustad, 49.

12. For more on Anne Hutchinson and her "antinomian" beliefs, see David D. Hall, ed., *The Antinomian Controversy 1636–1638: A Documentary History* (Durham, N.C.: Duke University Press, 1990); and Francis J. Bremer, ed., *Anne Hutchinson, Troubler of the Puritan Zion* (Huntington, N.Y.: Krieger Publishing, 1981).

13. For more on John Cotton's career and importance to seventeenth-century Puritanism on both sides of the Atlantic, see Larzer Ziff, *The Career of John Cotton: Puritanism and the American Experience* (Princeton, N.J.: Princeton University Press, 1962) and *The Correspondence of John Cotton*, ed. Sargent Bush Jr. (Chapel Hill: University of North Carolina Press, 2001).

14. Cotton to Williams, early 1636, *Correspondence of John Cotton*, 213.

15. Cotton to Williams, early 1636, *Correspondence of John Cotton*, 217.

16. Cotton to Williams, early 1636, *Correspondence of John Cotton*, 220.

17. Cotton to Williams, early 1636, *Correspondence of John Cotton*, 222.

18. *Mr. Cotton's Letter Lately Printed, Examined and Answered*, in *Complete Writings of Roger Williams*, vol. 1, 50.

19. *Mr. Cotton's Letter*, 42–43.

20. *Mr. Cotton's Letter*, 44–45.

21. *Mr. Cotton's Letter*, 95.

22. *The Bloody Tenent of Persecution for the Sake of Conscience*, in *Complete Writings of Roger Williams*, vol. 3, 96. Hereafter, *The Bloody Tenent* will be abbreviated *BT* in the notes.

23. *BT*, 80.

24. *BT*, 191.

25. *BT*, 131.

26. *BT*, 135.

27. *BT*, 219.

28. This anonymous tract was titled *Queries of Highest Consideration* (included in volume 2 of *Complete Writings of Roger Williams*). Williams published it as a contribution to the heated debate regarding the proper form of church government that was taking place in the English Parliament and Westminster Assembly in the early 1640s. The Presbyterians, with the support of Scottish allies against the king, held the upper hand in both bodies, but the Independents were a strong minority, and in 1644 a number of notable Independents made their case by publishing a pointed

defense of the principles of Independency, titled *An Apologetical Narration, Humbly Submitted to the Honorable Houses of Parliament*. The Scottish Presbyterian contingent responded with an apology of its own, and to this contest between intractable positions the anonymous *Queries* soon was offered. *Queries* criticized both parties, with particularly penetrating blows reserved for the Independents, whose hypocrisy Williams believed was exposed by the religious intolerance routinely practiced in New England and of which Williams had firsthand knowledge. Williams rejected both parties' interminable grapple for a national church after their own liking. Instead, he encouraged them to imagine religion and civil power in radically new ways, according to the principles of tolerance made more famous in *The Bloody Tenent*.

29. For an explicit example of this reading of Williams as religious relativist, see Jack L. Davis, "Roger Williams Among the Narragansett Indians," *New England Quarterly* 43 (1970): 593–604.

30. See Timothy L. Hall, *Separating Church and State: Roger Williams and Religious Liberty* (Urbana: University of Illinois Press, 1998), for a clear and concise discussion of the distinction between Williams's religious confidence and defense of civil plurality.

31. For an example of Williams's rejection of the religious views of both Catholics and Muslims, see *Experiments of Spiritual Life and Health*, in *Complete Writings of Roger Williams*, vol. 7, 51.

32. *Mr. Cotton's Letter*, 34.

33. *George Fox Digg'd from His Burroughs*, in *Complete Writings of Roger Williams*, vol. 5. For much more on Williams and the Quakers in Rhode Island, see chapter 5.

34. Robert Brunkow argues that Williams contradicted his advocacy of religious liberty with his rhetoric against the Quakers, although he does not tie the inconsistency necessarily to age; see "Love and Order in Roger Williams's Writings," *Rhode Island History* 35 (1976): 119–20. Edwin Gaustad accurately dismisses this interpretation of Williams's interaction with the Quakers as "nonsense" (*Liberty of Conscience*, 178).

35. In the course of these debates, one of the claims Williams wished to make was that the Quakers also threatened civil peace and stability by the anarchy they allegedly promoted and the religious persecution they theoretically justified. Williams wrote that one of his objectives was to prove "that the spirit of [the Quakers'] Religion tends mainly to reduce Persons from Civility to Barbarisme, to an Arbetrary Government, and the Dictates and Decrees of that sudden Spirit that acts them, to a sudden cutting off a People, yea of Kings and Princes opposing them, to as fiery Persecutions for matters of Religion and Conscience, as hath been or can be practiced by any Hunters or Persecutors in the world" (*George Fox*, 5). It was only in a concrete manifestation of this *civil* threat, and not in terms of their religious beliefs alone, that Williams would entertain the possibility of restrictions on any group.

36. *BT*, 197.

37. *A Key into the Language of America* (1644; reprint, Bedford, Mass.: Applewood Books, 1997), 127–28.

38. For an example of Williams's contention that even the best of God's people cannot totally escape the possibility of theological error, see *BT*, 70. Also Perry Miller, "Roger Williams: An Essay in Interpretation," in *Complete Writings of Roger Williams*, vol. 7, 23–25.

39. In this way, Williams practiced what contemporary political philosopher Michael J. Perry calls "apophatic Christianity." See *Religion in Politics: Constitutional and Moral Perspectives* (New York: Oxford University Press, 1997), 7, 96–102.

40. *YMB* 307.

41. For examples of Williams's use of the early church fathers, see *BT*, 34–36, and *YMB*, 368.

42. Perry Miller, "Essay in Interpretation," 21.

43. It is true that *The Encyclopedia of the Reformed Faith* does not include an entry for Williams, but it does have one for John Cotton. See *The Encyclopedia of the Reformed Faith*, ed. Donald K. McKim (Louisville, Ky.: Westminster/John Knox Press, 1992). The entry for John Cotton is on p. 84.

44. Henry Chupack is a good example of a scholar who vaguely recognizes Williams's religiosity but then goes to great lengths to read his as an alternative to, rather than a variety of, American Puritanism. See Chupack, *Roger Williams.*

45. Perry Miller, *Errand into the Wilderness* (Cambridge, Mass.: Harvard University Press, 1956), 48–98.

46. As quoted in Perry Miller, *Errand into the Wilderness*, 50, n. 1.

47. For instance, see Williams's use of Owen in his debate with the Quakers in *George Fox*, 466.

48. *BT*, 153–55. For Williams's response to Cotton's rebuttal of *The Bloody Tenent*, see *YMB*, 264–67.

49. *BT*, 3.

50. *BT*, 98.

51. John Calvin, *Institutes of the Christian Religion*, Library of Christian Classics, ed. John T. McNeill, trans. Ford Lewis Battles (Philadelphia: Westminster Press, 1960), 4.20.2.

52. See, for instance, *George Fox*, 140, 197–98, 230–31. If *George Fox* is at all valuable, it is as a clear indication of Williams's commitment to orthodox Calvinism.

53. *BT*, 125–26, 208.

54. *George Fox*, 58.

55. *BT*, 92.

56. *George Fox*, 140.

57. *George Fox*, 142.

2. INCARNATIONAL THEOLOGY AND RELIGIOUS FREEDOM

1. See Perry Miller, *Roger Williams: His Contribution to the American Tradition* (Indianapolis: Bobbs-Merrill, 1953); Edmund Morgan, *Roger Williams: The Church and the State* (New York: W. W. Norton, 1967); and W. Clark Gilpin, *Millenarian Piety of Roger Williams.*

2. Stanley Hauerwas, for instance, argues that pacifism is a Christian characteristic derived from Christ's example and normative for the church community. He insists on this point more than he justifies its priority over other aspects of the life of Jesus (e.g., Jesus clearing the temple with a whip) and other voices within the biblical tradition (e.g., the Pauline epistles), however. Hauerwas assigns priority to Jesus as moral pattern without sufficiently arguing for what he considers essential to the life pattern of Jesus, nor does he persuasively justify his apparent disregard for the more Chalcedonian aspects of the christological tradition. For an

example of the limited scope of Hauerwas's Christology and canon, see *A Community of Character* (Notre Dame, Ind.: University of Notre Dame Press, 1981), 36–52.

3. *George Fox*, 69–79, 405–8.

4. *George Fox*, 159–61.

5. It should be noted that Williams's commitment to the importance of Jesus as moral exemplar does not mean that Williams subscribed to an "exemplary" theory of atonement. Here and throughout this discussion of Williams's incarnational piety, we should take care to distinguish *atonement* theory (how God reconciled human beings to God) from *moral* theory (how Christ serves as inspiration and guidance for the sanctified life). On the former question, Williams gave every indication that he subscribed to a conventionally Puritan substitutionary theory of atonement. It is on the matter of moral theory, however, where Williams reserved so much priority for Jesus as exemplar.

6. *Mr. Cotton's Letter*, 33–34.

7. Chupack, 80.

8. *BT*, 219.

9. *The Examiner Defended in a Fair and Sober Way*, in *Complete Writings of Roger Williams*, vol. 7, 279.

10. Rosenmeier, "The Teacher and the Witness: John Calvin and Roger Williams," *William and Mary Quarterly*, 3d ser., 25 (1968): 419–21.

11. Rosenmeier, 415.

12. *BT*, 178, 220.

13. *The Hireling Ministry None of Christs*, in *Complete Writing of Roger Williams*, vol. 7, 159.

14. Rosenmeier, 419–21.

15. There was more to Puritan biblical exegesis than typology, though the relationship between Williams's typology and that of his Puritan colleagues is most significant to my argument. For the Puritan, however, not every biblical passage was of typological importance. Some parts of the Bible were better read literally; many biblical commandments were read this way, as were certain figures or episodes taken to be simply authoritative models for faithful living. The choices that an individual Puritan writer made for interpreting a particular passage often illuminated his priorities as much as the conclusions of the interpretation itself. James P. Byrd has written a remarkable study of the differences between Williams and his Puritan antagonists in their nontypological use of the Bible, in which he details Williams's use of the Old Testament, the parable of Wheat and Tares, and the book of Revelation to justify religious toleration. Though space does not permit further exploration of the subject here, Byrd successfully demonstrates how biblical interpretation, in all its variety, was of immense importance to the competing claims of religious uniformity and conscientious freedom. See James P. Byrd, *The Challenges of Roger Williams: Religious Liberty, Violent Persecution, and the Bible* (Macon, Ga.: Mercer University Press, 2002).

16. Miller's failure to understand Cotton's exegetical method led him to argue that Williams's typological method itself was his primary departure from the conventional thinking of Puritans like Cotton. Adopting Williams's biblical methodology as the sole definition of typology, Miller then contrasted it with Cotton's use of the Bible, which Miller viewed as simply an extension of Puritan "federalist" theology. He argued that Cotton's conventionally Puritan exegesis was based not in types but in covenantal theology. To a conventional Puritan like Cotton, the Bible

was to be understood as God's commentary on the single covenant between God and God's people, entered into with Abraham, sealed with Christ, and maintained among God's people until the present. Of course, one of the assumptions behind Miller's faulty interpretation of the Williams-Cotton relationship is his belief that typology and covenantal theology are somehow necessarily competing approaches to the Bible, mutually exclusive exegetical models. Miller's assumption led him to ignore the typology on which Puritan federalism depended.

Sacvan Bercovitch and others have long since demonstrated that Miller's understanding of typology contained significant errors. In contrast to Miller's contention that typology was "a peculiar method of interpreting the Bible . . . which makes unnecessary and actually irrelevant any concern for the literal, historical facts of Israel's career" (*Roger Williams: His Contribution*, 33), Bercovitch has shown that typology did not require the dismissal of the literal and historical significance of Old Testament events. The Puritans actually understood typology to act in interpretive harmony with other "levels" of exegesis, including the literal meaning of the text. Furthermore, in response to Miller's claims that Williams was unique among Puritans in his employment of typology, Bercovitch has demonstrated that typology was actually a method of biblical interpretation exercised by most Puritan preachers, poets, and theologians. Preachers like Thomas Hooker, New England leaders like John Winthrop, and early American poets like Anne Bradstreet and Edward Taylor deftly used typology to interpret the Old Testament with a characteristically Puritan christocentric focus. See Sacvan Bercovitch, "Typology in Puritan New England: The Williams-Cotton Controversy Reassessed," *American Quarterly* 19 (1967): 168–71. What Miller read from Williams and posited as definition was, then, simply one typological strategy. By accepting Williams's exegesis as the definition of typology, Miller was unable to see that Cotton himself read the Bible typologically and offered typological responses to some of the errors he believed Williams had made in his arguments. Miller's inability to see that Williams and Cotton held the typological approach in common also left him unable to explain where Williams had picked up his "maverick" exegetical method. For Miller, Williams's dedication to "typological lore" had little grounding in traditional Puritan education and training, and thus the source for his exegetical strategy was ultimately a "fascinating and probably impenetrable mystery" to Miller ("Essay in Interpretation," 11). But Williams was far from the first Puritan to prefer the treasures of typology. What is distinctive about Williams's biblical interpretation is the way he uses typology. His typological exegesis yielded starkly different results than Cotton's more conventional interpretation, but contrary to Miller's thesis, the difference between the two was not a distinction between "federalist" theology and "typological" theology. It was instead a distinction between two competing typological interpretations based in variant conceptions of the incarnation, and the implications of the incarnation upon the divine-human covenant, through which they read and interpreted the Bible.

17. John Cotton's Answer to Roger Williams, in *Complete Writings of Roger Williams*, vol. 2, 69.

18. Perry Miller, "Essay in Interpretation," 11.

19. Cotton, 29.

20. Cotton, 71–75, 129–42.

21. Cotton's typological interpretation accorded well with the standard Calvinistic approach to typology. Contrary to Miller's claim, Calvin explicitly rejected *allegorical* interpretations of the Bible, but not typology. Like Cotton after him, Calvin

employed typology in his own biblical exegesis. For instance, in his reading of the prophets, Calvin's typological interpretation allowed the prophetic literature to serve him both as a transition between the testament of the law and the covenant of Christ and in his refutation of the apparent Catholic preoccupation with legalism. See *Institutes*, 4.18.15. For perhaps Calvin's clearest use of typology to understand the relationship between the Old and New Testaments, see *Institutes*, 2.11.2–2.11.14. As Cotton illustrated, conventional Calvinist typology accented the continuity between the obligations of the Old Testament and the New, as details of a single unifying covenant of grace, represented first in the shadows of the Old Testament and then declared more fully in the incarnation of Christ.

22. Perry Miller, "Essay in Interpretation," 11.

23. Perry Miller, *Roger Williams: His Contribution*, 32.

24. *BT*, 30.

25. John 4:21–24 (Authorized Version).

26. *BT*, 317.

27. *BT*, 290.

28. Cotton's Answer to Roger Williams, 126. Williams chastised the churches of the Plymouth Colony, themselves separatists, for allowing their church members to attend Anglican services when they returned to England for occasional visits. See *Mr. Cotton's Letter*, 41, 109. Williams also refers to this objection of his in a 1651 letter to Governor Endicott in *Correspondence of Roger Williams*, ed. Glenn W. LaFantasie (Providence, R.I.: Published for the Rhode Island Historical Society by Brown University Press, 1988), 337.

29. John Cotton called it "no impeachment of church liberty, but an enlargement of its beauty and honor, to be bound by strict laws and holy commandments, to observe the pure worship of God" and claimed that the evangelistic objectives of religious compulsion served as a "great advancement" for both church and state. See Irwin H. Polishook, *Roger Williams, John Cotton, and Religious Freedom: A Controversy in New and Old England* (Englewood Cliffs, N.J.: Prentice-Hall, 1967), 27, 76.

30. *Mr. Cotton's Letter*, 102–3.

31. See Morgan, *Roger Williams*.

32. Gilpin, *Millenarian Piety*, 1–14.

33. *Christenings Make Not Christians*, in *Complete Writings of Roger Williams*, vol. 7.

34. William Ames, *The Marrow of Theology*, ed. and trans. John Dykstra Eusden (Boston: Pilgrim Press, 1968), 157–60.

35. John Bunyan, *The Pilgrim's Progress* (New York: Penguin Books, 1987), 71.

36. Gilpin, 46–47. Cotton was sensitive, of course, to the whole question of grace and works, especially after his involvement with Anne Hutchinson in the antinomian controversy.

37. Morgan, *Roger Williams*, 47–48.

38. See *The New England Mind: The Seventeenth Century* (Cambridge, Mass.: Harvard University Press, 1933), 365–462; and *Errand into the Wilderness*, 48–98. Perry Miller's description of the covenant concept is more contractarian and mechanical than it appears in the everyday use and arguments of the Puritan teachers themselves, and Miller failed to locate the basic ingredients for covenantal thinking in Calvin himself. But despite these shortcomings, Miller ably represents the importance that this emerging emphasis played in the Puritan understanding of salvation and moral motivation.

39. *Errand into the Wilderness*, 71.

40. Breen, *The Character of the Good Ruler: A Study of Puritan Political Ideas in New England, 1630–1730* (New Haven, Conn.: Yale University Press, 1970), 29.

41. Miller, *Errand into the Wilderness*, 89–92.

42. Hall, *Separating Church and State*, 51–55.

43. See, for instance, *BT*, 294, and *Christenings*, 40–41.

44. *YMB*, 258; see also *BT*, 295–99; *Hireling*, 160; *Correspondence of Roger Williams*, 188.

45. *Mr. Cotton's Letter*, 68–69; *Hireling*, 159–61.

46. *BT*, 184; see also *Mr. Cotton's Letter*, 68; *YMB*, 127.

47. *BT*, 187.

48. Gilpin, 133–34.

49. *Fourth Paper of Major Butler*, in *Complete Writings of Roger Williams*, vol. 7, 131.

50. *Hireling*, 158, 176.

51. Gilpin, 58–59, 84.

52. *Fourth Paper of Major Butler*, 131; see also *George Fox*, 340.

53. "This Prophecy [i.e., the vocation of the "scattered witnesses"] ought to be (chiefly) exercised among the Saints in the companies, meetings, and assemblies of the fellow-mourners and witnesses against the falshoods of Antichrist" (*Hireling*, 176).

54. Breen helpfully notes that despite the Puritans' agreement that political power derived from popular consent, they disagreed considerably regarding the nature of the power that popular choice conferred. Some early Puritans argued that civil leaders rightly enjoyed broad *discretionary* powers as the direct vicegerents of God (albeit humanly chosen). Others insisted that specific political authority was *delegated* through the consent of the people. Thus, the Puritans' common acceptance that political authority originates from popular consent and is ultimately accountable to it did not make their deliberations concerning the *nature* of such authority any less complex or heated. See Breen, 59–64.

55. Gilpin, 51.

56. Gilpin, 3.

57. Gilpin, 9.

3. PLURALISM AND NATURAL MORALITY

1. As Joshua Miller notes, "The Puritan political outlook cannot accurately be described as liberal," for they did not believe in many of the basic freedoms of belief and expression we take to be axiomatic today. Furthermore, "the Puritan lack of tolerance was, in part, a result of the seriousness with which they took their ideas. They believed that their own ideas about the correct form of worship were true, and they defined liberty as the right to put those ideas into practice. They feared that radical dissent which challenged the fundamental principles of Congregationalism would divide and destroy their fragile experiment" (Joshua Miller, "Direct Democracy and the Puritan Theory of Membership," *Journal of Politics* 53 [1991]: 61). Despite this general spirit of intolerance, however, Miller is correct to note that the stereotype of Puritan New England as an illiberal theocracy is more than a bit extreme. The established political structure preferred to discuss publicly any important social and theological concerns over which there existed significant disagreement, turning to

forced compliance with official decisions only as a last resort. This proclivity toward public debate encouraged the emergence of dissident voices like Roger Williams, who continued to serve as "voices in the wilderness" even after the magistrates and ministers in charge had put an end to official discussion.

2. See David Little, "The Indivisibility of Tolerance," an unpublished (to my knowledge) essay delivered at a conference on Freedom of Religion and Belief and the UN Year of Tolerance, at the Barbican Centre, London, September 18–20, 1995.

3. In this way, Williams demonstrated what Little calls a "weak" theory of ethical pluralism (and, we might add, religious pluralism). A weak theory of pluralism "would on normative grounds welcome the existence of diverse ethical positions, and propose procedures for accommodating them, without necessarily rejecting a monistic (or dualistic) theory" of belief. Little contrasts this with a "strong" approach to pluralism, which would hold that ethics is "in its nature incapable of being reduced to one (or two) comprehensive theories [sic]." See David Little's unpublished essay "A Christian Perspective on Ethical Pluralism," 1–2.

4. In comparing the arguments for religious freedom of Williams and Thomas Jefferson, interpreters commonly argue that Jefferson was interested primarily in saving the state from the church, while Williams was preoccupied foremost in safeguarding the church from the state. There is some truth nestled in this dichotomy, but like most attempts to categorize the philosophical perspectives of great thinkers, it is overly simplistic. Indeed Jefferson was worried about the abuses that established religion suffered on the civil rights of citizens and, as we have seen, Williams's first priority lay with the purity of the church as he conceived its apostolic mission. Drawing this distinction between these two men, however, often leads one who does not know Williams's work intimately to conclude that he had little interest in protecting the integrity of the state from an overzealous church, and, in fact, many scholars who otherwise demonstrate familiarity with Williams's writings fail to understand him on this point. While it is true that Williams's perspective on religious liberty originated in his concern for ecclesiastical purity, his theological mind-set caused him to be just as concerned with safeguarding the civil realm, for he understood civil authority as the protector of both the bodily goods of citizens and the freedom of belief and practice of religious communities. Williams's work suggests that he believed respect for religious and moral pluralism in civil society to be right in itself and the best means to preserve the physical and spiritual identity of its citizens, and that this respect for pluralism did not require an abdication of those truths and values that most distinctively mark a person as Christian.

5. See David Little, "Roger Williams and the Separation of Church and State," 9–11.

6. Throughout his several treatises, Williams is adamant regarding the inalienable nature of belief, insisting that a person cannot "betrust such a power to the civil Magistrate, to compel their Souls and consciences unto his" (*Examiner*, 218). For more on the inalienable nature of belief, see also *BT*, 13; *Examiner*, 206, 273.

7. "True it is, the Sword may make . . . a whole Nation of Hypocrites: But to recover a Soule from Sathan by repentance, and to bring them from Antichristian doctrine or worship, to the doctrine or worship Christian, in the least true internall or externall submission, that only works the All-powerfull God, by the sword of the Spirit in the hand of his Spirituall officers" (*BT*, 136). For the incompatibility between force and true belief, see also *BT*, 80–81; *Christenings*, 38; *Hireling*, 174; *YMB*, 384, 439.

8. *BT,* 138–39. As a vivid metaphor for just how repulsive a violation of selfhood Williams considered the coercion of belief to be, he frequently refers to the practice as "soul rape." See, for example, *Examiner,* 210; *BT,* 60, 182; *Queries,* 20; *YMB,* 325–27.

9. Of course Williams spent much of his life in this type of dialogue, first with the Native Americans with whom he maintained conversation on religion and other subjects his whole life in New England, and later with the Quakers of Rhode Island. Some critics have pointed to these latter disputes to argue that Williams retreated from his respect for religious pluralism in his old age, but his arguments with the Quakers captured in *George Fox* demonstrate quite the opposite. They demonstrate that Williams never wavered from his belief that the best response to religious pluralism was civil toleration mixed with spirited debate. His conversations with the Quakers were quite spirited, but he never suggested any response to them other than rational refutation, except in the instances when he thought certain of their practices may threaten the civil peace.

10. This mistaken reading has been encouraged in part by the application of a strict inner/outer dualism to Williams's thought. For instance, Ellis M. West argues that for Williams religion "pertains to the inner life of persons, that is, to their spiritual orientations or their attitudes and beliefs about God or gods, which, in turn, determine the 'everlasting welfare' of their souls." By contrast, West claims, Williams reserved the term "morality" for that realm that "pertains to the external or outward behavior of humans, that is, their dealings with one another." A careful reading reveals, however, that Williams did not employ the distinction as starkly as interpreters like West demand. Williams recognized that religion and morality were both a messy combination of conviction and practice, so that the boundaries to freedom of conscience occur not along some inner/outer distinction, but according to the nature of the beliefs and practices concerned. West is right to state that Williams sought protection for "religious beliefs," defined as matters of personal piety and salvific concerns, but among the religious "beliefs" that Williams sought to protect was also the refusal to take oaths, a religious *practice* that had a major social impact beyond the internal and private realm. Thus West is incorrect to characterize the values that Williams defended as simply "inner" piety. See Ellis M. West, "Roger Williams on the Limits of Religious Liberty," *Annual of the Society of Christian Ethics* (1998): 139–40. For Williams's rejection of required public oaths, see *BT,* 253–54.

David Little also locates in Williams's work a distinction between "inner forum" and "outer forum" that he ties to a similar dichotomy in Williams's theological predecessors, notably Augustine and Calvin. According to Little, though, Williams recognized that some matters of conviction occur as complex members of both jurisdictions, meaning that questions of conscience are often not so easily resolved as "inner" or "outer" matters. See Little, "A Christian Perspective on Ethical Pluralism," 11–21.

11. *Examiner,* 244. Williams here invokes circumcision and the single motherhood of the Virgin Mary as cases of apparent moral improprieties to which it would be morally wrong to respond with punishment.

12. These "universally" recognized norms constitute what Williams calls the basic values of "civility," which is the subject of chap. 5.

13. This is a misimpression that I shall revisit in the chapter on civility.

14. *New England Mind: The Seventeenth Century,* 64.

15. Perry Miller, *New England Mind: The Seventeenth Century,* 170.

16. Perry Miller failed to recognize the Puritans' indebtedness to Calvin on this point because he seriously misread the role of human rationality in Calvin's theology. Miller believed that Calvin included human reason among the victims of "the total and complete incapacity of nature," as a condition of the Fall. According to Miller, Calvin believed reason no longer operated effectively at all, a condition only "relieved occasionally by gifts of specific powers" endowed on a discrete number of special moral or political virtuosos. Miller contrasts Calvin's pessimism regarding the survival of reason with Puritans like John Preston, who considered reason to be "an innate and universal capacity, even though it was imperfect and could not attain to salvation." The Puritans' insistence that reason, though corrupted, survived as an operable human faculty indicated, according to Miller, "how far Puritanism of the early seventeenth century had already strayed from pure 'Calvinism.'" See Miller, *New England Mind: The Seventeenth Century,* 186–87.

17. Calvin, *Institutes,* 2:276.

18. Calvin, *Institutes,* 2:277.

19. Calvin, *Institutes,* 2:271.

20. Calvin, *Commentary on the Gospel According to St. John,* part 1, trans. T. H. L. Parker. In *Calvin's New Testament Commentaries,* vol. 4 (Grand Rapids: Wm. B. Eerdmans, 1991), 12.

21. Calvin, *Institutes,* 2:270.

22. Like Calvin, the Puritans counted scientific knowledge among the "natural gifts" partially corrupted by sin. See *Institutes,* 2:273–75, and John Adair, *Puritans: Religion and Politics in Seventeenth-Century England and America* (Phoenix Mill: Sutton Publishing, 1998), 274–78.

23. As Perry Miller points out, the Puritans believed reason to be unsuited for matters of faith and salvation in part because of the creation-redemption dualism that characterized their theology. The Puritans believed that God had endowed humanity with reason in order to equip people to "read" the inherent rationality of creation. Because the moral order was part of the natural order, reason also operated as a moral capacity. Matters of salvation, however, belong to the redemptive plan set in motion after creation and the fall. The order of redemption is not a part of creation and thus does not participate in the inherent rationality of creation. Therefore, reason cannot serve as a capacity for salvation. See Miller, *New England Mind: The Seventeenth Century,* 168–70, 185–95.

24. Perhaps no feature of Puritan moral thought demonstrates their recognition of reason as a legitimate moral faculty more than the preeminence of Ramist thought among Puritan thinkers, most notably William Ames. Though he stated it with characteristic exaggeration, Perry Miller was right to note in *New England Mind: The Seventeenth Century* that "the whole Ramist system, with its trust in direct perception, its immediate adjudication between doubtful alternatives through the divining rod of the disjunctive syllogism, its assurance that instinctive recognitions will lead to the right practice of method, was fundamentally a glorification of nature; it was an assertion that the cultivated mind, unexalted by divine influence, is competent to gather accurate knowledge of things, and to assign particular truths to the proper place in the universal system, because the mind is fundamentally commensurate with creation" (157). For more on Peter Ramus and his influence on the Puritans, including Ames, see Perry Miller, *New England Mind: The Seventeenth Century,* 89–180, 300–330; and John Dykstra Eusden's introduction of William Ames, *The Marrow of Theology,* ed. and trans. John Dykstra Eusden (1629; reprint, Grand Rapids: Baker Books, 1997), 37–47.

25. Little, "Roger Williams and Separation," 8.

26. *BT*, 6; *YMB*, 413.

27. *Experiments*, 99.

28. *YMB*, 443.

29. *BT*, 249–50.

30. *George Fox*, 99.

31. For evidence of Williams's orthodox view of sin, see especially *George Fox*, 197, 424–25, 484–85.

32. *Christenings*, 35.

33. *Key*, 49.

34. For instance, *Key*, 10. In claiming that Williams was as racist as the rest of the Puritans with regard to Native Americans, William S. Simmons not only misreads the general Puritan reaction to Native American culture and religion (see Bremer's *The Puritan Experiment* for a better informed perspective), but he also inexplicably ignores the very positive impression of the Americans that Williams gives in his *Key* and other writings, including of their intellectual ability and moral character. See Simmons, "Cultural Bias in the New England Puritans' Perception of Indians," *William and Mary Quarterly*, 3d ser., 38 (1981): 56–72.

35. Calvin, *Commentary on Romans*, 48–49.

36. *Institutes*, 2:281.

37. *Institutes*, 2:282.

38. *Institutes*, 2:367–68. The phenomenon of conscience and its connection with natural law is a subject that will be taken up in the next chapter.

39. *Institutes*, 2:367.

40. *Institutes*, 4:1504.

41. *Institutes*, 2:272.

42. *Institutes*, 3:698.

43. *Institutes*, 2:273.

44. *Commentary on Romans*, 48.

45. *Institutes*, 2:282.

46. *Commentary on Romans*, 48.

47. *Institutes*, 2:367–68.

48. William Haller, *Liberty and Reformation in the Puritan Revolution* (New York: Columbia University Press, 1955), 77.

49. The power of this double-headed appeal should not be underestimated. According to Haller, the lawyers and gentry of the English parliament sought to carve out their independence from royal power by committing to a political conception in which royal prerogative took a back seat to the inherent rights of subjects. This sense of natural rights was rooted in a commitment to Coke's common law, "but in the dispute which now ensued over sovereignty and obedience, the defenders of parliament supplemented and extended their argument with momentous if confusing results by appealing also to the doctrine of equity or natural law as expounded to English lawyers by Christopher St. German." The result was a major political and philosophical alliance, as "the preachers of the Puritan brotherhood and the lawyers and gentry of parliament were able to join forces against the king in 1642 in the name of conscience, law, and equity combined." For Haller's discussion of the Puritan and parliamentary employment of natural law, common law, and equity in the prerevolutionary period in seventeenth-century England, see *Liberty and Reformation*, 69–78.

50. Ames, *Marrow of Theology*, 109.

51. *Conscience, with the Power and Cases Thereof* (1643; reprint, Norwood, N.J.: Walter J. Johnson, 1975), 5. For more on the relationship between conscience and natural law in Ames, see the following chapter.

52. A. S. P. Woodhouse, ed., *Puritanism and Liberty*, 3d ed. (London: J. M. Dent and Sons, 1986), 189. For more on the relationship Ames perceived between natural law and rights and civil law and rights, see Woodhouse, 187–91.

53. In William Perkins's exposition of interpersonal virtues, for instance, appeals to natural law supplement the biblical base he constructs for his ethics. See *The Whole Treatise of Cases of Conscience* in *William Perkins: English Puritanist*, ed. Thomas F. Merrill (Nieuwkoop: B. De Graaf, 1966), 163–240 (in particular 178, 195, and 227). For the importance of natural law to American Puritans, see Perry Miller, *New England Mind: The Seventeenth Century*, 185–206.

54. *Examiner*, 241, 263; *George Fox*, 359; *BT*, 424.

55. *George Fox*, 290, 364.

56. *Examiner*, 263.

57. *Examiner*, 241.

58. *BT*, 358. Despite this correlation of natural law with the Decalogue, Williams thought it important to point out that his conception of natural law did not include any of the ritualistic or judicial laws of the Deuteronomic code. Just as interestingly, while he seems to acknowledge the existence of natural theology and suggests occasionally that a general awareness of a deity is an inherent part of human knowledge, he does not include any of the first table in his conception of natural law. Williams made a special point of countering John Cotton's effort to extend the parallels between Old Testament laws and natural law. Cotton justified the effort to govern the New England colonies according to Old Testament codes (e.g., civil punishment for blasphemy) by arguing that the Israelite codes were, in fact, biblical reflections of natural law. In response, Williams vehemently rejected the direct association of natural law with the laws of particular societies, even those of Israel. Mosaic law, he argued, is in its very essence particular; it articulates the ends of natural law but in language, culture, and rituals that reflect the needs of a particular community. In general, Williams charges Cotton with a major methodological error: Cotton insisted on implementing the particular traditions and codes of a society that no longer exists (i.e., Israel), instead of seeking to capture anew for Massachusetts the moral spirit, norms, and ends of natural law in laws crafted and designed for the particular people of New England. See *YMB*, 485–89.

59. *Examiner*, 263.

60. *YMB*, 368.

61. *YMB*, 414.

62. Many passages in the *Key* reflect Williams's recognition of natural morality in the moral accomplishment of the Americans. See, for example, *Key*, 53, 151. In his recognition of basic moral similarities between Europeans and Americans, and his attribution of this similarity to natural law, Williams was not altogether unique among the Puritans. See Perry Miller, *New England Mind: The Seventeenth Century*, 185.

63. *George Fox*, 30, 62, 134, 210, 359–61.

64. *BT*, 6. For a brief but insightful discussion of the importance of experience to Williams's attempts to both identify and practice the moral principles he thought to be conducive to the common good, see Clinton Rossiter, "Roger Williams on the Anvil of Experience," *American Quarterly* 3 (January 1951): 14–21.

65. *BT*, 206; *Examiner*, 216–17; *YMB*, 98.

66. *BT,* 206; *Examiner,* 211. Williams also pointed out the instability of established religion, which changed its allegiance to Protestantism or Catholicism as often as England changed monarchs. See *BT,* 136; *Examiner,* 205; *Queries,* 20 (206).

67. *BT,* 249–50; *YMB,* 242.

68. *BT,* 424.

69. For discussion of analogical imagination see David Tracy, *The Analogical Imagination: Christian Theology and the Culture of Pluralism* (New York: Crossroads, 1981), 405–56, and William C. Spohn, *Go and Do Likewise: Jesus and Ethics* (New York: Continuum, 1999), 50–71.

70. Tracy, 410.

71. See *BT,* 242.

72. See, for instance, *Mr. Cotton's Letter,* 53–54.

73. Spohn, 58–59.

74. Spohn, 50.

75. Gustafson, *Can Ethics Be Christian?* (Chicago: University of Chicago Press, 1975), 159.

76. David Novak, *Jewish Social Ethics* (Oxford: Oxford University Press, 1992), 70–76.

77. A comparison between my interpretation of Williams's natural morality and Gustafson's view on natural law may be helpful here. Gustafson affirms that "generalizations about the moral values and principles which provide the conditions *sine qua non* for human personal and social life can be made" (*Can Ethics Be Christian?* 158). He rejects, however, "the epistemological assumption" that underlies classical natural law theory "that there is a correspondence between the order of the human mind and the order of being." Instead, he proposes what he calls a "weaker" view, in which "almost universal" and "almost absolute" principles and values may be ascertained, "but the conditions of knowledge do not exist on which universality and absoluteness can be claimed without qualification." It is probably a stretch to think Williams would agree completely with this "weaker" assessment of natural law, because he inherited from his Calvinist teachers both their epistemological foundations and their confidence in universal truths. I do believe, however, that Williams also inherited enough of the Calvinist predisposition to observation (versus metaphysical musing) to be more comfortable with Gustafson's preference that "the necessary moral conditions for human life to be fulfilled in any satisfactory sense can be stated" as "inferences from experience" rather than "knowledge of being." I interpret a similar preference to be behind Williams's fondness for appeals to experience over metaphysics in virtually all of his arguments for religious liberty based in an appeal to natural morality, and therefore, in this limited way, I understand Williams's use of natural law to resonate with Gustafson's differentiation between "classic natural law theory" and his own work.

78. Novak, 77.

79. Lovin, *Reinhold Niebuhr and Christian Realism* (Cambridge: Cambridge University Press, 1995), 110.

4. CONSCIENCE

1. Of these casebooks, Richard Baxter's *A Christian Directory* is certainly the best-known today and was perhaps the most ambitious in its scope, considering thou-

sands of questions of conscience on issues from political involvement to family dynamics. The two most prominent casebooks within 17th-century Puritan circles were William Perkins's *The Whole Treatise of Cases of Conscience* and William Ames's *Conscience, with the Power and Cases Thereof.* In these volumes both authors actually combined the objectives of theoretical development and practical application, producing textbooks that offered both intensive analyses of the theology behind the concept and numerous examples of its experience and use in everyday living. Partially as a result of their exhaustive approach, these two works quickly became required study for generations of students in Puritan higher education.

2. Furthermore, the absence of concise theoretical analysis on the topic hardly surprises anyone patient enough to have read a couple of pages of his prose. While thorough, Williams was not at all systematic, and so the absence of a theoretical treatise on conscience does not stand out from among the other conceptual analyses we would like for him to have provided (e.g., his philosophical understanding of political power or his thoughts on the nature of belief). On the topic of conscience, as with these other topics, one gets the impression that Williams was too busy trying to change the world (or at least England, New and old) to explicate theory.

3. For example, see *BT,* 84–92. Here Williams presents his exegesis of Titus 3, in contrast to Cotton's interpretation of the passage as biblical support for religious compulsion.

4. Williams's liberality is unique enough among Puritans to make me wonder if Williams directly read Thomas on the subject of conscience. The plausibility of such a connection is reason enough to begin the trace of theological antecedents with Thomas, even if its historical verification is beyond the capability of this (or possibly any other) study.

5. *The Summa Theologica of St. Thomas Aquinas* (New York: Benzinger Brothers, 1948), 1, q.79, a.12; *S. Thomae Aquinatis, Opera omnia,* vol. 22, *Quaestiones disputatae de veritate* (Rome: ad Sancta Sabinae, 1972), as translated in excerpts by Timothy C. Potts, *Conscience in Medieval Philosophy* (Cambridge: Cambridge University Press, 1980), 124.

6. Potts, 48.

7. Potts, 128.

8. Potts, 127–28.

9. *Summa Theologica,* 1, q.79, a.12, ad 3.

10. Potts, 129.

11. *Summa Theologica,* 1, q.79, a.13.

12. Potts, 50.

13. For an excellent discussion of John Calvin's theology of conscience, see Randall C. Zachman, *The Assurance of Faith: Conscience in the Theology of Martin Luther and John Calvin* (Minneapolis: Fortress Press, 1993). Zachman is concerned primarily with how Luther and Calvin relate conscience theologically to the sufficiency of Christ and the experience of saving faith, so his study does not exhaust the important questions surrounding conscience as a moral concept. On the way to answering his own questions, however, Zachman provides useful background for what each Reformer understood the conscience to be, including the differences between their interpretations and some of the implications their theologies might have for considering conscience as a moral phenomenon.

14. *Commentary on the Epistle to the Romans,* trans. by Ross Mackenzie, in *Calvin's New Testament Commentaries,* vol. 8 (Grand Rapids: Wm. B. Eerdmans, 1991), 48–49.

15. Romans 2:14–16, as translated by Calvin in his *Commentary on the Epistle of Paul to the Romans*, 47.

16. *Institutes*, 4:1181.

17. *Romans*, 49.

18. Ibid.

19. *Institutes*, 4:1504. For more on the universality of conscience and its independence from soteriological status, see also p. 358.

20. *Romans*, 48.

21. *Institutes*, 2:367–68.

22. *Institutes*, 2:367–68, 4:1504.

23. Zachman, 114–19.

24. Perkins also shared Calvin's dependence on Romans as a biblical source for his thinking on conscience. See Perkins, *A Discourse of Conscience*, in Thomas Merrill's introduction of *William Perkins: English Puritanist*, 7–9.

25. *A Discourse of Conscience*, 5.

26. *A Discourse of Conscience*, 7, 99.

27. *A Discourse of Conscience*, 6.

28. *A Discourse of Conscience*, 66–67.

29. *A Discourse of Conscience*, 66.

30. Ames, *Conscience*, 1.

31. Ames, *Conscience*, 3–5.

32. Ames resists any pressures to identify a discrete list of particular principles as the natural moral law on which *synderesis* is based, but implicitly he does offer four norms—veracity, justice, nonmaleficence, and the commendation of divine worship—as a fair representation of the principles at work in the conscience. In addition, Ames also seems to locate room among these for a principle of limited beneficence as well. In a strong sense, the fifth book of *Conscience* demonstrates these principles in action via syllogistic consideration of specific moral problems.

33. Ames, *Conscience*, 4.

34. Ames, *Conscience*, 3.

35. *YMB*, 508.

36. *BT*, 89.

37. *George Fox*, 443.

38. *Examiner*, 241.

39. For a discussion of natural law in Williams's moral theology, see chap. 3.

40. *BT*, 369; *YMB*, 90.

41. *BT*, 89.

42. *BT*, 272.

43. *YMB*, 508–9.

44. *George Fox*, 443.

45. *Key*, x.

46. See, for instance, *Key*, 129.

47. Fiering, "Will and Intellect in the New England Mind," *William and Mary Quarterly*, 3d ser., 29 (1972): 537.

48. Fiering, "Will and Intellect," 532–36.

49. Ames's rejection of intellectualism in favor of a voluntarist moral psychology is obscured by the dominance of the Aristotelian, syllogistic structure in his discussion of conscience. Ames understood the conscience to be part of the understanding, and the intellect remained important to Ames's sophisticated consideration of

human reason, despite the voluntarist direction his moral anthropology ultimately followed.

50. *George Fox*, 370–71.

51. As rehearsed by Williams in *BT*, 42, 47.

52. *YMB*, 474.

53. *BT*, 89.

54. The matter of whether or not conscience is infallible is an important one, with implications for the question of respecting the freedom of conscience. It is also an issue with no clear consensus. The contemporary philosopher J. F. M. Hunter, for instance, takes as axiomatic that the conscience is "morally infallible," a position that Williams clearly rejected. By Hunter's estimation, "Like an English monarch, conscience can do no wrong . . . one would think." See Hunter, "Conscience," in John Donnelly and Leonard Lyons, eds., *Conscience* (Staten Island, N.Y.: Alba House, 1973). Hunter bases his assumption, however, on a confusion between the authority of conscience and the infallibility of that authority. Williams was able to defend the binding authority of conscience without arguing that conscience was somehow unique among the human faculties by virtue of an insusceptibility to sin and error.

55. For instance, in *The Bloody Tenent*, Williams explained that the abuses of some past political leaders were caused by "the light of the eye of conscience" being "darkened" in them, by which he meant that their consciences erroneously led them to commit actions they thought to be in the best interests of the church and consistent with the desires of God. See *BT*, 369.

56. Ames attempts to avoid the pitfalls of this contradiction by drawing a distinction between the power of conscience to bind and its authority to bind an agent *to do* an action, based on a differentiation between the formal and material authority of conscience. Formally, says Ames, we are bound to heed our consciences because they are the internal expression of divine judgment. Materially, however, conscience cannot bind us unequivocally to follow its imperatives because the commendation of something the "objective" law of God forbids violates the notion of divine perfection. This leads Ames to make the contradictory claim that an agent with an erroneous conscience is required at once to follow the dictates of conscience and to ignore them! See Ames, *Conscience*, 9–16.

57. *Examiner*, 218.

58. *YMB*, 509.

59. Williams's argument appears to anticipate Locke's in the latter's *A Letter Concerning Toleration* (1689; reprint, Buffalo, N.Y.: Prometheus, 1990). Here Locke argues against the coercion of conscience by appealing to the moral faculty. Belief is a matter of the intellect, insists Locke, not of the will. But force cannot be applied to someone's understanding; force only affects the will of a person. If force may only be applied to the will and matters of conscience are the domain of the intellect, Locke concludes, then the idea of coercing belief is, in fact, irrational. Without the care that Locke puts into his argument, Williams nonetheless seems to be arguing much the same thing, that the coercion of conscientious belief simply makes no sense, given what "force" and "belief" are.

60. I hesitate to invoke the popular internal/external distinction to describe the boundaries Williams draws around the jurisdiction of conscience, though some scholars like David Little point to such a dichotomy as a similarity between Williams's understanding of tolerance and Locke's (see Little, "Roger Williams and Separation").

As I read him, though, Williams's distinction has less to do with *location* and more with the *nature* of the issue at hand. What makes conscientious belief or practice susceptible to civil restriction is not its distance from public manifestation, but the effect that manifestation has on public good and the freedoms of others. The importance of the difference can be seen when a theory of conscience is applied to questions of religious practice. Strictly speaking, much that qualifies as practice is "external" or public in nature, including such things as a Native American's religious use of peyote or an Islamic policeman wearing religiously motivated headdress or facial hair despite department regulations. The complexity of questions of conscientious freedom, when it involves practice, is hardly captured by an internal/external dichotomy.

61. See *BT*, 139, 272, and *YMB*, 90.

62. *YMB*, 71. See also 476.

63. *YMB*, 209.

64. *YMB*, 230.

65. See Morgan, *Roger Williams,* 133–35. While rightly noting that Williams did not advocate an "anything goes" policy in respecting the freedom of conscience, Morgan overstates Williams's willingness to impose civil restrictions on erring consciences. Williams's concern was always the "common good," and arguments for coercing against conscience always required justification by appeal to public safety and welfare. While the practices that Williams considered dangerous to the common good more closely resembled seventeenth-century social standards than a present-day American stance on conscientious freedom, as a matter of principle Williams believed the presumption was against compulsion of conscience.

66. Morgan, 130–33.

67. See, for instance, Calvin's commentary on the book of Daniel, where he insists that citizens "ought rather utterly to defy than to obey [rulers] whenever they are so restive and wish to spoil God of his rights, and, as it were, to seize upon his throne and draw him down from heaven" by mandating behavior contrary to the will of God. From "Commentaries on the Book of Daniel," as excerpted in *On God and Political Duty,* ed. John T. McNeill (Indianapolis: Bobbs-Merrill Publishing, 1956), 102. Of course, the final chapter of the *Institutes* is also fascinating in part because of the way Calvin desperately tries to hold together his two priorities of individual liberty and institutional authority; see especially 4.20.8–4.20.10, 4.20.16, 4.20.31.

68. Richard Baxter, *A Holy Commonwealth,* ed. William Lamont (1659; reprint, Cambridge: Cambridge University Press, 1994), 29–30.

69. The Massachusetts Bay Colony also valued uniformity for its political importance, namely to keep the colony from catching the attention of the British monarchy. This is simply to say that the stereotypical Puritan drive for unity, purity, and order was not solely religious in motivation, nor was it at all the only possible product of a Puritan theological perspective (as figures like Roger Williams immediately make apparent).

70. *YMB*, 26.

5. CIVILITY

1. *YMB*, 207.

2. *YMB*, 207.

3. Little, "Roger Williams and Separation," 16.

4. *YMB*, 238.

5. *YMB*, 311.

6. *YMB*, 174.

7. *Letter Concerning Toleration*, 63–64. Williams acknowledges the political fears behind the English Protestants' suspicions of Catholics in particular, fears of disloyalty that played a significant role in Locke's restrictions on the religious freedom of Catholics (as well as Muslims). Williams even seems willing to entertain public laws that would require Catholics to wear distinctive insignias on their clothing to make them easily identifiable, a practice that brings to mind similar measures of segregation employed in Nazi Germany in the 1930s and that would strike many today as morally problematic. But besides this method of public identification, Williams rejects any arguments for the restriction of Catholic freedoms that depend on the mistaken belief that they are less capable of civility and moral citizenry than their Protestant counterparts. He even goes so far as to blame the instances of Catholic insurrection in seventeenth-century Britain not on Catholic ignorance of civility, but on the suppression of their consciences and religious practices by the Protestant political authorities. See *YMB*, 310–17; Little, "Roger Williams and Separation," 10.

8. *YMB*, 207.

9. *Hireling*, 190.

10. *Examiner*, 243.

11. Edmund Morgan, *Roger Williams*, 129.

12. Morgan, 128.

13. *YMB*, 203.

14. *BT*, 246.

15. *YMB*, 222.

16. *YMB*, 238.

17. *BT*, 73.

18. *BT*, 74.

19. *BT*, 251.

20. *BT*, 225.

21. *YMB*, 238. For this common theme in Williams's writings, see also *BT*, 80–81, 291, and 330.

22. *BT*, 398–99.

23. *BT*, 331.

24. *Correspondence of Roger Williams*, 537.

25. *BT*, 399.

26. Williams to the Town of Providence, August 31, 1648, *Correspondence of Roger Williams*, 238.

27. This is, of course, a major qualification and one that preoccupied much of the discussion between Williams and John Cotton, for precisely what constitutes a fundamental threat to public peace and order can be interpreted differently by different parties. Cotton, for instance, claimed that heresy itself was destructive. One of Williams's great accomplishments was his convincing argument that, contra Cotton, compulsion of conscience and not religious pluralism is the true enemy of social stability. Some of Williams's own suggestions of *behavior* that threatened public order, however, would certainly be considered illiberal today, a problem I take up in more detail later in this chapter.

28. *YMB*, 204–5.

29. *YMB*, 313, 476.

30. *YMB*, 306.

31. *BT*, 93.

32. *BT*, 178.

33. *BT*, 78.

34. James F. Childress, *Moral Responsibility in Conflicts: Essays on Nonviolence, War, and Conscience* (Baton Rouge: Louisiana State University Press, 1982), 17–18. Lisa Sowle Cahill agrees that the purpose of the Quakers' socially deviant behavior was to "challenge human pride, violate social expectations (especially those tied to political and class hierarchies)," and stimulate the conversion of their neighbors (*Love Your Enemies: Discipleship, Pacifism, and Just War Theory* [Minneapolis: Fortress, 1994], 167).

35. Boston printers had wanted nothing to do with Williams's treatises on freedom of conscience, so he had to wait for his occasional trips to London to publish them. His tirades against the Quakers, however, so satisfied the Massachusetts leadership that in 1676 they published *George Fox* themselves.

36. *George Fox*, 39.

37. *George Fox*, 307. I venture to say that Williams would be horrified with the routine violation of the procedural rules of civility in public discourse that is commonplace in the contemporary American political climate.

38. By "substantive" I do not mean to claim that these norms provided immediate moral guidance independent of a need to specify them and apply them to particular cases and contexts. I mean instead to identify them as norms concerned with how we might live, as opposed to the "procedural" norms that guide how we might go about talking about how we might live.

39. *Examiner*, 263.

40. *YMB*, 498.

41. *BT*, 396; *YMB*, 95–97.

42. *BT*, 71, 204–5, 396; *YMB*, 522.

43. According to Robin Lovin, twentieth-century Christian realists like Reinhold Niebuhr acknowledged seventeenth-century English sectarians like Williams as the originators of a philosophical connection between liberty and justice. The English radicals increasingly began to envision liberty as a regulative principle of justice that protected the natural human freedom of belief and provided a critical criterion for the restriction of overly ambitious political power. For Lovin's brief discussion of the relationship between liberty and justice in Christian realism, see *Reinhold Niebuhr and Christian Realism*, 227–30.

44. Henry S. Richardson, "Specifying Norms as a Way to Resolve Concrete Ethical Problems," *Philosophy and Public Affairs* 19 (1990): 279–320.

45. Richardson, 283. Richardson offers the notion of "specification" as an alternative to ethical approaches that relate moral principles to particular cases through either a strict practice of deductive application or the attempt to "balance" between norms by intuitively assigning relative weights to the norms in question. Richardson is careful to point out, however, that a sophisticated approach to moral principles combines more limited commitments to application and balancing with the practice of specification in order to establish midlevel moral norms and make connections between general principles and particular moral scenarios.

46. See Richardson, 294–300, 308.

47. Williams to the Town of Providence, ca. January 1654/55, *Correspondence of Roger Williams*, 2:423–24; *Examiner*, 203.

48. *Correspondence of Roger Williams*, 203.

49. Calvin argued that "equity alone must be the goal and rule and limit of all laws." In fact, he suggested that the principle of equity provided a comparative tool for evaluating the legitimacy of other laws, moral and civil. See Calvin's *Institutes*, 4:1504.

50. *Institutes*, 3:677, including note 16.

51. *Institutes*, 2:379–416.

52. *Institutes*, 4:1504–5.

53. E. Clinton Gardner, "Justice in the Puritan Covenantal Tradition," *Journal of Law and Religion* 6, no. 1 (1988): 51–53.

54. The idea of equity as a specifying factor in the exercise of toleration does appear occasionally in Williams's writings. For instance, in a letter to John Winthrop Jr., Williams expresses his hope not only that liberty of conscience would take hold in New England, but that "Equitie, Pietie," and the Christian spirit would accompany its implementation. Equity is particularly important, suggests Williams, in preventing conscientious freedom from begetting "licentiousness," for he is aware that "all Mercies are apt to be abused." Equity, it would seem, calls for a spirit of moderation in appeals to conscientious freedom that accounts for the common good and social ordering, as Williams makes clear in his treatises. See *Correspondence of Roger Williams*, 392.

55. *George Fox*, 308, 490.

56. *George Fox*, 308.

57. *YMB*, 207.

58. *Correspondence of Roger Williams*, 536.

59. *Key*, 7–10.

60. *Key*, 10.

61. *Key*, 99.

62. *Key*, 58.

63. *Key*, 70.

64. *Key*, 101–2.

65. *George Fox*, 59–62. Williams was convinced that the "incivilities" of the Quakers, insofar as they violated cohesive social practices and hinted at an underlying intolerance in the Quaker religion for all things conventional, ultimately would threaten political stability; see also *George Fox*, 307–12.

66. *George Fox*, 38–39, 306–7. In fact, Williams was quick to claim that the "savage" Native Americans consistently outperformed the Quakers in gestures of respect and general civility; see also *George Fox*, 211.

67. While other Puritan writers often used the notion of common good to restrict human freedoms or aspirations, Williams sought in the concept a balance between the priorities of the state and the pursuit of individual whim. Williams's conception of government, for instance, was that it was needed precisely to block the pursuit of private interest from threatening society's common good. But Williams strongly preferred a government based on the consent of the people, for he believed that the common good of a society was very much determined by the will and wishes of the citizens who constitute the society. In this way, Williams's consideration of the common good was both consistent with his advocacy of individual liberty and a curb against the excesses of toleration. See *BT*, 354, and *Key*, 142–45.

68. Gardner, 50.

69. Gardner, 50.

70. *BT*, 127, 252, 354.

71. *Examiner*, 203–4.
72. *BT*, 169.
73. *Examiner*, 203.
74. *George Fox*, 307.
75. *BT*, 299.
76. Morgan, 127.
77. Hall, *Separating Church and State*, 107.
78. Bellah, "Is There a Common American Culture?" *Journal of the American Academy of Religion* 66, no. 3 (1998): 613–25. Bellah levels this same indictment against Williams in "The Protestant Structure of American Culture: Multiculture or Monoculture?" *The Hedgehog Review* 4, no. 1 (2002): 7–28.
79. Williams to Henry Vane, August 27, 1634, *Correspondence of Roger Williams*, 2:397.
80. Hall, 103.
81. As Hall observes, despite shortcomings in both his conception of conscientious freedom and the specific norms of civility, Williams remains a corrective voice in the debate over moral pluralism, for "Williams looked beyond his age and recognized the potential for limiting religious freedom based upon overly generous characterizations of public interest in peace and civility" (111).

6. CHRISTIAN INTEGRITY, PUBLIC DISCOURSE, AND THE LEGACY OF ROGER WILLIAMS

1. For a collection of scholars who argue along these lines from many different methodological perspectives, see Michael L. Budde and Robert W. Brimlow, eds., *The Church as Counterculture* (Albany: State University of New York Press, 2000).
2. Stanley Hauerwas, *Against the Nations: War and Survival in a Liberal Society* (Notre Dame, Ind.: University of Notre Dame Press, 1992), 39.
3. *Against the Nations*, 41.
4. *Against the Nations*, 38.
5. *Wilderness Wanderings*, 4.
6. *Wilderness Wanderings*, 4.
7. *Wilderness Wanderings*, 2–3.
8. Gustafson, *Can Ethics Be Christian?* 123, 173.
9. *Can Ethics Be Christian?* 118. See also George Marsden, *The Outrageous Idea of Christian Scholarship* (New York: Oxford University Press, 1997), 63.
10. See, for instance, Gustafson's *Ethics from a Theocentric Perspective*, vol. 2 (Chicago: University of Chicago Press, 1984), 4–19.
11. Lovin, *Reinhold Neibuhr and Christian Realism*, 66.
12. Lovin, 67.
13. *Can Ethics Be Christian?* 129.
14. Lovin, 102.
15. Gustafson explores what he means by this and how his position on this question might be located among other historical and contemporary possibilities and types in *Can Ethics Be Christian?* 145–78.
16. *Can Ethics Be Christian?* 177. In his proposal for more forthright participation for religious perspectives in higher education and scholarship, George Marsden

similarly describes the effect religious piety may have in broader public discourse. To Marsden, the effect of Christian belief on Christian contributions to such conversations often remains at the level of commitments even while producing results that have much in common with those of other non-Christian perspectives: "Even on some questions of larger significance, distinctive Christian commitments do not necessarily produce agendas, questions, or conclusions that will not be almost identical to those of some other scholars. So Christians would do well to make clear that 'distinctively Christian scholarship' does not typically lead to scholarship that will set Christians apart from everyone else." See Marsden, *Christian Scholarship*, 69.

17. *Against the Nations*, 24.

18. Hauerwas, *A Community of Character*, 92–93; *Against the Nations*, 24.

19. Hauerwas, *A Community of Character*, 2.

20. *In Good Company: The Church as Polis* (Notre Dame, Ind.: University of Notre Dame Press, 1995), 216.

21. Gustafson, *The Church as Moral Decision-Maker* (Philadelphia: Pilgrim Press, 1970), 93.

22. *Church as Moral Decision-Maker*, 93.

23. Hauerwas does appear to have a point when he observes that, at times, Gustafson interprets the identity of the church in language devoted more fully to sociological existence and a general philosophical perspective than to the unique beliefs and practices of the faith tradition (especially in his later work). In particular I have in mind here the barely discernible role Christology plays in Gustafson's *Ethics from a Theocentric Perspective*. For Hauerwas's criticism of this work in particular, see "Time and History in Theological Ethics: The Work of James Gustafson," *Journal of Religious Ethics* 13, no. 1 (spring 1985): 3–21. (A revised version of this essay appears in *Wilderness Wanderings*, 62–81.) As a result, occasionally Gustafson fails to demonstrate adequately the distinctive contribution of the church to moral discourse beyond its service as an example of rational conversation and moral analysis. Hauerwas rightly reminds Gustafson that the church is as much a theological reality rooted in the unique beliefs and practices of the disciples of Jesus Christ as it is a sociological reality. At the same time, Hauerwas's theological commitment to the church frequently shields him from the recognition of the sociological realities of Christian existence and participation. As David Tracy observes, Christian thinkers like Hauerwas are so invested in the theological conception of the church that they fail to see the value of sociological analysis, fearing that to treat the church as a sociological entity will inevitably prove to be "reductionist." Tracy's comment is pertinent, that "so frightened by this reductionist prospect do some ecclesiologists seem that they are incapable of undertaking, or even appreciating, strictly sociological understandings of the reality of the church. . . . Any sociological understanding of the church—as voluntary association, as institution, as community, as social reality—will seem reductionist to some theologians." See *The Analogical Imagination*, 21–24.

24. *Against the Nations*, 44.

25. David Tracy argues that the biblical depiction of God, specifically the Yahwist and Johannine accounts, necessarily commits the believer to the recognition of "the realities of our common human experience" that opens Christian theology to relationship with a wider public than simply the church and compels it to account for our similarities and differences with the "world" on theological grounds. See Tracy, *The Analogical Imagination*, 49–50.

26. By contrast, Hauerwas by his own admission centers his theological ethics on the church. In his ethics, ecclesiology dominates and Christology, theology (in the literal sense of the term, referring to doctrines of God), and his view of scriptural authority play prominent and formative but ultimately secondary roles. As a result, his ecclesiological vision of a community of "resident aliens" at key moments limits and determines the development of other components of his theology. His failure to offer a clear and multifaceted Christology, the sparse development of any equivalent to the Christian doctrine of creation in his work, and his periodic, almost quasi-Marcion relegation of the language and concepts of the Old Testament to secondary status are choices that, implicitly or otherwise, come from his initial commitment to a radical separatist ecclesiology. Beginning with theology and Christology, Williams is better prepared to represent the "publicness" (David Tracy's term) of Christian belief and avoids a premature sellout to an ecclesiology that insufficiently respects the similarities-in-difference (also Tracy's term) that the church shares with the rest of God's world. See Tracy, *The Analogical Imagination*, 21, 62–64.

27. Calvin, *Institutes*, 1:35.

28. *Can Ethics Be Christian?* 172.

29. Gustafson addresses this relationship between "special ethics" and "ordinary" moral norms when he discusses the "natural law type" or approach to Christian ethics. In those Christian theologies, like Williams's, that depend in part on natural law, the natural law usually represents that conduct which ought to be recognizable and obligatory in ordinary human relations. What Gustafson calls "special ethics" consists of those moral obligations that specifically accompany the undertaking of the Christian life. They are moral in character, but they are obligatory only to those who choose to be Christian disciples. It is because of the existence of this dimension of "special ethics" that Gustafson insists that Christian ethics can never be converted to the "natural" or the "human" without remainder. The natural and the human are aspects of Christian ethics, on the theological grounds of the doctrine of creation, but Christian ethics always entails more than the simply human or natural (Gustafson, *Can Ethics Be Christian?* 153–54).

30. For instance, see the contributions from various religious and political traditions in *Religious Human Rights in Global Perspectives*, 2 vols., ed. John Witte Jr. and Johan D. van der Vyver (The Hague: Martinus Nijhoff Publishers, 1996). I understand the rich diversity in these two volumes to be a sign that analogous concepts for the largely Western commitment to "conscience" do in fact exist, even if substantial disagreement remains regarding the extent and nature of the freedom we grant to this human experience.

31. Karl Barth, *Ethics*, trans. Geoffrey W. Bromiley (New York: Seabury Press, 1981), 478.

32. Barth, *Ethics*, 485.

33. Barth, *Ethics*, 479. In more classically Protestant language, David Leal argues that, from a Christian point of view, an inordinate focus on conscience encourages a "works righteousness" that obscures our dependence on God for moral ability. Leal also argues that preoccupation with the casuistry of conscientious reflection undermines the importance of Christian character, insomuch as it hinders the development of a moral capacity that is "second nature" and does not require the incessant calculus of "cases of conscience." See Leal, "Against Conscience: A Protestant View," in

Conscience in World Religions, ed. Jayne Hoose (Notre Dame, Ind.: Notre Dame University Press, 1999), 21–61.

34. Barth, *Ethics,* 477.

35. For more on Barth's understanding of conscience, including what he sought to reject in the concept, see *Ethics,* 475–97, and *Church Dogmatics,* III/4, ed. G. W. Bromiley and T. F. Torrance (Edinburgh: T. & T. Clark, 1961), 3–19.

36. A participant in this philosophical renaissance, Guyton B. Hammond has undertaken a rehabilitation of the concept of conscience by drawing on the Frankfurt school, feminist psychoanalysis, and the theology of Paul Tillich. The result of his effort is an attempt to save conscience from its Puritan and Freudian formulations by reconsidering it as the internalization of well-rounded parental nurturing and thus the utopian voice of a perfected self in perfected community. See Guyton B. Hammond, *Conscience and Its Recovery: From the Frankfurt School to Feminism* (Charlottesville: University of Virginia Press, 1993).

37. C. D. Broad, *Ethics and the History of Philosophy: Selected Essays* (London: Routledge & K. Paul, 1952), 244–62; Leal, "Against Conscience: A Protestant View," 28.

38. Hunter, "Conscience," 80.

39. Hunter, 73–74.

40. Thomas Nagel, "What Is It Like to Be a Bat?" in *Mortal Questions* (New York: Cambridge University Press, 1979), 173.

41. Nagel, 178.

42. Hunter, 84.

43. Hunter, 75.

44. Gustafson, *Church as Moral Decision-Maker,* 93.

45. Pat Robertson, *The Turning Tide: The Fall of Liberalism and the Rise of Common Sense* (Dallas: Word Publishing, 1993), 48–49, 63, 66. Even Stephen L. Carter, a more careful thinker than Robertson, argues for an essential role for religion in the cultivation and standards of civility. Carter employs the term "civility" to argue for a return to mutual respect, a willingness to sacrifice our ends for the needs of others, and a spirit of social cooperation. Religion assists society in the cultivation of civility by providing the language and motivation for self-sacrifice and mutual regard. Although at times Carter claims that civility does not depend on religion to exist and flourish, he develops the relationship between "religion" and "culture" as such antitheses that it is difficult to understand from his analysis how "culture" may develop civility without the direct intervention of "religion." The dominant "culture" pushes citizens to emphasize self-regard and to principally view others as means to personal ends, while "religion" reminds us of the virtues that inhabit the soul of civility. Statements to the contrary notwithstanding, Carter's antagonism between "religion" and "culture" leaves his reader with little optimism that civility can germinate in society without the direct influence (perhaps the covert establishment even) of religious beliefs and values. See Carter's *Civility: Manners, Morals, and the Etiquette of Democracy* (New York: Basic Books, 1998), especially chap. 6.

46. Carter, 280.

47. Carter, 87.

48. Carter does include a caveat to his reliance on the current rules and norms of the community. Children should be taught that civility requires adherence to rules, writes Carter, "unless there is a good reason to make a different choice" (87). But by basing his conception of civility so deeply in social convention, Carter fails

to provide an adequate basis for the justified deviations he presumes to allow. Williams appealed to natural law, the conscience, and practical reasoning for the source material of civility, thereby connecting it with public consensus without tying it inextricably to convention alone. Carter lacks the independent source that allowed Williams to imagine civility as a cultural critic. One might ask of Carter's proposal: on what basis are we to evaluate social norms in order to decide that we have "good reason to make a different choice"? Carter's response seems to be simply that this kind of decision making requires "moral conversation," though he is unclear regarding the sources of authority for that conversation beyond the conventions of our time and place.

49. Carter, 284.

50. As David Little recommends, "Williams's belief in a shared moral standard independent of religious conviction, as the basis of civil society, . . . should particularly be retrieved and reexamined." Little, "Roger Williams and Separation," 16.

51. *BT,* 423.

52. Vernon Louis Parrington, *Main Currents in American Thought* (New York: Harcourt, Brace, 1927); James Emanuel Ernst, *The Political Thought of Roger Williams* (Seattle: University of Washington Press, 1929).

53. Roger Williams is often regarded as the patriarch of the American Baptist tradition, because he was involved in the consecration of the first Baptist church in the English colonies. What is less often remembered is that Williams remained affiliated with the Baptists in Rhode Island for less than a year before determining that they, too, failed to live up to his ecclesiological expectations. While his denominational affiliation was fleeting, however, Williams remained theologically within the Reformed tradition his entire career.

SELECTED BIBLIOGRAPHY

PRIMARY SOURCES

Ames, William. *Conscience, with the Power and Cases Thereof.* 1643. Reprint, Norwood, N.J.: Walter J. Johnson, 1975.

———. *The Marrow of Theology.* Translated by John Dykstra Eusden. 1629. Reprint, Grand Rapids: Baker Books, 1997.

Aquinas, Thomas. *Opera omnia.* Vol. 22, *Quaestiones disputatae de veritate.* Rome: ad Sancta Sabinae, 1972. As translated in excerpts by Timothy C. Potts, *Conscience in Medieval Philosophy.* Cambridge: Cambridge University Press, 1980.

———. *The Summa Theologica of St. Thomas Aquinas.* New York: Benzinger Brothers, 1948.

Baxter, Richard. *A Holy Commonwealth.* Edited by William Lamont. 1659. Reprint, Cambridge: Cambridge University Press, 1994.

Bradford, William. *Of Plymouth Plantation 1620–1647.* New York: Random House, 1981.

Calvin, John. *Commentary on the Epistle to the Romans.* Translated by Ross Mackenzie. In *Calvin's New Testament Commentaries.* Vol. 8. Grand Rapids: Wm. B. Eerdmans, 1991.

———. *Institutes of the Christian Religion.* Library of Christian Classics, 20, 21. Edited by John T. McNeill and translated by Ford Lewis Battles. Philadelphia: Westminster, 1960.

———. *On God and Political Duty.* Edited by John T. McNeill. Indianapolis: Bobbs-Merrill Publishing, 1956.

Cotton, John. *The Correspondence of John Cotton.* Edited by Sargent Bush Jr. Chapel Hill: University of North Carolina Press, 2001.

———. *John Cotton's Answer to Roger Williams.* Edited by Reuben Aldridge Guild. In *The Complete Writings of Roger Williams.* Vol. 2. New York: Russell and Russell, 1963.

Locke, John. *A Letter Concerning Toleration.* 1689. Reprint, Buffalo, N.Y.: Prometheus, 1990.

Perkins, William. *A Discourse of Conscience* and *The Whole Treatise of Cases of Conscience.* In *William Perkins: English Puritanist.* Edited by Thomas F. Merrill. Nieuwkoop: B. De Graaf, 1966.

Williams, Roger. *The Complete Writings of Roger Williams.* 7 vols. New York: Russell and Russell, 1963.

———. *The Correspondence of Roger Williams.* 2 vols. Edited by Glenn W. LaFantasie. Providence, R.I.: Published for the Rhode Island Historical Society by Brown University Press, 1988.

———. *A Key into the Language of America.* 1644. Reprint, Bedford, Mass.: Applewood Books, 1997.

Winthrop, John. *The Journal of John Winthrop, 1630–1649.* Edited by Richard S. Dunn and Laetitia Yeandle. Cambridge, Mass.: Harvard University Press, Belknap Press, 1996.

Woodhouse, A. S. P., ed. *Puritanism and Liberty.* 3d ed. London: J. M. Dent and Sons, 1986.

SECONDARY SOURCES

Adair, John. *Puritans: Religion and Politics in Seventeenth-Century England and America.* Phoenix Mill: Sutton Publishing, 1998.

Barth, Karl. *Church Dogmatics,* III/4. Edited by G. W. Bromiley and T. F. Torrance. Edinburgh: T. & T. Clark, 1961.

———. *Ethics.* Translated by Geoffrey W. Bromiley. New York: Seabury Press, 1981.

Bellah, Robert. "Is There a Common American Culture?" *Journal of the American Academy of Religion* 66:3 (1998): 613–25.

———. "The Protestant Structure of American Culture: Multiculture or Monoculture?" *The Hedgehog Review* 4:1 (2002): 7–28.

Bercovitch, Sacvan. "Typology in Puritan New England: The Williams-Cotton Controversy Reassessed." *American Quarterly* 19 (1967): 166–91.

Bozeman, Theodore Dwight. "Religious Liberty and the Problem of Order in Early Rhode Island." *New England Quarterly* 45:1 (1972): 44–63.

Breen, T.H. *The Character of the Good Ruler: A Study of Puritan Political Ideas in New England, 1630–1730.* New Haven, Conn.: Yale University Press, 1970.

Bremer, Francis J. *The Puritan Experiment: New England Society from Bradford to Edwards.* Rev. ed. Hanover, N.H.: University Press of New England, 1995.

Broad, C. D. *Ethics and the History of Philosophy: Selected Essays.* London: Routledge & K. Paul, 1952.

Brunkow, Robert. "Love and Order in Roger Williams's Writings." *Rhode Island History* 35 (1976): 115–26.

Byrd, James P. *The Challenges of Roger Williams: Religious Liberty, Violent Persecution, and the Bible.* Macon, Ga.: Mercer University Press, 2002.

Cahill, Lisa Sowle. *Love Your Enemies: Discipleship, Pacifism, and Just War Theory.* Minneapolis: Fortress, 1994.

Calamandrei, Mauro. "Neglected Aspects of Roger Williams' Thought." *Church History* 21 (1952): 239–58.

Camp, Leon Ray. "Man and His Government: Roger Williams vs. the Massachusetts Oligarchy." In *Preaching in American History,* edited by Dewitte Hollard, 74–97. New York: Abingdon, 1969.

Carter, Stephen L. *Civility: Manners, Morals, and the Etiquette of Democracy.* New York: Basic Books, 1998.

Childress, James F. *Moral Responsibility in Conflicts: Essays on Nonviolence, War, and Conscience.* Baton Rouge: Louisiana State University Press, 1982.

Chupack, Henry. *Roger Williams.* New York: Twayne Publishers, 1969.

Dargo, George. "Religious Tolerance and Its Limits in Early America." *Northern Illinois University Law Review* 16 (1996): 341–70.

Davis, Derek H. "The Enduring Legacy of Roger Williams: Consulting America's First Separationist on Today's Pressing Church-State Controversies." *Journal of Church and State* 41:2 (spring 1999): 201–12.

Davis, Jack L. "Roger Williams Among the Narragansett Indians." *New England Quarterly* 43 (1970): 593–604.

Ernst, James Emanuel. *The Political Thought of Roger Williams.* Seattle: University of Washington Press, 1929.

Felker, Christopher D. "Roger Williams's Uses of Legal Discourse: Testing Authority in Early New England." *New England Quarterly* 63 (1990): 624–48.

Fiering, Norman. *Moral Philosophy at Seventeenth-Century Harvard: A Discipline in Transition.* Chapel Hill: University of North Carolina Press, 1981.

———. "Will and Intellect in the New England Mind." *William and Mary Quarterly,* 3d ser., 29 (1972): 515–58.

Gardner, E. Clinton. "Justice in the Puritan Covenantal Tradition." *Journal of Law and Religion* 6:1 (1988): 39–60.

Gaustad, Edwin Scott. *Liberty of Conscience: Roger Williams in America.* Grand Rapids: Wm. B. Eerdmans, 1991.

———. "Roger Williams: Beyond Puritanism." *Baptist History and Heritage* 24 (1989): 11–19.

Gilpin, W. Clark. *The Millenarian Piety of Roger Williams.* Chicago: University of Chicago Press, 1979.

Gustafson, James M. *Can Ethics Be Christian?* Chicago: University of Chicago Press, 1975.

———. *Christ and the Moral Life.* New York: Harper and Row, 1968.

———. *Christian Ethics and the Community.* Philadelphia: Pilgrim, 1971.

———. *The Church as Moral Decision-Maker.* Philadelphia: Pilgrim, 1970.

———. *Ethics from a Theocentric Perspective.* 2 vols. Chicago: University of Chicago Press, 1981, 1984.

Hall, Timothy L. *Separating Church and State: Roger Williams and Religious Liberty.* Urbana: University of Illinois Press, 1998.

Haller, William. *Liberty and Reformation in the Puritan Revolution.* New York: Columbia University Press, 1955.

Hammond, Guyton B. *Conscience and Its Recovery: From the Frankfurt School to Feminism.* Charlottesville: University of Virginia Press, 1993.

Harkness, R. E. E. "Principles Established in Rhode Island." *Church History* 5 (September 1936): 216–26.

Hauerwas, Stanley. *Against the Nations: War and Survival in a Liberal Society.* Notre Dame, Ind.: University of Notre Dame Press, 1992.

———. *A Community of Character.* Notre Dame, Ind.: University of Notre Dame Press, 1981.

———. *In Good Company: The Church as Polis.* Notre Dame, Ind.: University of Notre Dame Press, 1995.

————. "Time and History in Theological Ethics: The Work of James Gustafson." *Journal of Religious Ethics* 13:1 (spring 1985): 3–21.

————. *Wilderness Wanderings: Probing Twentieth-Century Theology and Philosophy.* Boulder, Colo.: Westview, 1997.

Hill, Christopher. *Society and Puritanism in Pre-Revolutionary England.* New York: St. Martin's, 1997.

————. *The World Turned Upside Down: Radical Ideas During the English Revolution.* New York: Viking, 1972.

Hudson, Winthrop. "John Locke." *Journal of Presbyterian History* 42 (1964): 19–38.

Hunter, J. F. M. "Conscience." In *Conscience,* edited by John Donnelly and Leonard Lyons. Staten Island, N.Y.: Alba House, 1973.

Innes, Stephen. *Creating the Commonwealth: The Economic Culture of Puritan New England.* New York: W. W. Norton, 1995.

Irwin, Raymond D. "A Man for All Eras: The Changing Historical Image of Roger Williams." *Fides et Historia* 26 (1994): 6–23.

James, Sydney V. "Ecclesiastical Authority in the Land of Roger Williams." *New England Quarterly* 57 (1984): 323–46.

LaFantasie, Glen W. "The Disputed Legacy of Roger Williams." *Church and State* 42 (1989): 9–11.

————. "Murder of an Indian." *Rhode Island History* 38 (1989): 67–77.

————. "Roger Williams: The Inner and Outer Man." *Canadian Review of American Studies* 16 (1985): 375–94.

Leal, David. "Against Conscience: A Protestant View." In *Conscience in World Religions,* edited by Jayne Hoose. Notre Dame, Ind.: Notre Dame University Press, 1999.

Little, David. "Conscience, Theology, and the First Amendment." *Soundings* 72 (1989): 357–78.

————. "Reformed Faith and Religious Liberty." *Church and Society* 76 (May/June 1986): 5–28.

————. "The Reformed Tradition and the First Amendment." *Affirmation* 2:2 (1989): 1–19.

————. *Religion, Order, and Law: A Study in Pre-Revolutionary England.* Chicago: University of Chicago Press, 1984.

————. "Roger Williams and the Separation of Church and State." In *Religion and State: Essays in Honor of Leo Pfeffer,* edited by James E. Wood, 3–23. Waco, Tex.: Baylor University Press, 1985.

Lovejoy, David S. "Roger Williams and George Fox: The Arrogance of Self-Righteousness." *William and Mary Quarterly,* 3d ser., 62 (1993): 199–225.

Lovin, Robin. *Reinhold Niebuhr and Christian Realism.* Cambridge: Cambridge University Press, 1995.

Marsden, George. *The Outrageous Idea of Christian Scholarship.* New York: Oxford University Press, 1997.

Mead, Sidney. "Church, State, Calvinism, and Conscience." *Perspectives in American History* 3 (1969): 443–59.

Milbank, John. "Can Morality Be Christian?" In *The Word Made Strange: Theology, Language, Culture,* 219–32. Cambridge, Mass.: Blackwell Publishers, 1997.

Miller, Joshua. "Direct Democracy and the Puritan Theory of Membership." *Journal of Politics* 53 (1991): 57–74.

Miller, Perry. *Errand into the Wilderness.* Cambridge, Mass.: Harvard University Press, 1956.

———. *The New England Mind.* 2 vols. Cambridge, Mass.: Harvard University Press, 1933, 1939.

———. *Orthodoxy in Massachusetts, 1630–50.* Cambridge, Mass.: Harvard University Press, 1933.

———. *Roger Williams: His Contribution to the American Tradition.* Indianapolis: Bobbs-Merrill, 1953.

Miller, William Lee. *The First Liberty: Religion and the American Republic.* New York: Alfred A. Knopf, 1985.

Moore, LeRoy. "Religious Liberty: Roger Williams and the Revolutionary Era." *Church History* 34 (1965): 57–76.

———. "Roger Williams and the Historians." *Church History* 32 (1963): 432–51.

Morgan, Edmund. *Roger Williams: The Church and the State.* New York: W. W. Norton, 1967.

———. *Visible Saints: The History of a Puritan Idea.* Ithaca, N.Y.: Cornell University Press, 1965.

Morris, Maxwell H. "Roger Williams and the Jews." *American Jewish Archives* 3:2 (1951): 24–27.

Myles, Anne G. "Arguments in Milk, Arguments in Blood: Roger Williams, Persecution, and the Discourse of the Witness." *Modern Philology* 91 (1993): 133–60.

Nagel, Thomas. "What Is It Like to Be a Bat?" In *Mortal Questions.* New York: Cambridge University Press, 1979.

Neff, Jimmy D. "Roger Williams: Pious Puritan and Strict Separationist." *Journal of Church and State* 38 (1996): 529–46.

Niebuhr, H. Richard. *Christ and Culture.* New York: Harper and Row, 1951.

———. *The Kingdom of God in America.* San Francisco: Harper and Row, 1937.

Noonan, John T., Jr. "Principled or Pragmatic Foundations for the Freedom of Conscience." *Journal of Law and Religion* 5 (1987): 203–12.

Novak, David. *Jewish Social Ethics.* Oxford: Oxford University Press, 1992.

Outka, Gene. "The Particularist Turn in Theological and Philosophical Ethics." In *Christian Ethics: Problems and Prospects,* edited by Lisa Sowle Cahill and James F. Childress. Cleveland: Pilgrim, 1996.

Parrington, Vernon Louis. *Main Currents in American Thought.* New York: Harcourt, Brace, 1927.

Peace, Nancy. "Roger Williams—A Historiographical Essay." *Rhode Island History* 35 (1976): 103–13.

Phillips, Stephen. "Roger Williams and the Two Tables of the Law." *Journal of Church and State* 38 (1996): 547–68.

Polishook, Irwin H. *Roger Williams, John Cotton, and Religious Freedom: A Controversy in New and Old England.* Englewood Cliffs, N.J.: Prentice-Hall, 1967.

Reinitz, Richard. "The Separatist Background of Roger Williams' Argument for Religious Toleration." In *Typology and Early American Literature,* edited by Sacvan Bercovitch. Amherst: University of Massachusetts Press, 1972.

Richardson, Henry S. "Specifying Norms as a Way to Resolve Concrete Ethical Problems." *Philosophy and Public Affairs* 19 (1990): 279–320.

Robertson, Pat. *The Turning Tide: The Fall of Liberalism and the Rise of Common Sense.* Dallas: Word Publishing, 1993.

Rosenmeier, Jesper. "The Teacher and the Witness: John Cotton and Roger Williams." *William and Mary Quarterly,* 3d ser., 25 (1968): 408–31.

Ross, Richard. "The Legal Past of Early New England: Notes for the Study of Law, Legal Culture, and Intellectual History." *William and Mary Quarterly,* 3d ser., 50 (1993): 28–41.

Rossiter, Clinton. "Roger Williams on the Anvil of Experience." *American Quarterly* 3 (January 1951): 14–21.

Rutman, Darrett B. Review of *The Complete Writings of Roger Williams. William and Mary Quarterly,* 3d ser., 21 (1964): 303–4.

Simmons, William S. "Cultural Bias in the New England Puritans' Perception of Indians." *William and Mary Quarterly,* 3d ser., 38 (1981): 56–72.

Simpson, Alan. "How Democratic Was Roger Williams?" *William and Mary Quarterly,* 3d ser., 13 (1956): 53–67.

Spohn, William C. *Go and Do Likewise: Jesus and Ethics.* New York: Continuum, 1999.

Spurgin, Hugh. *Roger Williams and Puritan Radicalism in the English Separatist Tradition.* Lewiston, N.Y.: Edwin Mellen, 1989.

Staloff, Darren. *The Making of an American Thinking Class: Intellectuals and Intelligentsia in Puritan Massachusetts.* New York: Oxford, 1998.

Stout, Harry S. *The New England Soul: Preaching and Religious Culture in Colonial New England.* New York: Oxford, 1986.

Tracy, David. *The Analogical Imagination: Christian Theology and the Culture of Pluralism.* New York: Crossroads, 1981.

Walzer, Michael. *Revolution of the Saints: A Study in the Origins of Radical Politics.* Cambridge, Mass.: Harvard University Press, 1965.

West, Ellis M. "Roger Williams on the Limits of Religious Liberty." *Annual of the Society of Christian Ethics* (1988): 133–60.

Wills, Garry. *Under God: Religion and American Politics.* New York: Simon and Schuster, 1990.

Winslow, Ola Elizabeth. *Master Roger Williams: A Biography.* New York: Octagon Books, 1973.

Witte, John, Jr., and Johan D. van der Vyver, eds. *Religious Human Rights in Global Perspectives.* 2 vols. The Hague: Martinus Nijhoff Publishers, 1996.

Ziff, Larzer. *The Career of John Cotton: Puritanism and the American Experience.* Princeton, N.J.: Princeton University Press, 1962.

INDEX OF NAMES

INDEX OF SUBJECTS